"A piercing but achingly beautiful exploration of the individual, the grief, anger, and guilt of loved ones left behind, and an inquiry into what happens after death. While many religions profess that the soul of those who commit suicide are eternally damned, the author comes to the conclusion that all death—in whatever form it takes—eventually leads to light. A must-read for those whose lives have been touched by suicide as well as for those who would delve further into what happens to our souls when we die."

—Nancy Nelson, editor, *www.morethanpassingstrange.com*

"The biblical proverb, 'Physician, heal thyself'" is explored at the most profound levels in *Heaven is for Healing*. When clinical psychologist, Dr. Joe Gallenberger must confront, internally and externally, his own brother's suicide, an exquisite journey unfolds through grief, spiritual exploration, joy, love, and compassion. While an obvious 'must read' for anyone that has touched, been touched, or even knows someone who has been touched by the energies of suicide, this book also offers much needed insights for all of us, especially caregivers, spiritual seekers, and those who face (or even consider) the concept of death—which, oh, by the way, is each of us whether we are brave enough to admit it or not."

—J. R. Madaus, author of *Think Logically, Live Intuitively: Seeking the Balance*

"Gallenberger knows, first-hand, what suicide does to survivors. But *Heaven is for Healing* goes well beyond advice for coping. It shows that suicides receive assistance after the fact, so that even death becomes only one more stage of life."

—Frank DeMarco, author of *The Cosmic Internet* and *Rita's World*

"A sensitive, heartfelt exploration of realms that most of us can only imagine. If you accept the existence of an afterlife, this book offers rich details—consistent with spiritualist traditions—regarding the evolution of the soul. Even if you are in doubt or disbelief, Dr. Gallenberger's account remains an honest and penetrating effort to grapple with some of the deepest wounds life can offer. I highly recommend this book."

—Jeffrey Mishlove, Ph.D., host/producer, *New Thinking Allowed* video channel

"In *Heaven is for Healing, A Soul's Journey After Suicide*, Dr. Joseph Gallenberger offers perceptive insights and comforting support to those who have experienced the death of a loved one through suicide. He also gives hope to anyone who might be contemplating taking their own life, sharing his own story of how he has explored the spectrum from 'suicide to salvation.' This book is an excellent and encouraging choice for anyone who wants to heal and release the grief and guilt which often accompany dealing with a loved one's death."

—Nancy H. McMoneagle, president, The Monroe Institute

"*Heaven is for Healing* is a beautiful and heart-wrenching story about Joe Gallenberger's brother Pete, who committed suicide, leaving his entire family in agony and grief for many years. Personally, this book helped me tremendously in better coping with and understanding the depression and ultimate suicide of a friend. Reading this book, I cried and laughed, and emerged at the end with hope and understanding that there is no eternal damnation as a result of suicide, that heaven is for indeed for healing everyone, regardless of how they died."

—Andrea Berger, president, Association for Consciousness Evolution

"*Heaven is for Healing* is a beautiful love story of two brothers, Pete and Joe, and the deep pain associated with the loss of one through suicide. Joe's search for meaning is expressed beautifully in this book and will be a comfort to anyone dealing with grief from a suicide or death of a loved one. Thank you, Joe, for your willingness to be so open and vulnerable."

—Charlotte McGinnis, spiritual leader of The Namaste Center

HEAVEN

IS FOR

HEALING

A Soul's Journey After Suicide

JOSEPH GALLENBERGER, PH.D.

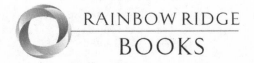

RAINBOW RIDGE
BOOKS

Cover and interior design by Frame25 Productions
Cover photo © Iakov Kalinin c/o Shutterstock.com

Published by:
Rainbow Ridge Books, LLC
140 Rainbow Ridge Road
Faber, Virginia 22938
434-361-1723

If you are unable to order this book from your local
bookseller, you may order directly from the distributor.

Square One Publishers, Inc.
115 Herricks Road
Garden City Park, NY 11040
Phone: (516) 535-2010
Fax: (516) 535-2014
Toll-free: 877-900-BOOK

Visit the author at:
www.SyncCreation.com
www.LiquidLuckbook.com

Library of Congress Cataloging-in-Publication Data applied for.

ISBN 978-1-937907-51-8

10 9 8 7 6 5 4 3 2 1

Printed in Canada

Nothing in this book should be construed as advocating, promoting, or endorsing suicide in any way. In fact if the book is read entirely as recommended, it will be clear that suicide usually causes untold devastation in the loved ones left behind and significant consequences for the soul that departs via suicide.

This publication provides the author's own opinions on the subject matter covered. It is sold with the understanding that the author is not engaged in rendering legal, medical, psychological, or spiritual services to the reader. If expert assistance is desired, the services of an appropriate professional should be sought.

If You Are Contemplating Suicide

There are people who can help. Each of us is born for a reason, and even the most difficult experiences of our lives have a purpose. Please reach out and find the support you need or refer someone who you think may need help. Crisis counselors can provide a safe way to talk about the challenges you face, and advice on how to handle them. It's free to call.

National Suicide Prevention Lifeline 1-800-273-8255, which includes help for veterans; (800) 799-4TTY for the deaf; and https://www.imalive.org/ for online chat.

In memory of those who have committed suicide
and their loved ones who miss them . . .

We can be shrouded by grief's dark cocoon
and re-emerge with great lightness
of heart and richness of spirit.
This is surely a sign that we are magical creatures!

CONTENTS

ACKNOWLEDGMENTS

I thank my family and friends who held me in a circle of love through the loss of my brother.

And I extend deepest gratitude to Elena, who later found me and resurrected me into full and joyful living again. I am becoming whole and holy within the cocoon of gladness you have woven with me.

INTRODUCTION

I want to tell you the story of the mysteries of life and death that my brother Pete, who committed suicide twenty-five years ago, and I are sharing. This true story speaks about a type of love seldom explored. It probes the rich interweaving of a lifetime of relating as brothers—at times close, at times distant, exchanging roles of giver and receiver, but ever deepening into a love that pierces through the veil of death.

We all experience loss. It is an unavoidable part of being human. When someone we love dies, it is natural to wonder whether the person we love is now at peace. Near-death experiences hint at what may go on during the process of dying but do not address what happens after that. Now there are new sources of information about what we experience after physical death. These sources suggest a rich, varied, and changing life of the spirit, with the possibility of at least some communication between those living in the physical and those who have died. The science of these links is beginning to be explored. This book provides an expanded view of life after death, particularly after death by suicide.

In addition, this book is about conquering the grief that follows a person taking his or her own life. Globally more than a million people a year commit suicide, which equates to one person every forty seconds. When we experience the suicide of someone close to us we feel the shock, denial, helplessness, and sadness of all sudden deaths but statistics suggest we also experience more depression, fear of aloneness, and relationship problems. When someone chooses death, that person renounces our power to help. This renunciation tempts the survivor to feel a persistent worthlessness and guilt. Many survivors are silent about their pain. Most would benefit from talking it out with someone who will listen and will not judge. I hope my book comforts you if you are ever affected by suicide and lightens your heart by hearing about the intelligent, respectful, and compassionate beings that await to help and guide us all after death, regardless of the method of our dying.

I feel my sharing in this book can counter the harsh, medieval attitudes about suicide that still permeate many cultures and religions today. My own mother, in addition to the devastation of losing her son, agonized about her treasured son spending eternity in hell according to Catholic belief. Within Christianity the unforgivable sin is the sin of despair. Suicide is also condemned in Judaism and Islam.

I will tell you of a recent experience to show how severe and superstitious our root culture stance is to suicide. Recently I was visiting New Orleans to give a talk at a conference. On a free afternoon my wife and I decided to take the city ghost tour. As we assembled in front of the old church by the river our guide told us this story. She said that a few centuries ago church and state were completely intermingled and that we were standing in front of the building that was that very seat of power. In those times, when someone committed suicide, their corpse was put into an inquisition chair in this church and then interrogated and tortured for hours. As the person was dead and could not put up a defense they were always condemned, and in response they were then tied to a wagon wheel with their hands, feet, and head protruding past the rim. They were driven around town for ridicule and dismemberment, then fed to the alligators, bypassing any chance of being buried in sacred ground. Sacred ground held protection, so this unconsecrated disposal of the remains was believed to subject the person's soul to eternal torment by the evilest of spirits.

This story illustrates the rush to judgment and a total discounting of the psychological, spiritual, and life-event forces that might drive a person to taking their own life.

In ancient Greek and Roman times suicide (with certain exceptions) was considered a heinous crime against the state. The theme of disallowing proper burial and confiscating all lands and property, which punished the loved ones left behind, continued through European cultures, and in current times suicide is still considered a felony in many countries. There is still much denial of suicide as the heart-rending community issue it is.

Today, many people consider suicide to be a selfish and insane act, even while acknowledging that the suicidal person may be responding to massive pain that they perceive as intolerable. I would guess that there is a near universal question at some point in most people's lives about whether it is worth it to keep going on. In that dark moment we may stay for religious reasons, to meet family obligations, from fear of the unknown, or from hope that things will change. We must realize that some people may lose all hope that things will change, cannot conceive of a good reason to stay, and just be too tired and discouraged to go on.

I feel that it is urgent to apply enlightened thinking to allow healing and comfort to be extended to and received by those who have suffered from the loss of a loved one through suicide. I want to present my understanding that there are many growth paths available to the spirit of a person who has committed suicide and that there is no way to be truly "lost for eternity." To this end I will be sharing my brother Pete's experiences on the other side for the last twenty-five years since he left his body.

I do not want to encourage anyone towards suicide and so I am starting this book in Part One with a re-publishing of an edited version of my 1996 book, *Brother's Forever: An Unexpected Journey Beyond Death*. It explores what happened to Pete immediately after his death upon reaching the other side. It also gives a clear and unvarnished report of the devastation that suicide produces in the loved ones who are left behind and reveals a way out of the grief. It was a difficult book to write but it helped me come to terms with my own loss and to move on. *Brothers Forever* has been out of print for many years, yet I still receive letters telling me how much the book helps when someone has experienced loss in their lives.

Part Two of *Heaven is for Healing* takes up the story twenty years later and explores what my brother Pete has been up to on the other side for these decades. We will see how helpers on the other side assist people in coming to grips with the act of taking their own lives. These helpers assist in planning the soul's continuing stages of growth, which may or may not include next experiencing another physical life. It appears that there are several different healing methods used, each tailored to individual circumstance and personality. I will also share the transformations that have occurred in my life, directly stimulated by Pete's actions. For example, my attitudes about death and my way of approaching life have both changed dramatically.

We might look at this book as an exercise in "Loving through the Veils": the veils that keep all of us from fully seeing our true nature and potential, the veils we put over our hearts to try to protect ourselves from pain, and the veil between this life and the other side. I know now that love can pierce any veil.

My life is currently happy and I am enjoying success from authoring two books: *Inner Vegas: Creating Miracles, Abundance, and Health*, and *Liquid Luck: The Good Fortune Handbook*. Yet writing this current book is awakening difficult feelings. As with many traumas, when surviving a loved one's suicide, the pain can eventually be healed and a good life can be led, but echoes of the pain never entirely vanish. I think that you will find that, though the subject is sometimes sad, there is much humor, heart, and healing within this book. And if I am successful, you will have a greatly expanded view of the power of the heart, the amount of help that is available to us from the world of spirit, and you will be inspired by the loving grandness that awaits us on the other side.

In a recent eighteen-month period I was in the circle of three more suicides. The first person was my wife's sister who had suffered from an intractable illness for decades. The second person was a woman who was in my opinion one of the best healers on the planet but suffered from a traumatic childhood and manic depression. The third person was my wife's boss, who left behind a wife and two young children. I have also experienced the death of my father, mother, and my dear brother John in these ensuing years. My perspective on death since my brother Pete's suicide has changed so much that I was able to handle all these losses in a strong, centered, and open-hearted fashion and return to joyful living much more quickly.

There is often a sense of uncertainty about what to do or how to be helpful to persons who are grieving a suicide. This can cause us to withdraw from them, under the guise that we want to respect their privacy, at the time they actually need us the most. What is one to do to be helpful? Deborah Greene lost her father, Lowell Herman, to suicide on April 20, 2015. She is a devoted advocate on issues of mental illness and suicide prevention/awareness. She blogs at *Reflecting Out Loud*. I am including a letter from her blog here to show just how much simple acts of kindness and connection can help with the shock of discovering that someone we loved has left by suicide. Here is what Deborah wrote:

My Dad Committed Suicide

"No matter how many times my mind takes me back to that horrible life altering moment, it is not all darkness; because you reached out to help."

> Dear Strangers,
> I remember you. Ten months ago, when my cell phone rang with news of my father's suicide, you were walking into Whole Foods,

prepared to go about your food shopping, just as I had done only minutes before.

But I had already abandoned my cart full of groceries and I stood in the entryway of the store. My brother was on the other end of the line. He was telling me my father was dead, that he had taken his own life early that morning and through his own sobs, I remember my brother kept saying, "I'm sorry Deborah, I'm so sorry." I can't imagine how it must have felt for him to make that call.

And as we hung up the phone, I started to cry and scream as my whole body trembled. This just couldn't be true. It couldn't be happening. Only moments before I was filling my cart with groceries, going about my errands on a normal Monday morning. Only moments before my life felt intact. Overwhelmed with emotions, I fell to the floor, my knees buckling under the weight of what I had just learned. And you, kind strangers, you were there.

You could have kept on walking, ignoring my cries, but you didn't. You could have simply stopped and stared at my primal display of pain, but you didn't. No, instead you surrounded me as I yelled through my sobs, "My father killed himself. He killed himself. He's dead." And the question that has plagued me since that moment came to my lips in a scream: "Why?" I must have asked it over and over and over again. I remember in that haze of emotions, one of you asked for my phone and asked who you should call. What was my password? You needed my husband's name as you searched through my contacts. I remember I could hear your words as you tried to reach my husband for me, leaving an urgent message for him to call me. I recall hearing you discuss among yourselves who would drive me home in my car and who would follow that person to bring them back to the store. You didn't even know one another, but it didn't seem to matter. You encountered me, a stranger, in the worst moment of my life and you coalesced around me with common purpose — to help. I remember one of you asking if you could pray for me and for *my father. I must have said yes, and now when I recall that Christian prayer being offered up to Jesus for my Jewish father and me, it still both brings tears to my eyes and makes me smile.*

In my fog, I told you that I had a friend, Pam, who worked at Whole Foods and one of you went in search of her. Thankfully, she was there that morning and you brought her to me. I remember the relief I felt at seeing her face, familiar and warm. She took me to the back, comforting and caring for me until my husband could get to me. And I even recall as I sat with her, one of you sent back a gift card to Whole Foods; though you didn't know me, you wanted to offer a little something to let me know that you would be thinking of me and holding me and my family in your thoughts and prayers. That gift card helped to feed my family, when the idea of cooking was so far beyond my emotional reach.

I never saw you after that. But I know this to be true: If it were not for all of you, I might have simply gotten in the car and tried to drive myself home. I wasn't thinking straight, if I was thinking at all. If it were not for you, I don't know what I would've done in those first raw moments of overwhelming shock, anguish, and grief. But I thank God every day I didn't have to find out. Your kindness, your compassion, your willingness to help a stranger in need have stayed with me until this day. And no matter how many times my mind takes me back to that horrible life altering moment, it is not all darkness. Because you reached out to help, you offered a ray of light in the bleakest moment I've ever endured. You may not remember it. You may not remember me. But I will never, ever forget you. And though you may never know it, I give thanks for your presence and humanity each and every day.

Part One

BROTHERS FOREVER

DEPARTURE

My first memories of Pete were formed just after we moved to a New Jersey suburb. During their house hunting, my folks feared that they would not find a decent place to raise their family of seven. Rural Midwest Catholic values strained to fit this new environment. And my parent's modest savings meant little so close to that pounding heart of commerce, New York City. They felt fortunate to find a large old colonial in bad repair in a stable neighborhood with maples and oaks overhanging the streets. I was five years old and Pete was thirteen when we moved in.

Our resettlement omens were not good. We arrived in the fall of 1954 just hours before the full force of Hurricane Carol came roaring through. I peered into the black cavern of the huge Mayflower van, eye-level to the floor of the truck, anxiously waiting for my bicycle to resurrect itself, as the wind began to howl. Strong men were struggling, tacking left and right toward the front door with the mattresses they were carrying. Once we were inside with our possessions, the power went off and we spent the first day and night listening to oaks crack and crash around our new neighborhood. Pete comforted me while my folks set up a base camp within the house.

Over the years, we worked hard to put the charm back into that old house. I can still remember that first winter, working in yeasty humidity, steaming off a mile of worn, dark maroon damask wallpaper, my knuckles scraping the rough plaster underneath. It felt five-year-old great to peel off a really long piece, intact, from ten-foot-high walls. As fresh mint-greens, whites, and creams transformed the walls, and light apricot carpeting went down, we knew we would win the struggle.

The woozy smell of wood-stripper and its bite on the skin accompanied restoration of the stairs and banister. As the weather warmed a bit, we attacked the outside. The fragrances of leaf mold, fifty years ancient, and of fresh-cut wood danced together deep into my lungs as we trimmed back towering rhododendrons that hid the leaded windows in front of the house.

Pete and I worked side by side around this house. He showed me how to make a game out of picking up vast quantities of shattered glass that rose shimmering to the surface each spring in the back yard. By the time I was ten, those shards had become as rare as treasure. Pete showed me how to sow seed evenly and care for the fragile lawn until it thrived. Our house finally became a beautiful home. We had learned the value of work and enjoyed its results.

My parents had four boys, each four years apart, followed by my sister two years later. Pete was the second child and I the last boy. All of us were born in the snowy season, which in Wisconsin lasts half the year. We moved to the East Coast when my dad started climbing his corporate ladder. Both my parents were very busy during that time, so Pete took up the slack and often served as my mother, father, friend, and mentor. In the flow of time, I have had the privilege of returning each of these blessings to him.

Eight years older, he volunteered to diaper me as an infant, play with me when I was a toddler, and counsel me on playground tactics as I started school. I don't remember him wasting time or expecting someone else to come up with his entertainment. He enjoyed competition and abhorred poor sportsmanship. I never saw him angry at our parents. He seemed always to be performing "up to specs." Perhaps he missed part of his own childhood—the chance to be at times weak, scared, petulant, or selfish. To me, he has been a magical interplay of dark and light, and always the adult.

During my childhood and his adolescence, Pete set an example of excellent appearance: dressing cool, building his body to perfection, and keeping his car gleaming. He would work summers, sunup to sundown, cutting lawns. Then he would come home, lift weights, shower, dress, and go out in his shiny chariot. He had many different automobiles as a teenager, mostly convertibles—all fast ones with perfect paint, paid for with his own money. These cars granted freedom, embodied power, and promised adventure—things he cherished at a soul level then and throughout his life.

The schools in our town had a reputation for excellence. Yet Pete cared little about school. When I was a kid, I had the sense that the classroom was a prison for him, as it was for me. His bright intellect was creative, playful, and Socratic. And he liked to see immediate results from his actions. He was a doer, and any knowledge had to pass the test of practicality. He sought fairness for everyone. Later, Pete confessed that he had found school agonizingly slow, dulling, senseless, and arbitrary in its application of rules. He may have been what is now called attention-deficit disordered: very restless when information is coming in too slowly and anxious when stimulation is coming in too fast.

What I most admired about Pete as I was growing up and what I still treasure is that he treated all life forms (human, animal, or plant) with an intelligent, quiet kindness and respect. And he did so in a very manly way. Adults, peers, and children all responded to him with a great attraction. So he set an example which seemed to me both worthy and reachable. If I could follow it, I felt guaranteed to become a good man, well-liked and successful. Of all my hand-me-downs, his were the best. Yet they also contained a dangerous shadow.

As he disappeared into college, his clothing remained as a tangible echo. His muscle shirts were stretched large at the biceps; I worked hard to have them fit my younger arms tightly. After Pete went away, I took over some of his chores, but each in our family missed his spark of bright, loving power.

Many years later, I learned that he had not wanted to go to college. He yearned instead to open a pool parlor and wanted my folks to use his college money to back him. He was eager to get on with life, to be where the action was and build something new and vibrant. But my folks stood firm. My Dad had been the first in his family to complete college. That education had taken him from farming to the vice-presidency of a printing company, launching him into the larger world. He was committed to providing a similar opportunity to each of his five children.

Pete, knuckling under to my folks' wisdom or fear, tried my Dad's alma mater, Lawrence College, in Wisconsin. Freshmen had to live on campus and could have no car. Pete suffered through a first year's snows, feeling isolated and restricted. He left college in the spring.

He escaped by joining the Army, presenting his enlistment as a surprise and expecting everyone to be happy for him. But Vietnam was heating up, and we worried that he would be killed. My folks also felt that he was wasting his talents. I think Pete felt that, if he could not follow my folks' wishes for him, he should pay his own way to follow his own dream.

I can remember a series of phone calls during this time, after which my folks seemed weakened, muted, and sad. They were torn between a deep commitment to give each of their children full freedom and a dread that Pete was digging his hole deeper. I know, however, that there was no "You are not making us proud" pressure. Rather, love and support were extended along with unheeded advice.

I was amazed at Pete's rebellion—his refusal to continue college. This stand did not fit my image of him. Our shining star further transformed into the black sheep when he announced that he was dropping the Church and planning to marry a non-Catholic. I watched this hushed family drama with great interest, sensing that someday I too might need to rebel. It was encouraging to see love hold but frightening to see the pain that this revolt caused. I attempted to ease family pain by trying to become as perfect as he used to be.

On a cloudy, quiet summer's day, two long years after he left us, Pete glided back home in a red Corvair convertible that purred perfectly at idle. He got out of the car and stood tall in dress uniform. He sported medals for marksmanship and a fiancée at his side. That fall their wedding took place in swirling gold leaves and bright sunshine. Then he disappeared again. He finished his tour working in Army intelligence.

Pete found me later, when I needed rescue. I was being kicked out of a monastery school at fifteen years of age—angry, lonely, frightened, and disillusioned. The headmasters felt that I wasn't monk material, being too challenging of authority. They were right. But from the time of fifth grade I had fiercely wanted to become a priest. I had a deep love of God and wanted to help people. At the moment my dream failed, I could conceive of no other life.

Pete came, got me, and took me to his world. It was a tiny, cinder block house in Utica, New York. The yard looked worn in late winter. The surrounding snow was dirty gray. But his house sparkled white. He seemed very pleased to see me. Pete was twenty-three years old at that time.

He had two German Shepherds, one pure white and one dark, that he had trained with a whisper. They guarded his two-year-old son silently, like library lions. Pete's wife and son were clearly devoted to him. My first night there, in the glow and the smell of the kerosene heater in his basement guest room, I felt safe for the first time in two seasons and slept peacefully. Before bed, he had joked that now the family had two black sheep. I was comforted that he had paved the way. If I was not a failure in his eyes, perhaps I could really face myself and go on.

I followed him around for a few days, as he made his way between two jobs: cigarette-machine route salesman and night clerk at a motel. He worked hard, and I was impressed with the caring and intelligence he applied to his work. Later, still in Utica, he would work three eight-hour-a-day jobs at the same time, after a try at establishing his own business had failed. He survived on almost no sleep for months as he strived to get back on sound financial footing. He bravely presented this period as an experiment in micro-sleep, where he learned to catch a moment of slumber every time he blinked his eyes.

Despite the pressure Pete was under as I came out of the seminary, he was eager to help me and shared all that he had. I wanted to try snowmobiling. He took me out, even though it was a windy twenty-below zero, and the locks were frozen on his car. Laughing together, we decided to end the adventure before we actually rode, when the reality of the cold sunk into our flesh. I felt close to him and very loved.

I stayed two weeks with Pete, and then it was time to go back to my parents. We stood by each other, bracing against the wind, at the small run-down train station, not saying much until we saw the engine's light. Then we exchanged smiles and a brief hug. When he put me on the train I was in much better shape than when he had picked me up.

Over the next twenty-five years we saw each other mostly during holidays when the whole family gathered. He seemed reserved during these visits—cordial but somehow uncomfortable. On the rare occasions when I visited with him privately, he would loosen up as we nestled under afghans at opposite ends of a sofa and share his deeper thoughts as we talked into the night. As I grew into adulthood, we bonded as brothers and friends. Still, he remained mostly a mystery.

After I married and moved down South, there were no private visits for many years. During family gatherings, I could sense his growing frustration over his own inability to capture the American Dream. Yet he was genuinely happy to hear of the blessings that others in our family were enjoying.

During these two decades, Pete's life didn't go well. Financial pressures were constant. It seemed that every job he tried resulted in failure. And he tried many occupations, usually in sales, sometimes in services—always hoping for the big score. When he sold cars, then motor homes, copiers, and real estate, he would be out of rhythm, hitting recessions and gas crunches at the wrong times. Sometimes people took advantage of his good nature. In other situations, he would lose confidence and sell himself short.

His marriage may have been impulsive; I am not sure. Over the years, the stress of finances and his deepening depression took a heavy toll on it, and the marriage ceased to bring him joy. His son was one bright source of love and hope. Yet even in that relationship there was tension.

The son's personality and interests were different from his father's in almost every way. For example, his son had no interest in cars, and still doesn't own one to this day. Pete did encourage his child to get an education, preferably in a trade that guaranteed a good living, such as plumbing. No doubt Pete felt his own unprepared path was a mistake. His son's path was to major in languages in college. Pete, despite subsistence-level income and his belief that language study was impractical, paid his son's way fully through college, including a master's program. He did so by running up massive credit card debt, and eventually he was forced to declare bankruptcy.

Pete's pain and bitterness began to surface more strongly, despite his efforts to shield us from it. He attended fewer family functions, but we could count on seeing him at weddings and funerals and at Christmas time. We were a family of high achievers, executives, and professionals. All his siblings had earned graduate degrees. It was obviously hard for him to listen to our conversations of success, not so much from jealousy, as from his sense of isolation—that his life experience had little in common with ours due to what he felt were his own failings. He was slipping away.

I suspect that our family is genetically prone to depression. My own despondency during college got me into psychotherapy. After therapy, my despair was controlled but still surfaced with unwanted regularity until it waned in my late thirties. My depression occurred in the context of outward abundance and loving friendships. When I was depressed, joy was suffocated by a great, dark, soul-quaking heaviness. I can only wonder at what that weight must have felt like for Pete, lacking the support of material and relationship success.

When Pete was in his mid-thirties, a kid in a speeding Cadillac ran a stop sign and smashed into the driver's side of his car. Pete was severely injured. He sustained a crushed left arm (he was left-handed) and a broken left thigh. We now had something traumatic in common.

When I was twenty-one, I had broken my left thigh in a motorcycle wreck and had spent nearly a year in the hospital. I had rods drilled through my leg without anesthesia, was strung up in traction for four months, and then was confined to a body cast. Roaches crawled in and out of my cast in the inner-city hospital. The immobility was maddening for me, as I had always been active as a swimmer and a runner. I was panicky and tearful often during my recovery.

When I heard the news of Pete's accident, I vomited, knowing what was ahead of him. When I saw him in the hospital, he appeared shaken but stoic. He was gracious to his guests and glad to see me. Pete's recovery was slow and incomplete. Some of his handsomeness and physical strength were taken from him; and physical pain became his constant companion.

Pete re-entered my life when he divorced and moved to the Carolina coast, within six hours of my home in the mountains of North Carolina. The warm climate allowed much outdoors time. He had always loved the ocean and the sun, and now he tanned darkly.

My wife and I had purchased a ridge-top ranch with a 360-degree view of the Smoky Mountains and the Blue Ridge and eight acres of rolling land. We had refurbished it lovingly and had added daffodils, roses, and all manner of grapes, berries, and fruit trees, as well as a big vegetable garden. At the beginning, we went overboard with the joy of country life and planted two acres of corn by hand. Needless to say, we had enough corn for years and the crows had an absolute feast. Our crows consider us their friends for life and appear immediately when we go outside even to get the mail, on the off chance that I'm ready to repeat the great corn experiment!

A few months after he moved to the coast, Pete came to visit with his new girlfriend. I couldn't believe the difference. He seemed relaxed, playful, and happy. He enjoyed the beauty of our mountain home, taking long walks through the woods hand-in-hand with his new life mate.

I remember one fabulous day when we flew a giant kite, chasing it to and fro in our pasture, then resting in the sun. Later we devoured a sumptuous cookout, enjoyed the twilight, then the stars, and finally moved inside. That evening, he surprised me by springing up to dance with his girlfriend to the Beach Boys music playing on the stereo. My wife and I joined in, laughing and dancing. There was no self-consciousness, only celebration of life.

I was hopeful that, with his girlfriend's obvious support and his better mood, Pete's luck would change. But his lack of work success continued through many new attempts at earning a living. The pattern was very puzzling. He was brilliant, hardworking, honest, personable, and fair. He was experienced in real estate, construction, and many different types of sales. The only drawbacks I could see were his slightly crippled left hand and leg and his lack of a college degree.

During job interviews, he tried to hide his growing insecurity. For the few days before an interview, you could see him building up his cheerfulness and confidence, making an effort to turn his nervousness into energy and excitement. After practicing for the session, he dressed perfectly, shoes shined to a military gleam, and went to slay the dragon. But within himself, Pete was developing a theory that he was somehow cursed and that any project he might be part of would also be cursed. Although he was a great poker player and could bluff with the best, his theory may have been telegraphed unconsciously to prospective employers, causing them to shun him.

After a few years, he began to realize that the woman with whom he was living was becoming tired of his work failures and his despair. She couldn't stand to see the man she loved, who seemed a better man than any other she had met, in so much constant pain. They separated. He accepted my offer to come to live in my town.

We set up an apartment for him in the upstairs of the old home where I had my psychology practice. It was humble surroundings, but he seemed genuinely glad to stay there. He put his bed, refrigerator, microwave, and a long table in one room. Dishes were washed in the bathroom sink. In the other room, he built shelves out of cinder block and scrap wood to hold his books. He was an avid reader. A sofa, TV, and his treasured miniature classic car collection completed the decor.

He kept the place immaculate and planted many flowers around the grounds. I would arrive at work to find him bent over and shirtless, glistening in the early southern sun, tending the plants. He would stiffly straighten with a smile. Filled with affection for him, I would try to keep my eyes from lingering too long on the scars which deformed his arm.

I was delighted and honored. I was having a chance to spend extended time with my older brother for whom I had the deepest respect. I went upstairs to his apartment whenever I had a break in work. He would greet me with his gentle smile and fresh orange juice, pretzels, or pizza, depending upon the hour. We would sharpen our intellects together, then talk from the heart. His thinking was deep and probing, and his interests ranged widely.

One of our mutual interests was the work of Robert Monroe. We both had read *Journeys Out of the Body*[1]. Mr. Monroe was a businessman who had experiences in which he felt his consciousness float away from his body. He traveled freely in this non-physical state. The book excited us because Pete and I had both enjoyed such experiences in childhood. Mine often began when I would awaken enough within a dream to be conscious of what was going on.

I would find myself, filled with excitement, rocketing down a big hill on my bike. Slowly and silently, the handlebars would separate and begin to rise, with me holding on, as the bike dropped beneath on its path downhill. At that point I would begin to have control within the dream. I'd let go of the handlebars and feel as if I were flying low over the treetops with great freedom and joy. I could cruise the town's streets, just above the telephone wires, and land at friends' houses or favorite places in the woods. Then I would fly home, feeling a jarring sensation as I re-entered my body on the bed. For days after one of these experiences, I would be filled with energy and a sense of well-being.

Many people report having some type of out-of-body experience (OBE) spontaneously a few times in their lives, particularly as children. Mr. Monroe had them nightly as an adult and had learned to induce and control them at will. Research of the OBE phenomenon has since been undertaken by others, including Keith Haray, Ph.D., and Pamela Weintraub at Duke University and the Institute for Advanced Psychology in Los Angeles.

When Pete came to live with me, he brought Monroe's sequel, *Far Journeys*[2]. It renewed my interest in this area, which had been quiescent since graduate school.

I had experienced a vivid OBE when I was twenty-one during my motorcycle accident. When the car hit me, I felt enormous pain that awed me with its totality. It had a terrible beauty, much like that of an atomic blast. It overwhelmed the senses and entranced my consciousness. This moment of pain was followed by complete surprise at finding myself floating peacefully and completely pain-free, about ten feet above my body. I looked down with complete unconcern at my body in spasms in the street and the motorcycle strewn nearby. Looking back in the direction from which I had been traveling, I could see three lanes of traffic fast approaching. I found it an interesting show and was detached from what would happen when the traffic arrived. My perception of the physical world was crystal clear; my thought patterns were fully cogent and logical. There was no doubt that this was real and not just some biochemically-induced hallucination after trauma.

Then I felt what seemed to be an angelic presence because it was emanating unconditional love. Its will was that I return to my body. I resisted, telepathically argued, and lost. As I re-entered my body, the pain was no longer beautiful; rather, it was agony tainted with severe worry about how damaged I was and the hurt that was sure to follow. Then I blacked out and continued to go in and out of consciousness as the paramedics did their caring work and I was transported to the hospital. I remember screaming some, too.

During my hospital stay and for a few years after that, I attempted to consciously induce OBEs with some limited success. I then dropped my experiments in the fullness of marriage and parenting. OBEs have much in common with near-death experiences. Both are often transformative and leave the person knowing—not just believing—that there will be survival after the death of the physical body.

While he lived with us, Pete challenged me to take carefully considered risks in business. For me, money had always been tied to hours of effort—throwing papers, cutting lawns, painting houses, and, later, working as a psychotherapist. He had a different perspective. As a salesman, he could put in countless hours with no pay-back, and at other times be at the right place or take the right gamble and make money quickly and easily.

Although Pete encouraged me to reach for my dreams and take risks, my witnessing his life situation paradoxically made me more fearful in some ways. I did take greater risks in terms of trying new things and risking small amounts of money, but I became more cautious of anything that could leave me jobless.

In many aspects of life, Pete was my mentor during this period. He taught me billiards. Playing pool, I entered into a space with him where competition was light and playful and both of us celebrated a good shot regardless of who made it. I'd leave the pool hall feeling centered and peaceful. He taught me how to enjoy the simplest things of life with more patience and gracefulness. He celebrated my gardening successes and complimented me on anything that I did well. He reminded me of my blessings and confronted me whenever I was being less than honest with myself or was blocked by fear. Yet, the most precious offering he gave me during this time was to let me help him.

So, Pete's living with me was a great gift. I had looked forward to getting to know my brother and ended up in deep friendship with him, finding myself talking more frankly about some things with him than I ever had with anyone else. It felt reassuring and connected just to be with him. Much was discussed and re-experienced about our childhoods—both the commonalities and the differences. Vietnam and the peace movement had taken place between us, and the culture had changed dramatically during the eight years that separated our travels through adolescence and into adulthood.

When he first came to live with me, I don't think he had much regard for clinical psychology as a profession, but he did respect the effort it had taken me to get there. With his own feeling about school, he admired me for sticking it out through four years of college then five years of graduate school, studying subjects such as human personality, abnormal psychology, neurophysiology, research design, and psychotherapy.

Pete admired me for all my efforts and accomplishments, but his nature was to respect workers who produced something more tangible than I had to show for my work. He tried to understand my profession, however, and eventually appreciated the difficulties and satisfactions involved in the therapist role. This appreciation pleased me greatly, as his respect was important to me. His probing questions helped me sort out the wheat from the chaff delivered to me in all that training. He made me more aware of the importance of mundane practicalities in my patients' lives—how busyness, tiredness, financial strain, and responsibilities hampered one's quest for self-understanding and change.

Pete would particularly challenge any assumption he felt was too New Age or too liberal. He did not necessarily disagree with these philosophies but was on guard against any thinking that he considered illogical, "mushy headed," or not consistent with real-world experience. He would get almost angry when he felt people were using the word "love" too frivolously.

Despite all the richness I felt from his presence, he felt that he was mooching off me by paying no rent. Employment for middle-aged white males was drying up as the country headed toward its long late-80s recession. His job search went no better in my area. And he was running out of money.

About two years after he had moved in with us, it became apparent how depressed and anxious he was. He seldom slept peacefully. Weekends during which he avoided all human contact were increasing. Pete refused therapy and medications despite much urging. He acknowledged their value for others but didn't see how they could help him. He felt that without a mate and without work, his life was truly depressing. And if anything made him content in the face of that, it could only do so at the expense of having him be out of touch with grim reality.

This stance was extremely frustrating for me, as I believed that psychotherapy and medications might help him. I repeatedly related to him all kinds of counseling success stories and went over the intricacies of how antidepressants work, trying to show him how they did not drug away selfhood, consciousness, or willpower. We replayed versions of the same conversation:

He would respond, "Well, how would talking to someone help me? What I need is a job."

I would propose, "Therapy could give you support, and let you vent your feelings instead of keeping them inside. It might even generate some new options you haven't thought of."

"I don't want to be humored or pitied. And all I do is think of options day and night. I have talked to you guys, friends, and job counselors about this over and over. Do you really think I could have missed anything that really would make a difference?"

"Why not try anyway? What have you got to lose?"

"How about the last of my self-respect and money!"

"Well then, how about trying medications? They may help you to sleep better and help with the pain. You are depressed. That impairs your concentration, creativity, and energy. You need to be at your best when you look for work. Medication can help with that."

"Of course I'm depressed. I would have to be crazy not to be depressed. I don't have the money to go to doctors and besides I just don't feel medication will help me get a job. Having that on my record might even keep me from getting a job and health insurance later."

If I pressed on, the final retort would be: "I tried therapy a long time ago. The shrink was well-meaning and skillful but it didn't help. Can we please just drop it?"

And so I would drop it with a final entreaty: "Please think about it."

One thing Pete did try was meditation. Through my seminary experience with centering prayer and, later, studies of an Egyptian system of focused concentration[3] and practice of Buddhist meditation, I could relax and enter a peaceful state where creativity was enhanced and options became apparent. I could then return energized and more calmly implement positive changes in my life. I felt this skill could help Pete. But regardless of the meditation system he tried, he would get restless instead of relaxed. I think that he was holding too much emotion to let his defenses down. He got most of his relief through long walks following the train tracks out of town and into the woods.

To appreciate Pete's view on life and on his chances for happiness, you need to understand the great importance he put on productivity and the string of frustrations he experienced in this area. From his point of view, his thirty-year work history was a string of disasters. Here are just a few examples. He gradually added one cigarette machine after another to his route in Utica. When he owned about twenty machines, he found them all smashed in one night. He had entered into Mafia territory without knowing it.

Desperate for quick money, he then purchased a race horse. The bottom fell out of a trailer as he was transporting it to its first race, killing the horse instantly. Large real estate deals he had worked on for years were finally consummated, only to have him cut out of the commissions by politicians who took bribes. He worked cleaning carpets—often on his knees, scraping gum off of barroom floors after closing time, until his damaged arm and leg could stand it no longer.

His last business before moving in with me was a used furniture business. It struggled through its first year, began to show promise, then collapsed when a fire forced him to move to a new location, undercapitalized.

It is hard to comprehend his efforts each time to start over in some new business, scraping up funds through menial jobs that barely allowed for food and rent. No employer would hire him at a salary above minimum wage; the only other offers he had were straight commission jobs that offered no benefits.

It was eerie how far and long his bad luck, if that was what it was, seemed to extend. When he came to live with me, the first job he tried involved selling computerized pay telephones. I bought his first one and installed it at a local golf course. It got struck by lightning the very first day, one day before the insurance on it took effect. He wouldn't have let me invest unless he was certain that I would enjoy a nice secure return, and now he felt guilty that I was out three thousand bucks. This weirdness was typical of what happened when Pete accepted help from someone.

Pete did nothing that I could see to directly sabotage his own efforts. He worked long and hard for thirty-five years, and his luck just continued to be amazingly bad. Picture keeping up your confidence in that situation and pulling deep from the gut to try once again. Now imagine doing it while burying most of the bitterness deep within yourself.

He felt that he could not get and keep a girlfriend until he had money. I doubt that he ever went Dutch on a date in his life. Perhaps his hopelessness was infectious; after a year of his living with me, I saw no option which he was willing to take that had a good chance of success. No option except that he find a job at a living wage.

As his job efforts in my small rural town reached a dead end, he began to mention suicide as his only way out. He was concerned that, if he lived much longer, his debts would finally wipe out all his life insurance, which was his only way to leave something for his son. He did not want to be a financial burden to anyone, particularly our folks, who were approaching eighty. He did not qualify for disability, yet he was unable to find health insurance because of his injuries.

He resisted going back to college, feeling that his employability would be very low when he graduated as a fifty-four-year-old white male with his physical limitations. He felt he couldn't risk other peoples' money on such a long shot. He looked into trade schools, but most programs involved manual strength and dexterity he no longer had, all cost money, and none guaranteed work.

Pete's thoughts of suicide ran to creative ways which would not be detectible, so that life insurance benefits would not be jeopardized. He considered hanging himself while standing on a block of dry ice in the woods so that it would look like someone else hanged him once the ice melted. I would counter that if he were far enough from people for this to work, he might never be found.

He then speculated that he could wait at a rest stop with a gun. When another car stopped, he could tie a string between the gun and the car bumper and run a short distance into the woods. As the car pulled away, the gun would fire. After the shot, the string would carry the weapon away and the string would wear out miles up the road, letting the gun tumble into the brush along the side of the road. It would look like murder, not suicide.

I took these dark fantasies seriously and yet understood that in the face of the intolerable current pain, he needed to have hope that there was an eventual way out of struggle. Most times he said these things in a way that allowed us to think he was just letting off steam. I would try to assure him of his value and help him generate some hope. Much of what they taught me in school—that suicidal thoughts were often anger turned inward; to help the person see past the current pain and realize that life continually changed; to encourage support systems and action to reduce stress and dissatisfaction—these were all shadowed by the knowledge that depression could be lethal.

The examples of suicide we were given in school were too easy: the teenager whose life would probably improve if he just hung on for six months, the terminally ill woman who most felt had a right to go, the elderly man who had lived a full life and wanted to join his departed spouse of sixty years. The teachers never mentioned what to do about the middle-aged adult who felt emptiness and despair despite support of loved ones, or was buckling under the weight of decades of joblessness.

Pete wasn't committable to a mental hospital against his will. By law, he would have to be an immediate danger to himself or others. His suicide plans were only a remote eventual possibility. Even if he had been committed, under the present state system he would be out in a few days, more depressed and humiliated than before. More lengthy private psychiatric hospitalization might have provided adequate care.

But that cost about $20,000 per month. Without insurance this route was impossible, given that he could not bring himself to burden his family with such an expense.

After two years of living with me, he decided to try to make a life in Las Vegas. He had some possible friend-of-a-friend contacts there. And the Las Vegas area was booming. His body was hurting nearly all the time in the humid Carolina mountain climate from his old car accident, and he felt that the desert heat might help with his arthritis. I remembered that he had joked when he came to live with me two years before that he would never commit suicide in my town, as it might damage my professional standing in the community. I worried that this last reason might be his strongest motivation for leaving. But I did not ask him point-blank about it, feeling that there was nothing positive to be said that hadn't been repeated many times. All of us who had come to know him in my town conveyed to him how much we treasured him. We made it clear that he would be welcomed joyfully, if he ever decided to return.

As Pete left for Las Vegas, I was greatly concerned that he would continue to hurt, but also hoped that things would be different for him there. I knew he had the potential to be an amazing worker if given a chance. He knew the gambling and hotel businesses well and would make an excellent personnel, hospitality, or gaming employee. He was ready to take a minimum wage job to start. But he was already so tired and beaten down.

With all his possessions packed into his car—now a worn, black, hand-me-down Ford sedan—he headed out after nervous smiles and heart-welling hugs were exchanged. Just as when he had left me at our parents' home to conquer life with his bride, once again swirling leaves suggested an ending of our close communion. This time we parted as men, knowing that men often hold wounds deep within the heart.

I sorely missed the delight of our daily contact. His quiet example and gentle love had nurtured my soul. But I was also relieved by his leaving. His pain, close at hand, was sharp and at the same time stiflingly heavy. It had been so hard to see him force himself up for each new job interview, put on the impeccable suit, pretend to be a winner, come home with hopes, and wait for the call to work that never came.

The initial news from Las Vegas was good. He liked desert living. It did help his arthritis. He let my folks "supplement his income," and he found a pleasant apartment with a pool. He was determined to relax and make a fresh start.

Time passed slowly for him, however. He continued to look for work vigorously, but his job hunting yielded nothing but growing disappointment. He discovered that in Las Vegas even convenience store clerks were credit-checked, and his past bankruptcy eliminated him from consideration.

I went to visit him in springtime. He seemed so pleased to see me and showed me the town. His apartment was bare, save a few pillows, a small TV, and a bed. He said he liked it that way. We took long walks with me gawking at the neon reds, blues, and greens dancing on hundred-foot signs. The contrast with country life couldn't have been more dramatic. He watched and advised as I gambled some, and we had many good laughs over my neophyte errors. Again I felt protected by him. It was wonderful to see him again—to remember that he was real.

Although not eagerly, Pete talked a little about his situation. He desperately wanted things to work out. I sensed that he was developing a timetable for his effort, with a deadline past which he would not go. Again the concern was that he would need more money from others, and he couldn't stand to take it. As I left, I felt his need for me and his isolation, although he bravely smiled. It was very hard to go.

As summer approached, the news worsened. When I called and pried it out of him, all he reported was a series of back-breaking straws. For example, he had landed a construction job on Friday. On Sunday he read in the newspaper that his new company was accused of unfair hiring. When he reported for work on Monday, they told him "Sorry."

They had to hire minorities to get the press off their backs and could not use him at that time.

Soon after this incident, he called me to borrow five hundred dollars. He wanted to get his car running so he could date a girl who had asked him out. He sounded upbeat and eager for her company. I sent the money to him. She stood him up three times before he gave up on her. My family, friends, and the therapists I knew could give me no alternatives to present to him, aside from what he had already tried or what he had refused to try.

About a week after his son received his master's degree, Pete called me on a Thursday. I wasn't home, and he told my wife it was not important. When I got home, she told me she was concerned. I called him, and we talked for an hour. I asked him if he needed help for car insurance, due the next day. He said he was going to let it lapse; he would renew it if he found work. He was friendly and warm, but kind of quiet. I promised to come out and see him again soon.

The following Monday night at about seven o'clock, I was home with my daughter watching TV when the phone rang.

"This is the Las Vegas police. Are you Joseph Gallenberger?"

"Yes."

"Your brother Pete is dead. It appears he committed suicide. Can we ask you some questions?"

"Who are you? Give me your number and I'll call you back."

"Certainly."

I ran upstairs, mind numb and heart racing. Maybe it was a creditor's scheme to track Pete down. Shaking, I dialed twice. I did not get through. I was more hopeful that this was a hoax. I dialed a third time carefully.

"Las Vegas police."

Oh, God. I am caught.

"Your brother shot himself with a thirty-eight in the right temple. It was a clean wound. I never have seen someone leave his apartment so clean. He left a note saying that he sold his car Friday and prepaid funeral expenses. He also sent a note to the funeral home telling them to pick him up at his address. He requested cremation and no funeral services. We were called to investigate. Your business card was found with instructions to call you. He has shipped all his belongings to your address. This is so considerate. You know most people who commit suicide in Las Vegas leave no identification and it's so hard to trace them. Did you know if he was depressed?"

"Yes, he was depressed."

"That's all we need to ask. Let us know who will be coming in to deal with his apartment. All that is left is his bed. He has cleaned out all the kitchen cabinets and refrigerator. He even took the sheets off the bed, put plastic down, and wrapped his head in a towel so as to not leave a mess."

I had to stop these inane comments about cleanliness. I had to stop the whole thing. I thanked him, asked if I could call him if I had questions, and hung up.

My six-year-old daughter Sarah, downstairs watching TV, was especially close to Pete. I started downstairs and reversed direction. I couldn't face her yet. I dialed my parents, fearing that they would hate me forever for telling them this news. My mother dropped the phone, wailing in grief. My father was stunned to silence. I shared what I knew and told him to go to Mother, that I would call the others and then call him back. I hung up and wept.

I called a neighbor who babysits Sarah; she agreed to come over. I told my daughter. She yelled, "No, That can't be! No, No, No!" and "Why, Why, but Why?" and we rocked each other and wept. My neighbor arrived. She held us both. Then she took Sarah while I went back upstairs. I called my brothers and sister, Pete's girlfriend, and his ex-wife.

Pete's son, feeling a strong need to call his Dad and suspicious of all the busy signals, called my father and found out.

About two hours later, my wife came home, and I told her the news. Each telling slashed deep. Adrenaline still surging, we rushed to my office and searched his papers left in the basement—hoping for a letter or something. Midnight now, I called back my parents and brothers and plans were made. My eldest brother would go out, identify the body, and take care of things. I couldn't sleep and found myself at the computer, writing his eulogy. Nobody was going to mispronounce his name at the funeral or tell untruths about him.

My wife and I went through the next morning frantic and worn from too little sleep and too much stress. But that afternoon, while waiting to fly to my parents' home, we took a half-hour to meditate. A tremendous peace filled us both. There was no sense of contact with Pete, but more of an angelic consolation. The sunset flight was filled with beauty. Our serene mood lasted and spilled into peace for our family once we arrived.

Pete's son and I planned the services and what would be said, sitting under an oak in a park. I told him that I was never able to have a son and if he ever felt he needed a father . . . He said he felt that he had three fathers now, in me and my two living brothers.

He and I went to the local priest and for my parents' sake we negotiated a full Catholic service, despite the suicide and cremation. We won but at a cost; I will always remember the discomfort of trying to explain my brother to the priest who sat in judgment. It felt like a violation to share intimate details with this stranger. I recall that part of what I said was that Pete was loving to everyone and yet in the end would have been happy to see the whole world blow up. The priest showed his uncomprehending disapproval. I wondered—didn't he sometimes get that frustrated?

The day of the funeral I woke up feeling a low but rising terror—a monster slowly waking within my gut. My daughter picked up my foreboding and didn't want to go. I feared I might die from grief, going through Pete's funeral. At the service, I saw my family ripped by sorrow. My daughter, thinking that she would throw up, left the church for a while with my wife. They returned as I delivered the eulogy.

A community of well-wishers waited in the back of the church, ready to console us. We didn't even register that they were there; we exited through the front of the church. We bled from the church to the gravesite, then we all went home—except my dear brother, Pete.

At my parents' home, we gathered with close friends. That afternoon we planted a Bradford Pear. It was Pete's favorite tree, and this specimen symbolized him well. It was not a sapling, but rather a strong, young, fifteen-foot-tall tree. It would have a delicate, lacy beauty in the spring when it bloomed with white flowers, but first it would meet fall wearing a strong ruddy crimson.

I saw my mother look out at the tree from the house later when daylight was waning. She said, "I can't wait to see it bloom next spring." Those words were sweet to hear, for I feared Pete's savage death would rob her of all determination to live. None of us there—mercifully—comprehended what it would take from us to live until spring.

PETE IS FREE OF TIME/SPACE
EULOGY FOR PETE

Dancing to Beach Boys
Flying the kite.
Lying in the sun here.
Enjoying a good joke.

Building book shelves
Out of block.
Pleasure and love
In simple living.

Fondness for cars
Kept shiny and bright.

DEPARTURE

Out-of-body excitement
Always aim for the light.

Roaming the mountains
On long limping walks.
Tending earth gently.
Harvesting sunflowers.

Teaching me Blackjack,
Poker, and people.
Always inviting me
To be my best.

Fiery curiosity
Old fashioned values.
Loving to family
Ever eager to serve.

Truest of friends.
Caring to strangers.
World's briefest letters.
Talks until two.

Sun-bronzed example
Of kindness, grace,
Endurance—
Yet couldn't keep pace.

Protecting us until now
From your great pain.
I love you, brother.
I need to see you again.

TURBULENCE

I didn't know that I could cry so much. And that tears would provide so little relief. Crying was just what I had to do. There was no control. The shock of suicide is total, yet shock only slightly buffers the pain. Denial steps in to help.

There is an intermixing of, "It can't be," that extends long past the burial. Then the questions start: Why didn't he go back to college when he first found it difficult to get a job? Why did he have such a hard life when he was such a good man? Why didn't he keep trying? Why didn't someone help? How did we fail him? How did he fail life?

Pete's death was inconceivable from many angles. I had a six-year-old daughter who was closely attached to him—what was she feeling? Neither could I imagine what his suicide meant from his parents' perspective. I dwelled upon this often in those first few weeks and many times since. I have never dared ask them for a detailed, blow-by-blow description of their most private experience. My parents' loss remains unknowable.

Because he had lived with me and confided in me, and because of my background as a psychologist, many looked to me for answers. I had no real answers. I was drowning in my own questions.

My parents couldn't believe that he had been that depressed. I didn't know if it was more consoling to tell them of his decades of pain, so that his act made some sense, or to tell them less and let them think he acted out of temporary desperation. I voted to tell the truth as I saw it to anyone who asked. Truth seemed more important now, and secrets more deadly.

Family members called each other daily during those first few weeks. We pulled together. Living connections were appreciated anew. In the immediate family, no anger was expressed toward Pete. In-laws and others wondered out loud, "How could he do this to his dear parents?" That comment deeply offended me, even as I was beginning to brood, "How could he do this to me?"

Mostly, I felt that I had grievously failed him in some unclear way. I strove to renounce this feeling, knowing that I had loved him powerfully, intelligently, and consistently; but my feelings of guilt persistently slinked back into my being, time and time again.

Everyone in our family was careful to avoid even the hint of blame toward another. We shared ways we felt responsible. We reviewed what we had done—offering a place to stay, lending money, drumming up business connections, and visiting Pete. We knew that we had loved him. Now we agonized as to whether we had loved him in the correct way—the way that was best for him. We tried to wash away the stains of guilt for each other. Each knew that the others' actions did not cause this terrible act. But the stains would not vanish, only fade. My guilt first focused on wondering whether, by being both a friend and an unofficial therapist to him, I had ruined my chances at being useful to him as either.

I regretted that I had not gone to visit him again that summer. We all regretted unintentional rejections of him toward the end of his life—little things, such as saying, "Can I call you back later?" and calling back within an hour; slight impatience with his urgent requests for us to follow up job leads, expressed as, "I'm doing the best that I can. The person I need to contact for you is out of town." These were little, normal incidents, insignificant amid the consistent regard and support the family had extended him for so long; yet we recalled them in our agony.

During the years of trying to help him, I had tried to prepare for his possible suicide by telling myself that every human being has the right to decide whether to live, that his pain was deep and decades long, that his options were few, and that he deserved peace if he couldn't have success. But such thoughts would always be followed by revolt. He just had to make it! He was such a good man that somehow he would break through this impasse. After all—he was my hero.

A deeper secret began to surface. I perhaps had known when Pete was going to end his life. In the last weeks before his death, I had been unconsciously releasing him. How else to explain that I had become very dense for a perceptive individual trained as a therapist. I had missed the mounting signs that he was planning his death. I evidently acted upon my thoughts of helplessness and hopelessness about him. I acted by omission. I didn't struggle any longer to brace him up for yet another try at life. Now he had actually done it. He had killed himself.

After working as best I knew how to save him, in the end I had let him go without interference. I had let him know that my love and respect for him would endure, whatever he decided. In letting him go, had I committed the most terrible sin of my life by giving up on him? Or had I performed the most loving act of my life by granting him his freedom to choose? This was the kind of three-in-the-morning dilemma that could drive a person crazy. The question came between moments of restless sleep because during the day I didn't have time for it. I was mostly supporting everyone else and running away from the full impact of my own pain.

When I concentrated on Pete and focused past the brutal questions, it seemed that my heart went continually to our relationship: Who was he? Who was I? How were we the same? How were we different? The feeling that both of us were failures clouded out more positive memories during this time. I turned to writing and poetry to express my heart. I tried vainly to get my bearings in this storm of grief. I seemed to swirl with the randomness of a leaf in this whirlwind of bitter feelings and desperate questions.

Why did my brother have such bad luck? Was it luck, did he fulfill his fate, or was it consistent self-sabotage by a rebellious nonconformist? These questions seemed pivotal. It was obvious that he would still be around if his fortunes were different. He deeply enjoyed conversation, nature, helping others, and building things. He wanted to stay alive to experience all the wonders of this planet and of being human. But he couldn't find work.

The only explanation that made some sense was pure conjecture. He may have been suspicious of personal power. He could have been unconsciously so afraid that he would use it unwisely, or felt so undeserving of it, that he would not allow himself to gain even the minimum of personal power needed in order to live.

Many of us unconsciously limit our power to a level that is comfortable for us. Our society gives us such mixed messages about whether power is good or bad that sometimes we distrust the abundance that brings it. Some abuse their power so glaringly that we fear becoming like them, especially if we have been their victims in our youth. And now, in our culture, there is a deep distrust of male power in particular.

We start as children deeply wanting to please, to do well, and to enjoy power. But many raised in a perfectionist American and religious context begin to feel undeserving of true power and happiness. Most of us work out an uneasy compromise with these issues that allows us to live, although short of our full potential. Pete couldn't work out that compromise; he was never one to compromise principles.

It is curious that almost everyone who knew Pete felt that he was one of the most personally powerful people they had ever met. Without his saying anything, his mood would set the tone of the room; usually it was a wonderful tone of warmth and peace. He did countless good deeds that shaped others' lives. Yet he remained convinced of his own impotence. Much as the skeletal anorexic can look into the mirror and see a fat person, his self-perception was wildly divergent from reality.

I try to find lessons in Pete's experience. It helps make his death seem less senseless. His life suggests to me a message that earthly rewards don't necessarily come to the good. Abundance comes to those who feel entitled to it and take risks to allow their potency to grow. Goodness is of great value, and it is its own reward. But it is essential to feel deserving at a deep level for abundance, in the form of love, money, meaningfulness, or grace, to be fully received. Free will demands this. We are free to reject any or all benefit that could come to us. I try to raise my daughter to do good deeds and to feel worthy of all blessings, regardless of outside measures of performance.

The paradox of suicide emerges from its being at the same time the ultimate act of free will and the most radical surrender of will. Suicide can be an act of self-sabotage. But it can also be an expression of anger, a self-release, or a decision to go home. It often contains components of each. Its mystery is wrapped within the enigma of life and of death. Suicide penetrates deep into the nature of who we really are; it touches on issues of soul and spirit. And it brings up issues of life and afterlife.

Part of the dilemma of letting go of Pete is "What exactly must we surrender?" Clearly, he is no longer here in the physical. Obviously, we want to keep the good memories we have of him. Preferably, we can jettison the sorrow and defeat. Beyond these generalities, we enter unknown territory. Will we meet again in eternity? In our transformation, how much of our personality will be left—enough to know and care about each other? Religious and philosophical theories abound. Most suggest a going on—into heaven, or reincarnation, or as just a drop of consciousness added back into the cosmic ocean. Traditional science will have none of these approaches, but this matter is not within conventional science's domain. It is the realm of spirit, defined in the Random House Unabridged Dictionary as (1) the principle of conscious life; the vital principle in humans, animating the body or mediating between body and soul, and (2) the incorporeal part of humans.

So Pete died on July 15, 1991. As to the questions of why his life went the way it did, there are probably no clear answers known with certainty by anyone here.

Accessing the other side of the veil, if there is non-physical existence, is difficult, but my brother's death demanded that I take a careful look into any source of information or experience that would shed light on what happened. My heart demanded that I seek contact with him and help him if it were possible. My compassion requires that I share what I found with others.

For the reader to understand why a modern man, trained as a scientist and psychologist, now knows that there is non-physical life requires presenting considerable background. Please forgive the interruption of this story as I back up to do so in the next two chapters.

RECONNAISSANCE

After I read Pete's copy of *Far Journeys* by Robert Monroe, the out-of-body expert, I discovered that Monroe had started a research and educational facility in Virginia and offered workshops in changes of consciousness such as out-of-body experiences (OBE's). The Monroe Institute also had home study tapes which could facilitate OBE's and other meditative experiences.

I had been exposed to many other tapes in my work as a psychotherapist and, in fact, had for years used hypnosis in my practice when it was appropriate. I purchased some Monroe tapes and found them to be powerful. They were much different from standard relaxation and subliminal tapes, although they had some features in common with other tapes, such as verbal guidance and relaxing surf sounds. For me, Monroe tapes had a much deeper effect, allowing greater freedom and clarity during meditation and opening up new experiences of consciousness.

The tapes work through a principle now also used by other neuropsychological researchers, such as biofeedback expert Dr. Thomas Budzynski[4] . Sound is employed to lead the brain into special brain-wave rhythms associated with meditative states, much as waltz music is used to lead the dancer to waltz. These states are accomplished with great assistance from the Institute's patented sound-wave technology, called Hemi-Sync® for the hemispheric synchronization of the brain it encourages. One listens through headphones. Special tones help the brain learn to quickly balance its right and left hemisphere activity, and then to deeply relax. After relaxation is achieved, various states of consciousness are introduced and experienced[5].

By the time I purchased the Monroe tapes, Pete was in pretty bad shape. He listened to the tapes a little, but found that he was too restless to relax during them.

In the spring of 1989 I went to The Monroe Institute's week-long introductory Gateway Voyage workshop. That week still ranks as the most profound of my life. To give a sense of what happened is difficult, but here are some highlights of the magic. On the way to the Institute I was so excited that I drove until 3 a.m. and stopped, exhausted, in the blackness of the Virginia countryside at a shoddy motel. I tried to sleep but was too excited and got up after an hour, waking up the sleepy clerk to check out.

As I left the building, I had the thought that I wished I didn't have to pay the $19.95 motel bill and immediately found a crisp, dry $20 bill, folded into thirds, lying on the cold damp outside step of the motel entrance. It was four in the morning. No one else was around, and I had looked at the same step just three minutes before on my way into the office. I never fold my own bills into thirds.

I arrived at The Monroe Institute later that morning to be greeted by Helen Warring, the Registrar, who was beaming excitement. She hugged me, laughing warmly, and showed me around the beautiful building and grounds. The Institute nestles into a knoll-top pasture in the Blue Ridge foothills, surrounded by taller peaks. Later that day, with twenty-four strangers and two trainers, I began an adventure in exploring consciousness that formed us all into life-long friends.

More than 20,000 participants worldwide have taken the Gateway Voyage, and it has been written about recently in the *Wall Street Journal*,[6] in *Omni* magazine,[7] and in many other books and periodicals such as *Healing Myself* by Gari Carter,[8] *Mind Trek* by Joseph McMoneagle,[9] and *Traveling with Power* by Ken Eagle Feather.[10]

Through the introductory Gateway Voyage program, one first must learn how to meditate deeply and to shed much fear of death. The program helps the participant do so through use of many Hemi-Sync tapes, through education and discussion, and through the gentle, accepting encouragement of the highly experienced Monroe trainers. As the participants free themselves from fear and unleash their creativity, many states of consciousness are explored.

The Institute uses numbers to designate these states to avoid previous associations to any names (such as "bliss" or "nirvana") given to these states by other disciplines. The state of balanced brain synchrony is referred to as Focus 3. Then one learns Focus 10, described as a state wherein the body is asleep or profoundly relaxed, while the mind is awake and alert. Few people realize that we can be highly conscious when completely relaxed or even while asleep. It is strange to feel wide awake and yet hear yourself snoring!

Next, the participant learns Focus 12, defined as a state where stimulation from the five physical senses is nearly absent or ignored, and information becomes more available through one's "sixth sense" or intuition. Here, participants often see visions and hear voices which do not exist in physical reality. Sometimes information is obtained through an instant knowing. Communication with one's own unconscious becomes much more available. Non-physical energies (whether termed the Higher Self, guides, angels, or God) often "speak" to the person through words, images, or knowings in Focus 12. This state is probably most similar to deep prayer and mystical states enjoyed by the devout. There is often a great deal of humor and creativity in these exchanges. These impressions can be subtle or intensely vivid.

In Gateway Voyage, one then moves on to Focus 15 consciousness. This is defined as a freeing from all adherence to the construct of time. Linear thought ceases. Everything seems to be occurring in an eternal now. Other disciplines refer to this state as experiencing the Void, both everything and no-thing, or the point of infinite potentiality. It is often blissful. In this state of consciousness, one can move through time easily, back to the past—or receive glimpses of the future.

Gateway Voyage concludes with teaching people how to experience Focus 21 consciousness. This is harder to describe. One can think of it as a bridge between physical and non-physical reality. It is usually experienced somewhat like the bright light of near-death experiences and with the same sense of profound peace and safety. In this state, communication with loved ones who are deceased, as well as with other non-physical "friends" is often clear and complete.

In my group, there were participants from around the world: three from Australia, one from Denmark, and two from Canada. Most were peaceful but powerful, multi-talented introverts. They were passionate and knowledgeable talkers if approached one-on-one. Many worked in the information or engineering fields, others in consulting or the healing professions.

The trainers' talks centered upon reducing our fears of the unknown and suggested we suspend struggle, impatience, and competing to have the most interesting experiences. They encouraged us to be willing to playfully explore new perceptions. During the program, listening to Hemi-Sync tapes resulted in much more profound relaxation and higher energy states than when I used them at home prior to coming to the Institute.

I experienced a variety of OBE states during Gateway Voyage, as well as clear knowledge of contact with intelligences much greater than my own conscious mind. It was as if I repeatedly prayed and received back as clear a message as I had sent. This bathed me in blissful and loving feelings. I felt my compassion for others expanding and even felt this physically as a dinner-plate-sized warm glow over my heart area.

My fellow travelers and I became increasingly intuitive and then often what I can only call telepathic. During a tape exercise, I would suddenly become aware of another participant's presence in my mind. In these deep meditative states it was easy to relate with the other person, to instantly know important things about them, to pass thoughts, feelings, and tremendous energy back and forth, and to understand one's connections with them that often included past lives together. The program changed forever how I viewed myself and the world.

When I returned home, Pete listened to my experiences at the Institute with great interest and some skepticism. He renewed his own efforts, and he found that he could occasionally induce the OBE state for himself by trying to remain conscious as he fell asleep. But, whereas I experienced the exhilaration of freedom from the physical body and found upon returning that the physical world was more pleasing and exciting as well, OBE experience was different for Pete. He used it to escape his physical and emotional pain and was understandably savaged by the return—much as when we awaken from a beautiful dream to confront some ugly reality.

My Gateway Voyage immediately created great changes in my life. Results flowered on many levels—from an increased self-awareness to a winning attitude. At times it got pretty spooky. For example, within the first few months of attending Gateway Voyage, I won several contests, including a prize of thousands of dollars worth of compact discs and stereo equipment. This was particularly sweet because music is one of the greatest joys of my life.

I was concerned that the effects of the Gateway Voyage would wear off. I had been to many seminars where one became flushed with enthusiasm and insight, only to become "normal" within weeks of returning home. Voyage was different. For me it seemed to start a catalytic reaction that continued to increase in depth as time went by.

That summer I attended The Monroe Institute's graduate program, Guidelines[11] and found it also of great value. Soon after, I became a trainer of Monroe programs both at the Institute and in my local community. I liked the fact that there was no dogma that one had to accept in order to benefit from the programs. And the Institute's sound technology made it relatively easy to reach deep meditative states that had eluded me during decades of standard meditation practice.

This affiliation with The Monroe Institute energized my life. It lifted the residuals of depression and enhanced my creativity. So, in one way it widened the gap between my brother's experience and mine, as he was still stuck and suffering. Yet it also deepened our bond. Pete was highly interested in my dramatic changes and very curious about the "other side"— possible non-physical realities and peak states of consciousness. Therefore, we had something fascinating and fresh to talk about, as opposed to continually problem-solving about his situation.

My wife also joined our conversation because she was attending Institute programs as well and having her own amazing stories to tell. Pete, in his graciousness and acceptance, was becoming a brother to her. He fed her deep desire for family fellowship. And he supported her venturing forth into the new areas she was exploring, such as Karate and public speaking.

Given how much I benefited from Gateway Voyage, I strongly encouraged Pete to go to one himself. He declined—I think for at least four reasons: (1) his experience with tapes at home had produced only restlessness; (2) he was a private person by nature and felt such shame about his situation by then that revealing himself to strangers was not a pleasant prospect; (3) he was not comfortable with what he thought would be an atmosphere where hugging and the word "love" would be bandied about freely; and (4) he felt that he couldn't spend the money it would have cost to go, even if the family had chipped in to provide it.

I still wish that he had gone and wonder if it would have made the key difference. I know that his privacy would have been respected, that his situation and his person would have been accepted, and that the money was unimportant relative to his own value. Perhaps in a week-long setting with the support of others, he would have been able to let down his guard and move into the open states encouraged by the program. All I can do is accept that either it was not meant to be, or that it was just too uncomfortable for him to attempt.

In one of the strangest synchronistic mysteries of life and death that Pete and I are sharing, I had just returned from The Monroe Institute's first offering of a program called Lifeline and had also recently trained Pete's son in a weekend mini-Gateway Voyage when I received the call that Pete had died.

Lifeline is a program designed to teach one in deepest meditation how to help the dying or the dead make their journey safely to the other side—pretty wild stuff! That is quite an assertion for me to make, and I think I owe the reader more of an explanation of how such a thing might work.

Again, Lifeline is a graduate program. To prepare for it, first one must take the Gateway Voyage program. The Lifeline program assumes that one is familiar with accessing the states of consciousness already referred to as Focus 3 through Focus 21. Lifeline's purpose is to help the experienced meditator access deeper realms of non-physical reality for the purpose of helping others in those realms. And in doing so, the person learns much about his or her greater self and the nature of higher realities.

To describe Lifeline is a bit complicated. Lifeline starts with a quick review of the lower focus levels and then, through different brain-wave signals, facilitates the exploration of Focus 22. This is the state of "dissociated consciousness" where dreams and strong drug experiences take place. When in a Focus 22 meditative state, one can also communicate with the consciousnesses of people who are in coma. It is more "there" than "here."

Lifeline then helps its participants to experience Focus 23. This state is defined as the vibration or phase of consciousness of those who are newly deceased and not yet released from the physical plane. We can call them "new goners" rather than "new comers"—the universe allows a sense of humor. In some systems, Focus 22 and 23 are referred to as the lower astral planes. It is here that one "meets" souls who are needing assistance to move on.

Often those who need assistance have experienced violent or unexpected death. Some do not realize yet that they are dead. They seem caught in the emotional shock/trauma of their passing. Thought seems to be reality in this state. So his thinking can deceive the person into believing that he is still alive in the physical. Again, most people die and transition to a new existence quite easily, depending on their faith. It is rare that a soul needs assistance of the type provided by Lifeline. But given that about a half-million people die each week on planet Earth, there is ample need for such assistance.

Lifeline next presents Focus 24 through 26. These are the "belief system" areas where consciousness is narrowly focused on a particular idea of an after-life, such as nirvana or heaven. Finally, Focus 27, the farthest reaches of consciousness that still has primarily human characteristics, is experienced and the Park is introduced. The Park is a place within Focus 27 designed to make newly deceased persons feel comfortable. There one is surrounded by everyday, Earth-like images such as trees and buildings.

After the meditator is familiar with these higher Focus levels (22 to 27), he (or she) is trained to go rapidly to Focus 27 and ask for a non-physical helper to assist him. He then goes with this assistant back to Focus 23 and waits until he feels pulled to connect with a consciousness in need of his help. When contact is made, the meditator helps the consciousness calm down, orient to the fact of his death, and offers to take him to the Park by linking energies and willing himself back to Focus 27. There the meditator leaves the deceased person in the "hands" of loved ones or helpers.

As can be imagined, this is a very interesting process and stretches what one thinks is real and possible. To me, Focuses 12 through 21 feel wonderful—each in its own way light, calm, and free. In contrast, Focus

22 and 23 feel chaotic and "darker." But Focus 27 and the Park feel incredibly clear, clean, and peaceful. It is as if there is no mental chatter there. The Park for me is experienced in detail with beautiful flowers, grass, ponds, and trees. While Focuses 12 through 21 are powerful mind states, they do not feel physical. Focus 27, on the other hand, feels like I am in a Shangri-La on Earth. Strangely, when you are at any focus level you may spontaneously "meet" a fellow meditator there, and when you get back independently confirm your joint experience.

When you wait in Focus 23 for someone in need, it seems as if nothing is going on. Then you feel a pull, like the pull that causes you to turn your head to find someone staring at you. You then "see" (as in perceive or just know) a situation—for example, a person killed in a motorcycle accident. That person may be trying to pick up her bike over and over, with her hands passing right through the bike. She is confused and often frightened or angry. You approach and ask if you can help. She notices you sometimes only after considerable effort to get her attention. You can hear her thoughts. You can feel her emotions. In your high, calm meditative state, her emotions feel low-energy and painfully agitating. You don't really speak, you just read each other's thoughts. It may go something like this:

"Can I help?"

"I can't get this damn bike up!"

"What happened?"

"A stupid drunk ran me right off the road and into that tree."

"What are you doing?"

"I got to get to school—have a big test today."

"You may not be able to."

"Why the hell not?"

"What did you feel when you hit the tree?"

There is now a strong sense of pain and fear radiating off this person.

"I hurt all over and then I was fine."

"Don't you think that is a little strange?"

"Come to think of it, yes."

"You may feel good now because you've changed. See your body over there?"

"Yes. What's happening? Am I dead? I don't feel dead. I can move and everything."

"Of course, only your body dies; you don't die."

"I can't be dead. I'm too young."

"Now, stay calm and think it through. Could you have survived hitting that tree?"

"No . . . my God! What do I do now?"

"Well, you can come with me."

"Where?"

"I'll take you to a place where you can rest and think. There will be people there to help you, perhaps even someone you know."

"Okay."

"Just hang on to my hand and stay with me. Here we go."

Other people have been in Focus 23 for a while by Earth-time standards, for there is really no time outside of physical reality. When I was leading a Lifeline program, one participant reported coming across a man who seemed very low in energy. She knew him and knew that he had died a few years before. He seemed to realize that he was dead.

She asked, "Hasn't anyone been by to help you?"

He replied, "There have been many beautiful angels coming by but I have hidden from them."

She asked why he would do this.

"Because they were going to take me to judgment and I don't want to go." She was able to help him move on only after considerable assurances to him. This situation points to how our beliefs may cause us to get stuck after we die.

Young children who have died while being severely abused are often very hard to reach—their fear is so great. Sometimes other souls are so angry or distressed that the meditator simply cannot tolerate the emotional radiations emanating from the person. The meditator cannot get close enough to help. Yet this emotional distress may be one reason that non-physical intelligence needs the help of Earth-bound meditators to work with the souls of some of the dead. If physically alive meditators have trouble handling the agitation, perhaps non-physical energies of an even finer vibration just can't penetrate the dense agitation of the distressed. There are certain meditators that specialize in difficult areas, such as working with victims of Satanic cults.

The easiest retrievals are often elderly people who have been ill a long time. The following dialogue is typical of these situations:

After entering Focus 23 during meditation, I felt a pull and found myself at the foot of a bed in a hospital.

"Oh, thank God you're here. What took you so long? All my pain has stopped. Boy that feels good! I'm ready to go."

"Fine. I'll help you."

"Could I ask a favor?"

"Sure."

"Could we just go by the hotel across the street? I want to say goodbye to my wife."

"Sure. Just remember to keep holding my hand."

Then, as we progressed to Focus 27, I asked some questions. To these questions I received impressions. For example, to the question, "Where are you from?" I received a rapid series of pictures of a modest middle-class house, his favorite cat, his children, the inside of his living room, and the words, "Dayton, Ohio."

At this time over a thousand meditators, in groups of twenty-four at a time, have gone through the Lifeline program. There have been efforts to verify some of the experiences by researching whether someone died with the name and in the manner and time that the meditator reports. There have been several confirmations.

Perhaps the program sounds grim, with its focus on helping people still reacting to the pain and violence of death. On the contrary, participants are usually very joyous because they often experience the intense delight of reunions on the other side between loved ones in the Park and the new arrival.

My experience with my own mother provides an example of the beauty of this process. I had been concerned that her intense feelings of guilt and strong fears of Judgment Day would cause her to have difficulty passing smoothly through the process of her own death. I was not immediately anticipating my mother's death, so my concern was out of my awareness most of the time; but it was there fairly constantly nonetheless.

Lifeline retrievals involve operating in non-physical states, where time does not exist as we know it. They usually occur in the present, but they are actually free of time constraints. Therefore, it may be possible within these meditations to tap into situations that will occur in the future. Of course, there is no way to verify such experiences—at least until Earth time catches up with them! The adventure with my mother may involve such a time-jump; on the other hand, this experience may have been a simulation, designed to help me with two concerns. The first, of course, was my worry that my mother would have difficulty passing over when the time came. This adventure replaced that anxiety with a sense of deep peace, a trust that she will successfully transition when she eventually dies. Secondly, the information I had read about Lifeline at this point, prior to any experience with it, was so foreign to my belief systems that it triggered concern. I worried that the Lifeline process may not be possible, or at least may not be possible for me to accomplish. My experience with my mother showed me how such a process can work and what it might feel like.

This experience occurred about two weeks before I participated in the Lifeline workshop, bringing my reading about the Park to life. One day, after ten hours of client work, I was extremely tired and lay down to rest and meditate. As I moved deeper into the meditative state, I felt pulled into the future. The experience went something like this:

I felt that I was at the opposite end of the tunnel that people describe in near-death experiences. Someone was coming through. I recognized that it was my mother. I calmed myself. She seemed to begin to recognize me. I felt the beginnings of her confusion at seeing me (from her point of view I was not supposed to be there) before she was even conscious of recognizing me. I masked my identity at once—surprised that I could do this. I beamed out radiations of peace and love. She immediately calmed down and moved forward. I greeted her. She asked:

"Are you an angel?"

"I'm here to help you."

"Have I died?"

"I guess you have left your body."

"Can I go with you?" (I felt she had doubts about her worthiness.)

I beamed acceptance, support, and love. "Sure you can. I will take you where you need to go."

I didn't know what to do next and felt a little panicky. Instantly the thought occurred to me that in this state I could create reality. I put some roses in her hand, knowing that she loved flowers. She brightened instantly and seemed absorbed with the roses. This diversion gave me a split-second to think. Ah! I sent her the thought-form of a newborn baby. Immediately a baby appeared in her arms and I felt tremendous love radiating from her. We stayed this way for a while.

Then something else seemed to take over the scene. I seemed no longer in control. The baby became me. I felt her love for me as an infant. I sent her memories of all the loving times we had had together: running through freshly hung wet sheets until I found her and hugged her legs—

reminded her how she stopped her work, picked me up, and hugged me until I laughed with delight. I let her see her devoted smile through my child eyes. Dozens of memories flooded through me and to her. I had the thought that I was helping her with her life-review and that that was the right thing to do. During this while, I was also willing us to travel to the Park. I was entranced at watching her life review as the baby in turn became each of her children.

Suddenly I was aware of another presence with us. It was her mother. The bliss of their reunion overwhelmed me as I felt their emotion. I steadied myself as best I could, feeling their joy myself. Others joined us—I recognized her father and sisters. The feelings just kept mounting to new heights of ecstasy. It was the ecstasy of love unbounded, of coming home, of true safety at last.

I began to realize that my part was done and began to move away. As I did so, and their radiations faded, I began to feel the loss of my mother and was at once overcome with grief at the rending. I cried out for help and instantly felt a calming presence that guided me back to consciousness of the physical with great gentleness and love. In clock time, thirty minutes had passed. My sense that we live in an intelligent and planned universe—loving beyond our bounds of understanding—becomes forever my knowing.

So the experience of helping on the other side profoundly changes the meditator. After several experiences, the participants know that they are much more than their physical selves, and understand much more about the love, intelligence, and beauty that exists everywhere in the universe—on both sides of the veil.

By now I suspect that my readers will have some important questions which I will attempt to anticipate.

What are other possible explanations for what is going on in the Lifeline program?

There seems to me to be no possibility of fraud. I have experienced the process directly myself, not just heard reports of it. It also seems very unlikely that it is some form of group hysteria, for several reasons. The process occurs spontaneously on an individual basis (for example, the experience I had helping my mother, which occurred a few weeks before the first Lifeline group even met); experiences have occurred in those who are very skeptical of the process, such as professed atheists, and there has been independent verification of the facts collected concerning the circumstances of some of the deaths.

But before concluding that Lifeline represents, at least at times, actual contact and interaction with humans who are no longer on the physical plane, two other explanations need to be explored. One possibility is that somehow the meditators are picking up the emotional-mental echoes left behind after the person has died. The problem with this idea is that the experience is so interactive. It is not fragmentary. It is not like "listening to a broken record." Another idea is that some non-physical intelligence uses the meditator's own unconscious to gather information and then simulates being the soul that needs help. This idea also seems unlikely in that often the meditator is pulled to work with perfect strangers rather than loved ones, and the process yields information that the meditator does not previously know and which can be verified.

Could this process be evil or unnatural?

I discussed the process with a fundamentalist Christian friend. He felt that anything psychic was evil and that if these meditators were communicating with anything, it was with demons. He was sincerely concerned for my welfare, and I appreciated his concern. However, I believe in the Biblical adage "By their fruits you shall know them." Because of the meditators' uniformly positive and integrative reactions to their work and because of the tremendous feelings of love and inspiration experienced, I am very confident that this represents a "gift of the spirit."

Why would I, as a trained clinical psychologist, give credence to any process that claims to be able to reach beyond death?
I can say with scientific certainty that distinct meditative states exist and that sound, by affecting brain waves, can induce these states. I can point to work being done at advanced physics and engineering laboratories, such as Princeton Engineering Anomalous Research Laboratory,[12] and previous work at Duke University and Stanford University which suggests that human consciousness is not dependent on physical matter. This body of research also suggests that we can move through time, perceiving and affecting events in the past and future.

I can offer Charles Tart's article "Compassion, Science and Consciousness Survival"[13] as a good summary of evidence for the survival of consciousness after death. I can also point to the eons of intuition embedded in religions, that submits that we exist after physical death.

I know that what occurs in Lifeline is practiced in a variety of forms in other disciplines such as shamanism. Christians and others pray for their dead, seeking to aid their loved one's progress toward peace and to God.

Recently a Lifeline group at The Monroe Institute was filmed for the entire week's program for a television show called *The Unexplained*. The producers were then able to use a noted library archivist to verify many of the details of people's lives for some of the soul rescues, as far back as the 1800's. There was no way that the Lifeline meditator could have known these details before the rescue.

What I cannot do is point to scientific proof of either an afterlife or the Lifeline process. But I feel that is the deficiency of science, not the data. Science at this time is restricted to the at-least-indirectly observable. Questions of afterlife go beyond its ken. Science is valid, but there are other ways to find truth as well—ways such as through mutually-verified experiences and through the human heart. Furthermore, the concept of how one can pierce the veil and what one can do there is consistent with leading-edge science in the field of quantum physics.

Why is such tremendous news not more widely known?
First, much of the data and scientific conclusions to which I refer are very recent (occurring within the past ten years). Secondly, traditional science is capable of behaving as a religion when confronting new thought: it suppresses data that doesn't agree with its current belief system, chiefly by ignoring it.

True story: I am aware of a prestigious university laboratory that completed an exhaustive, fully-controlled study that showed that humans can affect physical matter through thought alone. When the researchers sought publication in a peer review journal, they were told, "When you can send us the data by telepathy we will look at it." Inability to publish equals inability to get major funding.

Thirdly, the scientists doing this work are often very introverted by nature and fear they would be thrown out of their universities if they went to the popular press. Most universities tolerate this type of inquiry under the principle of academic freedom only if it is kept quiet, meaning no "wild" claims are made.

Why do I feel comfortable trusting The Monroe Institute?
It is primarily due to my considerable personal experience with the place. I have used The Monroe Institute as an extensive example here because it is a unique institution, a nonprofit "university" studying human consciousness. In my opinion, it is at the leading edge in its

field. It is a place where the farthest reaches of the human mind are explored and where what is learned is taught compassionately. In that special atmosphere of intelligence and love, great creativity and human potential flower.

While the Institute's budget is fairly small, its ethics and dedication are above reproach. It accepts no government funds. There is no guru there. There is no agenda of power or greed. It has a stellar board of advisors, and more than a hundred professional members, including many Ph.D.s and M.D.s. Its tape technology is being studied by major universities such as the University of California at Davis (for its use in surgery) and the University of Virginia (for its usefulness in healing). At the time of this writing, I understand that The National Institutes of Health are interested in exploring Hemi-Sync's potential in medicine. For further detail about the many uses of Hemi-Sync, I refer the reader to the book *Using the Whole Brain*, edited by Ronald Russell,[14] which contains more than forty articles on the application of Hemi-Sync in education, medicine, and meditation.

The Institute's use of valid principles of reverse engineering—using brain-wave patterns of talented subjects to create new Hemi-Sync signals—puts it at the cutting edge in assessing, duplicating, and teaching specialized brain-wave states that are at the current limits of human potential. The Institute possesses its own research division which has a 24-lead EEG neuro-mapper and other physiological monitoring equipment and is dedicated to objective reporting of results.

Perhaps my readers can't accept everything that I am suggesting. But it is my truth, derived through my own background, training, and experience. (I should add the disclaimer that my words are my own opinions and not necessarily those of The Monroe Institute.) All I ask is that one keep an open mind. Remembering that the best way to know anything is to directly experience it, perhaps the best that my readers can do, as my story progresses, is to see if what I am saying is logical, coherent, consistent. And discover whether it resonates not with what you have been taught, but with your own mind, heart, and experience.

The night Pete died, when I went to my office to search for a note from him (or probably to run away from the place where I had heard the news), I called one of the trainers of that first Lifeline that I had attended just the week before and asked her to go look for Pete on the other side and help him if she could. Teena graciously agreed to try to help. I wanted to search for Pete myself, but loved ones immediately after experiencing a death are usually too agitated to meditate that deeply; I was no exception. The following are excerpts from my personal journal written at the time.

7/17/91 Teena's Report:

[I called Teena 11:00 p.m. 7/15/91, the night of Pete's death and asked her to find and help Pete. Teena is experienced in soul rescue work. She feels that, going into an altered state of consciousness, she can contact the part of us that survives physical death. She called me back the next day.]

Teena reports that she easily found Pete on the non-physical plane—that he was glad to see someone who recognized him. His energy was scattered. In deep meditation, she spent about twelve hours with him, helping him to gather himself together, to calm down and to focus.

She introduced him to Focus 27 guides. He is surrounded by many protecting spirits. Focus 27 is The Monroe Institute term for the highest plane that still has relationship to human existence. Located in Focus 27 is a place called The Park, that was constructed and is maintained through human mental creativity, to duplicate the environment of Earth on a non-physical plane of existence.

The Park is used to help souls newly released from the physical body to calm down in a familiar environment.

These souls then can rest, review their lives, and make decisions about what to experience next. Some souls appear to choose to go to their idea of heaven, some to reincarnate. Other options also exist. Many souls go directly into heaven or another physical life without ever going through The Park. It is a place designed more to help those who are unaware that they are dead, are confused, or who have no strong prior belief system in a given afterlife.

Teena said that the main thought Pete sent her was that he was so happy to be out of the physical. By the end of this initial twelve-hour period he was calmer. He really wants to make contact with me. He really wants to talk to me. He is doing fine and is plugged into a very nice healing process. He was humorous about the traumatic energy that was released by the shooting, commenting, "That was not the way to make an easy transition."

Teena recommends that, for me to make contact with him, I should slow down (I was very upset at the time), get comfortable, and allow myself to feel subtle energy and sensations. Just allow the process to happen and stay aware of nuances. That I am powerfully psychic but need to calm down and open up. (It was after receiving this report that I took the half-hour to meditate before taking the plane to Pete's funeral and felt the great sense of peace that gentled my family's initial grieving.)

7/19/91 Teena's Report:

[Teena again contacted Pete five days after his death, at my request.]

"At this time Pete is more involved with whom he needs to be involved—undergoing a group orientation. He is losing attachment to the physical quickly. He is working on what has been learned in this life. He is engaging in much remembering of all that he is beyond his immediate last Earth incarnation. He is very comfortable with everyone's acceptance of his transition and feels very good about that acceptance. He was concerned about his loved one's reactions. He will continue to be available—more so as he integrates his energy."

Teena feels that this is an excellent opportunity for me, and that I am getting communication from him on an unconscious level. To make communication more conscious, I need to let go of a screen of beliefs that are in the way and be aware of the subtle stuff.

I questioned Teena: "What is in the way?"

She responded, "Traditional understandings of how the mind works stand in the way. Usually what one is best at in the physical gets in the way in this type of communication. You, Joe, are best at understanding the mind and have many conceptions as a psychologist about how the mind works. Loosen your preconceptions for a while. Let go of the need to understand for a while and just perceive.

"Pete at this time is very homed in on what we are thinking of him. He can easily understand us and 'see' what is going on. He is trying to extend thoughts of peace, love, and fun. Also, he wants to convey that he has experienced a state change, that it is not life versus death. That there really is no separation, that he is still connected and we are with him."

7/20/91 Lu's Report:

[Lu, a member with me in the first Lifeline group, had had many years' experience with psychic impressions before attending Lifeline. She had not been informed of Pete's suicide, but she called five days after his death.]

Lu called me, unsolicited, saying that Pete had some messages for me. She felt that he had committed suicide and had been ill for a long time. She saw him dressed in soft gray slacks and shirt. That he looked good. He wanted his parents to know that his way of life had been chosen beforehand. He stated, "Do not grieve. Time is nonessential. Life exists forevermore."

She saw rays of light emanating from his hands and heard the thought, "I am sending my family love, strength, and health." Lu saw a heavy gold ring with a large square stone in it. She also got the feeling "release me." Lu got the impression that for Pete, it will not be necessary to re-live this life. That even though there was a suicide, he is released from repeating this life's experience because he had been in such pain for so long with very restricted options. He will learn the lessons needed without re-experiencing them in the physical.

Even with what I feel is a decent amount of scientific support for the principles involved, and this data coming out of association with a reputable organization, The Monroe Institute, my skeptical mind still sought independent confirmation of the things being said about Pete and the afterlife. The next chapter introduces the background for that part of my journey.

GUIDANCE

When Pete came to live with us, he brought another exotic experience into our lives. He told us of a channeler in Ohio named Pam Hogan. Pam (who had no affiliation with The Monroe Institute) allowed a non-physical energy to speak through her while she was in a trance state. Pete had heard that she would give a one-hour reading by telephone, with the caller giving no information besides his first name. She would be extremely accurate as to one's life situation and predictions concerning the future. This was before channeling became more well-known, and to believe that such a thing was possible was a stretch of our belief systems and felt dangerous from our Catholic and scientific perspectives. We were skeptical but intrigued.

Pete and I had separate channeled sessions, and I have had many readings since. I am not sure what to make of these sessions, but several excerpts from them speak to what happened with Pete and with me.

But first a brief digression about the phenomenon of channeling. There appear to be at least three ways to get information during deep meditation. In the first, the person goes into meditation, has an experience, comes back to normal consciousness, and reports it. In the second way, an experienced meditator learns to talk while in a deep meditative state and report what is going on as it happens. This is particularly useful because many meditative experiences fade quickly after returning to normal consciousness, much as a vivid dream can fade upon awakening. In this meditative condition, if the experience is one of communicating with another intelligence, the person can report the dialogue while it is actually occurring. The third way information is obtained involves the meditator allowing the intelligence with whom he or she is communicating to speak directly to a listener (who is in normal waking consciousness and can record what is said). Here the meditator lets his own personality or ego fade and permits the other intelligence to use the meditator's own vocabulary and vocal cords to express thoughts directly. This third way of getting information is called channeling.

Some channelers report "going somewhere else in consciousness" while this is happening and have vivid and separate experiences while the channeling is going on. This type of channeler has little or no memory of what is said by the intelligence who is communicating. Other channelers are conscious of what is being said during the meditation. These are referred to as conscious channels. Pam Hogan is a conscious channel.

The phenomenon of channeling is now being studied neurophysiologically through brain-wave analysis. Most reputable channelers when channeling exhibit a distinct and unusual brain-wave pattern. The pattern is consistent with deep meditation. Several books now out are reported to be channeled works, including the copious Seth material,[15] the Emmanuel Books,[16] the Michael material,[17] and *A Course in Miracles*.[18]

There is much debate about the reality of the phenomenon. The first option to consider is that it is faked. This possibility is unlikely due to the rapidness and complexities of answers to questions spontaneously posed and to the accuracy of information otherwise known only to the questioner. Furthermore, the brain-wave patterns of a monitored channeler are very different from what one would expect from a person consciously faking.

If the phenomenon isn't a pretense, what is this other intelligence that is contacted? Some speculate that it is the channeler's own unconscious mind. But the channeler often speaks in a way that differs considerably from what one might expect if the unconscious were driving the thoughts; in other words, channeling does not proceed in a manner similar to either Freudian free-association or hypnotic speech.

Other skeptics hypothesize that the channeler accesses his own supraconscious mind, which then may access Carl Jung's Universal Unconscious—the human collective intelligence. This explanation would account for the cogency of answers. However, channelers are convinced that they access and relate with another intelligence or group of minds that have their own personality and higher emotions such as love, concern, and compassion. With repeated sessions, channelers often come to know and love the other intelligences, relating much as one might to good friends. What these intelligences say about themselves is that they exist outside of normal physical reality and that some have experienced physical life at some time.

Most channelers report that it is important to move into this skill carefully and to always be discerning regarding the quality of the other intelligence and be in dominion concerning one's own life choices. They feel that playing around with a Ouija board, for example, with the intention of contacting another intelligence, can instigate contact with intelligences that are of fairly low-quality motivation. These energies may pretend to be a loved one, gaining information through a telepathic link with the channeler, or may seek to control the channeler and live vicariously through the channeler's life experience. Channelers feel that they can determine the motivation of the intelligence through a sense of the energy's power and love, and the constructiveness of advice and perceptions given over time.

An interesting variant of channeling is having nonverbal information pour through without conscious control. Handel felt his personality was moved aside and that angels directly wrote the music to

The Hallelujah Chorus. Many other artists have reported similar experiences, that their inspiration came from somewhere outside of themselves. In fact, there are now channelers living who seem to be directly accessing the skills of some of the greatest painters and musicians who have ever lived. It is reported that highly skilled art critics who are trained to detect forgeries often claim that the channeled works are indistinguishable from the styles of, for example, Van Gogh or Bach.

Pam Hogan, who has relocated to Taos, New Mexico, since she first crossed my path, is by far the highest-quality channeler whom I have directly encountered. She communicates with a non-physical intelligence she named ARGO for "Ascending Rays of God's Oneness." Pam has a degree in social work and worked as a traditional therapist before starting to offer readings. Her story is an interesting one and can be found outlined in Appendix Two of this book. But now let's return to the story of Pete and me.

My initial session with Pam was highly individualized and extremely accurate as to central issues of my life. There were very few statements that I could dismiss as applying generally to everyone. It was also 100 percent accurate in predictions made for the behavior of gold and a few stocks. These predictions were specific as to exact dates that prices would rise and for how long the rise would continue. And most of these predictions went against conventional market wisdom at that time. With Pete's encouragement, I bought some stock options following the channeler's advice and acquired some of the most exciting money I have ever made! I was impressed by—and mention here—the market predictions because they were scientifically verifiable. Unless one was going to accuse Pam of insider trading in several companies simultaneously and of fixing the international market in gold, it was hard not to be in awe of the quality of this information.

More important was how I felt after this first session. There was a tremendous sense of energy and well-being that extended for about a week after the session. I felt that I was being filled with grace or being prayed for by a powerful angel.

In subsequent sessions, I encountered a reluctance to give more financial information. The exception to this was warnings about when the market was about to take a serious downward turn, apparently given to allow me to protect my self-administered pension fund. These subsequent predictions were usually, but not always, accurate. I have the sense that the initial specific market predictions were given to get the attention of the scientist in me so that I would listen and consider more important messages concerning the direction and meaning of my life.

The channeled readings which I received before Pete's death give insight into the deeper aspects of my brother's life. The excerpts presented here have been edited for increased clarity but left essentially in their original form. Given that they represent communication from a non-physical intelligence or entity—beyond the veil, if you will—I ask for tolerance of the somewhat odd style of expression. Such unusual language is common to all channeled material of which I am aware, including the works cited above.

Sometimes Pam puts her impressions in her own words. At other times, Pam lets ARGO speak directly through her without her conscious control. At times, ARGO sends Pam images to convey the meaning of their information. I think of ARGO as an angel, for want of a better word, due to the lovingness and wisdom of the message. I find that talking with ARGO is profoundly different than talking with a typical human person. I have never sensed the qualities of wandering attention, triviality, impatience, judgment, criticism, hostility, or defensiveness—so common in human communication—when speaking with ARGO. Instead, ARGO communicates with consistently exquisite discernment in an atmosphere of full attention and compassion.

Another startling difference is that ARGO responds not only to what I am saying but also to what I am thinking deep within my heart—and it may be an exact response to what I was thinking yesterday or will think in the future. ARGO does not always say what I want to hear. For example, when I had completed my first novel, I excitedly asked how it would do. The response I got was that it would not be immediately successful, but that its writing was good preparation for doing a second book. This prediction turned out to be true.

I listen carefully to the channelings, but I swallow nothing whole and at times have gone against recommendations. My feeling is that just because intelligences may be disincarnate ("dead") doesn't mean they are infallible or always right. This attitude seems fine with ARGO. Free will and personal sovereignty seem highly respected. Additionally, as in any communication, there is a possibility of distortion—what is said may not be what is meant, and what is said may not be what is heard. There are at least three sources of potential error in channeled information: error in the intelligence communicating; error through the channeler's mediumship; and error in the receiver's understanding of what is heard. I found, however, that when I went against the channeled guidance there would frequently be less-desired outcomes. Yet those experiences were also useful for my continued learning and growth. The school of hard knocks is an effective way to learn, just not the most pleasant one.

The channeled material which follows may be relevant to all of us who are "too nice," who self-deprecate, and who become discouraged. The excerpts concern issues in Pete's personality and soul which were operative in his life. It also discusses my relationship with him over many lifetimes. I did not provide Pam any information about Pete's situation. Nor, to my knowledge, did she have any way of obtaining knowledge about my personal life. In fact, I did not even mention having a brother in the initial channeling. I simply called her up and said, "This is Joe. I want to know if I am doing all that I am supposed to be doing with my life."

June 1989

[This was my first session. It was held
soon after Pete came to live at my office.]

*Now with the dear man who I want to call Peter, who is in your life,
you can give him great feelings of goodness and peace. He is your
brother. In past lives there was a real hand-holding between you.
There was a time when complete pleasure was impossible for him,
as well as you. You did suffer much along the way with him. This
sad man's childlike happy ways were lost for a very long time. On
the road to bliss, you did comfort him somewhat, gave over to him a
stroke, a comfort, a ray of light—awakening him to what the happiness of play can do, to make a real man walk straight and proud
in the world.*

*Now within himself, he self-deprecates much. And it is because
of this that you have reached out a weary hand once more, to touch
the controls of your dear brother's life—to bring him to the answers
of childlike peace for which he does so struggle now, and seeks.*

*It is in essence a peculiar twist of fate that you happened on your
brother's complexities at this time. For you have forgiven yourself
little for some of your own. And so now it is in gaining, within, a presence of self-esteem, that you can come through your own fears about
growing too powerful in your world.*

August, 1989

[This next session occurred two months after my brother
moved in with me and about two years before his suicide.
My questions concerned options for Pete at this time, as
I was disturbed by his depression and unemployment. I
did not mention any concern of suicide. The channeler
uses the word "they" to refer to ARGO, the non-physical
entity with whom she communicates.]

It is this kind of approach: "I will give back to myself what I gave to many others so that I will remember the pain of that." He is still consumed with so much guilt, and, at this point, so much self-deprecation that he can't feel that he could possibly deserve anything good in his life. He is to be the great giver and never to get a return on it.

So, that's the kind of thing that we are up against. He needs to see that it is his way of making amends. It is not the universe that says it must be this way. But there is just no way then to get a good job and manifest other good things when he is totally unable to see himself worthy of receiving anything and have any pride in his maleness nor pride in himself as a human light.

They were talking to me before you called about the need for you to lose a sense of responsibility about any decision of suicide, because you know in your profession that if someone decides something like this, there is really nothing one can do if they absolutely decide it. Okay?

You've done your piece. They were showing the cord of light between Pete, the universe, and you—and it going as a triangle. They were cutting the cord between you and Pete. I think what they were talking about was the feeling of responsibility. But let's have them talk some more.

Dear child, you are indeed the window of relief for your dear son, Peter. See how it is in the window. Even now, he cannot get a clear view of a loving self. The window needs washing, not by your dear open hands, but by his own feelings of self-worth. The cleaning rag is already in his hands but he is too tired to rise to the windowsill to offer his first stroke. Self-will here is the determiner. The enjoyment he does feel now, of growing past the pain of physical life by giving self over to the order of things, is indeed what you are in vision of this day.

He does not wish to belong on the earth plane. However, the mild-manneredness of this dear child does not want death by violence. He has within him many components of fear, lashing out at self mostly about powerlessness, and also a great struggle, a will to survive this present crisis.

The opening at the other end of (they are showing me a corridor) now does lead him to brighter light, if he can accept that feeling good about life comes from believing in the living processes—that the enjoyment of sweet power comes from knowing who he is despite the angry retorts of the powerless who do surround him also.

He has been confronted by this kind of issue many times before and he cannot, even with anger about this, rush to the light with any feeling of capacity about how he is to gain entry in the doorway of loving. It is indeed a way of seeing self complete and whole that will end this tired man's anguish.

But you, within the circle of light, must hold on to the winner's circle. For you do feel in your own great integrity how your great power of mind and love have grown to show the world another order of things. And by remaining by your brother's death bed, you are reminded of how great the glory of light is, and how dark the narrow corridor of suffering is.

Grow more to show your sweet brother how the intensity of light gives off an ever-shining effervescence. And this can indeed be an example of how one lives when the will of God is allowed entry into one's soul. However, he is not presently equipped in his darkness to understand all of this.

Peter was your son many times before in past lives. And you did, in many ways, wish to teach him how to give great loving within a family, and how to be a great beacon of stability and honor. He sold the truth about this, though, during these times when he was your only son.

And you did not bend to his darkness but allowed his own trials and mistakes to address the currents of disbelief he held about loving. So, truly you were the winner of many matches during those currents of time when loving was shown between you.

Indeed, as you are holding his hand once more, you are not the brother so much as you are the father. And as you watch this dear suffering child lose a hold on his chance for re-birthing, the natural tendency of father's pride is to override the strict rules of give and take within the universal plane of light and to allow one final wash of cleansing love to give this dear child a chance to overcome what would be his last mistake.

As you rush to your brother's bedside to show him another washing light, he may consider the power of death greater than the power of light. For death gives him, as he sees it, a chance of accepting a droplet of loving from a Father far greater than anyone here on the earth plane. Through God the Father's eyes, he may, as indecent as he feels, see one shining chance at believing in loving.

He will instantly awaken from this dream state of earth-plane activity and ask to walk more directly on the proud roadway to heaven's loving gates. If you do see him becoming more despondent, give him a chance to talk with you about pride as a male. For if he feels power through this, he can answer his own unholy, anguished cries about being a demon who must be lost.

We are most blessed angels truly. We do walk through the winter months with your dear son, Peter. He has been so cold, yet he would not allow us to throw the great blanket of life around his bent shoulders. (They are showing me pictures of a child freezing, of them trying to comfort him with a blanket, and of him rejecting it. Then they show you coming in to try to do the same thing.) Realize that he is rejecting of light.

Certainly I feel no judgment on the other side about his decision, or panic about his decision. I really do not feel that. I feel more peace about this than I do about other things. I feel more compassion from them, as far as understanding the complete sense of loss he has— about who he is, as a soul. It goes so deep and, you know, I've heard them talk about other people who struggle but never with the same feeling that this man really has such a slim chance on this side, of hope.

He does have, as they say now, the window cleaner in his hand. He just doesn't have the strength to even begin it. I just don't feel this is all that imminent, possibly because he also is a very mild-mannered man and that he really doesn't like the idea of doing himself in. So that is an obstacle to it. It's the fatigue, it's the fatigue . . .

If he could feel what I feel on the other side for him, the gentle, compassionate, loving of him, he could possibly understand that he is loving. I guess I just wanted to translate to you the tenderness I feel from them—it's pretty powerful.

In the past lives, you learned to let him take his lumps so that he could grow. But I think that as he took his lumps, he got angry and bitter and it just never worked well. But what I am hearing them say to you is that, as he has the opportunity to see you working as a light male, he at least has a vision of how that works and of the peace that it can bring. So he studies it. He also keeps you steady.

My dear son, the working is so hard to do now, that this dear child simply cannot believe himself holy enough to pull himself up by the bootstraps and take life on as a quest of joy. The amount of drainage is so great and his faculties so low for understanding, that neither the brother, nor the father, nor the sister, nor the mother could call him from where he sits. His ego is in displacement now.

The power of light is extraordinary surrounding him. As you have been about the place where he lives cleansing and powdering it, you have created indeed a holy castle.

A long-term effect of brain damage also is a part of your dear brother's problem. There lies within him a . . . (They are showing me pictures now. They are showing a graying area in the brain—small, not a big deal.)

This does not show as a powerful problem in this dear child's life. But it allows some erratic emotional responses to take place. Accord-

ingly, he is not able to respond as positively as you would wish. So please be certain also of this behavior pattern, as it was a current growing through his life from early childhood. They are just showing a very, very sensitive little boy. Worrying easily about things, and then responding. And it is part of the current problem.

When he goes to relate with anyone (and they are showing from work into personal relationships) there is a piece of him that can't accurately read what is given to him. And because he can't read it, he will frequently withdraw and be very nice, so that things can be smooth, and he won't get into an interaction that seems to him to be out of control.

Instead of sympathizing so much, listen with another ear and then run through with him what might really be happening. Although he feels very betrayed by many people, he has brought a lot of this on himself. Sometimes he asks something of them, misinterprets the response, and then reacts to that. So he makes himself a victim, where sometimes he wasn't. On a psychological level, that is what is going on with him now. On a spiritual level, it is the other piece that we have been talking about.

You and your dear wife struggle to hand self-worth to this dear child. Please know that as you work with him in such an intense fashion, you are really getting a one-sided story when he tells you what has happened to him. Give him loving support always with a clear-eyed vision that you believe in his power.

Now they show a picture of the two of you walking down a roadway and for you to let his hand go. And I think that means as far as the responsibility for keeping him here.

Much of the information conveyed in these first two channelings seemed true to me at some deep level. It felt very strange to hear it. The material about past-life interactions with Pete felt like a dream you can almost remember, that calls to you to remember.

My wife and I had indeed been trying to shower him with love, encouragement, and playfulness since he had come to live with us. The parts of the channeling that spoke of his feelings of lack of self-worth resonated with our understanding of him. The brain issue sounded to me to be what psychologists call a receptive aphasia, wherein one has difficulty interpreting the nuances, particular emotional meaning of complex speech. I wept as I heard how tired he was and that I needed to let go. But I put that part behind me as fast as I could and defiantly renewed my efforts to help him. Two months later, we had another session, followed by occasional sessions in the two years that followed.

October 1989

Now, it doesn't look good for Pete job-wise almost anywhere until he works through these issues. As he continues to put himself out there, he is going to become more depressed because of the same blocked doorways.

Dear child, it would be most important for you to know that although your dear son, Peter, does indeed live in great respect for the spiritual mind, he does create the limit of what he can expect for himself, when he is contained in a physical form. (While Pete believes in the goodness of the soul, he doubts the goodness of man on Earth.)

Please let him know that he does transfer great light within self when he does enjoy his excursions into the paranormal (out-of-body experiences). Please know that man is equipped with light, that man is given the boundaries of his own physical world only because he chooses to understand limit. As Peter and you become limitless in your excursions out-of-body, please do also know that man is of great light, that man is of great love, that man can be carried in his fullest expression, to the outer boundaries of joyous receptivity.

The theme that they are showing me is that somewhere in Pete's belief system there is a split between the power of light and the beauty of human, and that, as these are separated, it separates man from receiving his light.

February 1990

The way your sweet brother Peter does work through his rejection is an example for you. Realize how that kind of belief in karmic destiny does make a man impotent. It is important, however, for you to realize also that some of these suicidal tendencies came from an early chemical imbalance. There is a history of this within your entire family, not just within you or your brother.

Be brave, my son; the work with the chemical imbalance within yourself is almost completed. It is because you were interacting more proudly and willingly with the male energy that you were able to light the fires of a more exacting hormonal base than was he.

June 1990

[Pete requested before he went out to Las Vegas that I ask in this session whether the Vegas area would be good for him.]

Okay, I'm trying to get a little clearer because they are showing a cyclone around him. Just a cyclone. Oh boy, they just show him being blown with the cyclone.

Charge Pete more completely with the feelings of being responsible for himself. And release yourself also from personal responsibility of him. Now coming up your way is a breach of contract. Realize that, at times, in your over-commitment to heal others, you fail to grant to them their own freedom to choose. So it would be again that in the letting go, you arrive at God's love.

I feel that the breach of contract is more of a friend letting you down. I think it's somebody that you believe you would help and then they fall apart. I would suspect that it is Pete, but I do not know that. And that's where you are really going to learn to let go. It is someone you've poured a tremendous amount of energy into, who chooses differently.

The dear child, Pete, does not have the desire intensely enough to heal self—to release the unworthiness he feels in his heart. He has at this time broken with the commitment, however, to die. So we do not see yet a departure from the earth plane. But the unkindness this dear man had shown toward others in past lives does still haunt the inner beings of his soul.

He must know that as he works his way westward, hard times would be coming. He is a man without a center of grounding, or knowing where his home lies, and the turmoil of a city like Las Vegas leaves him feeling much more the same.

He is now seeing most of man as gross. Without the details of living securely on this earth plane, he is consumed by fright of defeat. Tell him to watch out for addictive behavior, as it could be aggravated in such a place. However, desire on his part to move ahead is being honored by all of us. As you do know, we are eager angels of love waiting to hear his call of friendship and light.

By understanding more how this child is power-driven to destruction, you may leave him alone to his journey of choices, and know that your love does go with him. He will live a singular life for a while. He is trying. But he is not out of the cyclone yet.

July 3 1991

[This session occurred about ten days before Pete died.]

Now, allowing (I think this must be Pete they are talking about) others to travel on their own way right now is most important. This man has decided to become self-taught and must learn the lesson of letting go of all judgment. (They show him out in the desert; is he still out around Nevada?)

As he is a man walking through the desert, he has the time now to take off the old clothing, to view the nakedness of his true self, and learn how to draw his own succulence from the dry desert sand. He is not as afraid to receive his succulence as he once was. Because of that, he feels that he can ask of himself much forgiveness now. And on his own, he can complete much of the self-healing work that was attempted on your glorious farmland.

Set him free and, as you feel the warm brotherliness next to him, see how you responded to your own lack of self-respect in a very different way. He chose to torment himself, through lack of forgiveness, for being powerless. You used it to challenge others to find their light.

I feel really good about Pete [First time you have said that.] Yes, it is and I am thrilled! There is hope in him. They are showing this tunnel of light piercing through some very dark funnel clouds. He can see the light there. The path is crooked, but I really think Pete will make it to a place where he is comfortable about who he is, where he can say "Okay, I've landed now."

This was the last channeling concerning Pete before his death. There were many sessions after his death, and those were a source of understanding and comfort for me. They led me to consider possibilities and hinted at the reasons why I felt such an intense connection with him beyond what I knew consciously. We'll return to those sessions later.

In the only channeling Pete had directly, he reported that he received information that in a past life he had been a powerful king who had been fair but not merciful. Many people were severely punished at his hand to keep order and safety in his realm. This fit what I knew of him. While I have literally seen him give the shirt off his back to a person in need—as well as his last five dollars—he also believed that those who repeatedly or severely hurt others should be shot.

The channeling stated that he now felt the need to pay back this debt and to stay far away from power. They suggested that Pete imagine himself going down a flight of stairs to a doorway and see himself opening the door and viewing a king counting his money inside of the room. In the exercise, Pete was to forgive the king and release him and all karma from that lifetime.

ARGO suggested to him that the way of karma (cause leading to effect) is a slow and hard way to learn the route back to the Light. The Law of Love, however, allows instant redemption and is available to us all at any time. Love surrounds us in any plane of existence we may inhabit. Yet free will is at all times respected, even our choice to turn away from the Light. But love will fulfill its intent to include and embrace all in the end.

The perspective gained from Pam's channeled information provided some comfort during those last years with Pete, and also after his death. But after he was gone, there were great oceans of grief to swim through.

DAMAGE CONTROL

The first months after my brother's death, much of my focus was a form of damage control—taking care of others and struggling to function myself. I went back to visit my mom and dad, fearing what I would find. We sat on their screen porch for several cool Berkshire summer evenings, listening to the wind in the pines and the crickets chirping. We talked. They were indeed deeply wounded, still in shock. Staying in shock could be fatal. And if they came out of it, the impact might also kill them.

Despite his unhappiness, Pete had always looked terrific in our parents' presence. He was ruggedly handsome. I had always thought that he looked and carried himself a lot like James Garner in *Maverick*. Pete wore his soft, dark brown, wavy hair combed back on both sides with no part. He never changed this style, and his hair was never mussed. His bright blue eyes carried a mischievous sparkle that was softened by his friendly smile and suggested a playful intelligence. He kept himself fit, tan, and trim. His clothes were always clean, neat, and of good quality. He had an amazing body grace. In short, whenever he was around my parents he looked like a million bucks in a happy and gentle way.

My mother talked openly during my visit about her son, Peter, the man she remembered as so handsome and fit. She would try to stop the conversations before crying, but she was only partially successful. The talks tended to be short, with her beginning again an hour or

two later, after regaining some composure. Mom couldn't believe it;
couldn't believe that the precious infant she had held at her breast
was gone, that the bright, eager, and helpful boy she had taken so
much pride in was gone, that the strong, kind man with whom she
had spent the wee hours of the morning talking was gone. He was
her shining jewel. She had spent her life, like most mothers, worrying
often about all the things that could happen to her children. Yet never
had it crossed her mind to prepare for this.

Mom knew that somehow this was her fault. She politely listened
otherwise but secretly repeated the chant: "How did I fail him? It must
have been something I didn't give him, my most beloved son. Oh God!
It cannot be true that he is gone." In her desolation, nearly eighty years
of devout Catholicism offered no comfort. The Catholic training also
set her up for dreading that her lovely son was in hell for eternity, for
the Church had taught her early in life that suicide was a mortal sin.
She struggled. Faith equaled terror. Rejection of faith meant the possibility that he was at peace but that there may be no God.

My dad deflected most inquiries about how he was doing or what
he was experiencing with brief answers. He went daily to Pete's grave
site to tend the flowers. He was fairly even on the surface. I think he
was also the first one to feel any anger. I think his anger came from
Pete wasting the precious gift of life and from seeing how grievously
his suicide was hurting others. When he thought he was in private, we
heard my dad at times sobbing deeply. That was harder to bear than
my mother's tears because it was difficult to know how to try to console him without invading his privacy. I did go in once to hold him
and he accepted it for a few moments.

I looked to my parents as models of how to deal with my own feelings. But neither parent's approach seemed right for me at the time,
although both were to be admired for coping at all. Strangely, a blend
of their styles seemed right for me, a blend of grief and going on with
daily life.

On the plane back home from this visit, I became aware that my relationship with Pete as I had known it had ceased to exist. To find him again in spirit, I had to throw previous conceptions away and search for a transformed Pete and perhaps a new me.

This newness felt true in my relationship to my parents also. Lost were our old roles. We were now marked by a common wound that no longer allowed the illusion of a big strong parent and a responsibility-free child. Yet it was obvious that we valued each other even more than before. I wanted a new relationship with them—an intimacy that had room to grow even through the veil of eventual death. I jotted this poem down as the plane floated me home.

My father is a gentleman.
My mother a sad angel.
Well, they have lit my way.

As I open my heart to them
Tonight
A radiance warms my chest.

It is joy to treasure them
And know they love me.
But now we grow further.

One last shell to crack
Before we go clear
Into deeper intimacy.

It is time to stop "sonning"
And fathering and mothering.
We release, to meet again as equals.

To see each other, truly
We release forty-year patterns
And find eternity.

This direction felt like the right one for me with these two dear people. I was so glad that they had each other. In their fifty-five years of marriage they had created many ways to know and convey their regard for each other. Love is often a celebration. Now it would be their anchor.

On the other side of things, I still was a parent of a young child. And my child needed me to stay in the father role for a good while longer. The hardest thing was that I could not promise what she felt that she needed the most—for me never to go away from her. Seven-year-olds let themselves clearly feel the distinction between "most probably" and "yes."

My daughter was devastated. Pete had been her loving companion. I remember him holding her tenderly for hours when she was a baby. Later he teased her gently in a way that made her feel big and proud. He would delight her with tricks such as putting cigarettes in each of his nostrils and ears and acting as if nothing was unusual no matter how much she reacted. After he was living with us, he would take her for a full day's adventure and bring her back smiling and safe.

Now she was worried that everyone would die. She didn't want to go to school, or on field trips to the zoo, or anywhere out of our sight. The nausea she had experienced during the funeral continued. Fearing she would get sick, she carried an airsickness bag wherever she went. She began wetting the bed.

Her questions were constant and often upset the fragile equilibrium her parents were attempting to maintain. Unexpectedly she would ask the hard questions. Was the undertaker sad when he picked up Pete's body? How come Pete was depressed? Why couldn't the doctors help him? Do you feel it when you are cremated? Why do people have funerals, if it makes everyone so sad? Is it allowed to kill yourself?

While we gathered blueberries, she would ask, "Who found Pete?"

While we were folding laundry, she would be talking about school and suddenly say, "How did Pete hold the gun?"

As I was putting her to bed, finally thinking I had her peaceful and settled, she would look me directly in the eye and ask, "Wasn't Pete scared?"

On and on.

Yet my daughter also stated firmly that if Pete wanted peace, it was his decision. She insisted that Pete came and talked to her the night we heard the news and also on the plane going up to the funeral. She said he spoke clearly, talking inside her head and telling her that it would be all right, that he was fine, that her Mommy and Daddy would stop being sad after a while.

Pete's son had just graduated with a master's degree a week or so before his father's suicide. I suspect that Pete had waited until he discharged all the responsibilities that he could toward his son. Pete had often talked with a warm pride about the chance at a good life that his son would have. But his son was blind-sided by the suicide. You could see him falter within the pseudo-sureness of young adulthood. A very private person by nature, he was now caught between loyalty to his dad and confusion at the ugliness revealed.

I cared powerfully for my family and they for me. I found myself being so grateful for them and proud of how all were striving to do the best that they could under the burden of grief. There was no trace of pettiness (Whom did he love best?), no hint of nervous, macabre humor—only dignity, suffering, and compassion.

Toward the end of the first month, I was beginning to understand the magnitude of my personal loss. He had become my best friend in the two years he lived with me. I began remembering all he did for me as a child. He used to let me hit him as hard as I could in his rock-hard stomach. He never budged or grunted, yet each year he said I was getting stronger. I would tell him to hit me back, but he never did so with humiliating force.

He tried repeatedly to get me to learn how to shoot a gun for protection. I always declined because I feared violence. Finally, after I had a daughter to protect, I let him show me how to use a pistol. The lesson was short. On a bright summer's day, he carefully went over the rules and safety procedures and then aimed at a tree about thirty feet away in our front yard. The bullet buried deep, right on the mark. He gave me the gun. I fired and then swept the still-loaded pistol right past him as I gestured at something. He quickly paled, stepping backward in surprise, said, "Maybe you'd better leave guns alone," and took back his pistol. I agreed. I think that was the gun he used to leave us.

I dreamt of him about three weeks after his death. In the dream, I was trying to put a window screen on a window. No matter what I did, it would not fit. Pete came up gently behind, put his hands on mine, and guided the screen to a perfect fit. I turned and asked him if he could now talk about what he had done. He turned his face away sadly and said, "No." Then he faded away.

I began to know the hope and dread of mourners—to encounter their lost loved ones in their dreams. Here contact was completely real, an incredible sense that he was here in the flesh. Then I would wake, realize I was "only dreaming," and experience the freshness of the wound all over again.

It was so difficult to express what was going on. Hell, it was hard to even feel it, let alone try to share it with others. The sense of isolation was acute. My clients were very caring of me in the weeks after I got back from the funeral. But they had their own pain, and I was supposed to be helping them. I found that I had zero patience for pettiness, trivia, or issues of vengefulness or violence. It took all I could do to sit there and not explode when these human feelings surfaced in my clients. But it was even worse when my clients or friends had some sorrow to express. Then I would be overwhelmed with grief at all the pain in the world. All of a sudden, it seemed like everyone was grieving somebody or something.

In my two decades of clinical work, I had counseled many who had lost loved ones. From this work I knew that although they usually kept the incidents private, many experienced contact with their departed. The typical pattern of contact was a fleeting sense of presence within the first hours or days after the death, then months of no contact, and finally, if they were lucky, a re-establishment of connection that would be felt at unpredictable times. I now tried to meditate and use Lifeline and other techniques to reach Pete myself. My desire for contact was powerful, but I felt no clear response, no real sense of him. Knowing the usual pattern of contact did not console me. I began to fear that I was unworthy and would never be skilled enough, and even that the reports of such connection were all nonsense.

I stopped watching television—couldn't take the news reports of the inhumanity of man, the triviality of sitcoms, or the constant commercials for unneeded products. In self-defense, I dove into numerous projects. I had a novel, three professional articles, and several seminars all going at the same time. My personal energy has always been high. Now it was becoming hard to just get up and get breakfast, but, once I was going, it was hard to stop. I have never been through anything so draining in my life.

About a month after Pete died, I realized that I had yet to spend a day fully alone with myself and my feelings. I scheduled it in. It began with my waking up at 4:00 a.m., unable to sleep. I opened a book someone had given me about surviving a loss by suicide. I read it from cover to cover, finishing by 7:00 a.m., and found myself furious. The book was filled with platitudes and trite observations, or at least it seemed so at the time.

I spent the day raging around the house—defeated, depressed, and confused. This wasn't the neat and clean grief that I had always read about in which you feel sad, cry, and then feel better. There was no sense of contact with Pete, no felt comfort from God, no sense of closure. So much for getting in touch with one's feelings! After that day, I went back to being overly busy, and took my grief in small hard chunks that, while they burned terribly, at least didn't choke me going down.

A different variety of experience was also building within me, as I came out of the initial shock. My grieving seemed to be feeding a part of my soul. I would be caught by the beauty of the most ordinary objects, and become absorbed and transported by the exquisite loveliness of small things in nature, even rocks and pebbles. I think that I was moving so often to thoughts of my brother and the world of the physically dead, searching so much for him in the beyond, that I had loosened my moorings to the physical world. This separation allowed me fresh appreciation of the magnificence of our physical world each time I re-entered it from my thoughts of faraway.

Through my experience of beauty and more often, through pain, I was acutely aware that I was alive. The pain gradually changed. Somewhere in the second week, I went a day without crying. Somewhere in the second month I went a day without thinking of my brother. There was an emerging commitment to live my own life more fully. The pledge involved being more honest with myself and with others about who I was and what I wanted.

While it was part of being fully alive, I found it was not easy for me to be honest about all that I really wanted. It brought up fears that I might not fulfill my dreams, that I might lose other things I valued in the trying, and that maybe I was being selfish. By facing these fears, it became possible to discover that life can be a win-win situation and to know that pursuit of happiness is indeed a birthright. Such pursuit needs to be balanced with responsibility, not weakened by fears of hurting self or others. It can be a dynamic balance between vigorous self-fulfillment and vital brotherhood.

All this was a quiet counterpoint to the dragging upward from shock and loss. I mention it here because these issues of aliveness and soul are, I suspect, part of the core nature of the grieving process as much as the tears are. Deep grieving changes us forever. It is different from the small unsettlement we experience when we hear of strangers' deaths, different even from the genuine sadness and uneasiness that the death of someone closer produces. In these situations, we eventually go back to pretty much who we were before. But the death of a parent, sibling, or one of our children is not dismissed so easily. It transforms us—breaking us apart. We put ourselves back together in a new way or not at all.

Suicide highlights how much choice we have as human beings and how little of that awesome freedom we usually use in our daily lives. We have near-total freedom of attitude, freedom of how we treat ourselves and others, freedom of what to focus upon, freedom to coast, tear down, or build up.

Suicide also highlights our power as human beings. When we see the death of another affect so many people we love in such radical ways, we are brought to an undeniable awareness that each person has a profound influence on the well-being of others. When we drop the stones of our actions into the waters of the Earth community, the circles cross the planet and echo far into future time. This is a power that we often like to deny. I began wondering how many of my stones were jewels and how many were millstones.

When we become aware of both our freedom and power within the precious days of physical life, it is hard not to feel that we've been lazy, stingy, or cowardly in our use of such gifts. We feel an urgency to finally live up to our potential, before our ending. Suicide shines as a lighthouse beacon, warning of unmet potential, false perceptions, and life-denying self-deprecation—too late to correct. To the extent we are guilty of these same crimes, suicide makes us uneasy.

Life also demands surrender—letting go of fears and attachments. To live well we must die each day to what is no longer useful, living, and vital in our lives. Releasing necrotic thoughts and behaviors allows rebirth each morning to the infinity of possibilities. Few people practice and are good at these mini-deaths. My brother surrendered his life with a gunshot rather than surrendering his deadening thoughts and behaviors. How many more of us slowly and quietly lose what makes us feel most alive, rather than give up an attitude or behavior that is no longer productive?

We like to call it a rut we fall into. It is really more accurately described as a grave. So, I had to learn how to surrender my brother. Maybe after I could do this, letting go of all that is dead in me would be possible for the first time.

I keep a personal journal sporadically. In the weeks after Pete's death, I recorded my observations and opinions, and also reports from family members concerning their feelings of connection with Pete after his passing. Here are some samples of what we were experiencing.

My Own Experience:
[These are excerpts from my journal in the
period immediately following Pete's death.]

Pete died yesterday. I felt great agitation after hearing the news until, at Teena's suggestion, I lay down for a half-hour at 3:00 p.m. today and attempted to calm myself and open to Pete. I felt an immediate sense of lightness and well-being that carried into the rest of the day including the flight to Massachusetts and meeting my family. The lightness was different in quality than ever experienced before. It was subtle yet powerful, and allowed feelings of joy at the beauty of clouds and sunset. The lightness seemed to bathe me both from above and from within.

✲

Through great agitation in the few days after Pete's death, until after the funeral, whenever I made time to lie down and relax, this same feeling of lightness was present and lasted for a few hours each time. At the funeral, though I was very sad, I felt supported by good energy. I was able to read Pete's eulogy in a strong and calm voice.

It was strange to see a white 1962 T-Bird convertible outside the back of the church when we exited from the funeral—best of my recollection, it was Pete's favorite car. [I have not seen that car, before or since, in that small town of three thousand people. The next time I was there I asked about town and could find no one who knew who owned the car.]

⚬─⚭─⚬

After the tree planting, when I meditated, I felt a very strong wave of gratitude toward me. It didn't feel directly like Pete (none of his personality seemed present). I had the feeling then that I was looking for the old Pete, that now he was transformed to an extent that his energy was much lighter and more delicate, happier, cleaner.

⚬─⚭─⚬

We have returned home after the funeral. When we got home to North Carolina from the funeral, our new BMW started immediately at the airport. The next morning the truck battery was dead. I went to start the lawn mower—the 2-month-old battery was also dead and had a hole in the top with acid bubbling out. The next morning my electric razor battery was dead and would not recharge.

We went to the office. My wife heard noises upstairs (where Pete had lived) in the evening when she was alone in the building. She went to leave and found that the BMW's battery was dead. The next morning we checked the upstairs of the office. The room used by a massage therapist was locked from the inside. It had never been locked before, and we had to hunt to find a key. That night, when we returned home, the garage door opener battery was dead.

Was Pete signaling us through all the dead batteries, or was he pulling energy for his own use? Were we pulling energy for our own use? Was it just a series of coincidences? Strange that so much of this had to do with cars, which were one of Pete's favorite things.

My Wife's Experience:

My wife also wondered at the battery experiences. Additionally, she meditated at the same time I did on the day after Pete died, and had the same feeling of lightness afterwards, despite great agitation beforehand; the lightness extended the same amount of time as mine.

My Daughter's Experience:

After being home a few days after the funeral, my daughter volunteered that when I had told her the news of Pete's death and we were crying together, she had heard Pete's voice saying, "It is going to be all right." The morning after his death, she seemed very calm when she woke up, and she told me that if Pete had called her before he died and told her what he was going to do, she would not have tried to stop him—that it was his choice.

Then, on the plane to the funeral in Massachusetts, she heard him again, saying to her, "I love you—don't be afraid." She heard him again another time when she closed her eyes and felt that she could talk to him easily.

At the family gathering she was exceptionally good, positive, undemanding, and helpful. She seemed agitated only at contemplating the funeral and then during the funeral. She says she misses him often but seems to feel still connected somehow. When she talks with a friend, it is with a great deal of acceptance about what has happened. In my clinical experience, this is unusual for a six-year-old.

My Brother John's Experience:

On the morning after Pete's death, before he had heard the news, John woke up to find blood on his pillow and no injury on his body that could account for it. Pete had shot himself in the head on his bed in Las Vegas only hours before.

The Sunday after Pete's death, while in church, John experienced a strong wave of energy that felt as if it would push him right out of the back of the church. At this time, he heard the words, "He is with me." These words seemed to come directly from God. The words were accompanied by a profound sense of consolation that lasted at least into the next few days. John is aware of no psychic experiences in his life before then.

Pete's Girlfriend's Experience:

She reports many small things, such as complete strangers coming up to her and starting to talk about things that are unusual for people to talk about, yet seemed consoling and relevant to her grieving process. She reports feeling Pete's presence strongly much of the time, so much so that she is having trouble being focused on the physical plane.

Three days after Pete's death, I contacted Pam Hogan, the channeler. Here are notes from that session.

Pam was reluctant to focus on Pete's transition, as often she feels the person's agitation and physical experience at the time of death, when she attempts to focus so soon after transition.

Through ARGO, Pam was fed the following information: That the final straw for Pete was fear of abandonment and aloneness with respect to an exclusive adult partnering relationship. That his connections with family were well and good but he needed more. That energies set up from long past pulled him to a choice of repeating old patterns even more intensely. He felt he had to break out of those patterns somehow.

His need to borrow so much money, and a deep sense of indebtedness and hopelessness about changing this, also weighed on Pete heavily. There was nothing anyone could have done to help at this point.

After a short initial period of scattered energy right after his death, she felt Pete settling down quickly, so that by 5:00 p.m. yesterday she saw him as jubilant, tucked in, resting, and very glad to be home. He has a feeling of being in a very child-like, trusting, sleep—finally having a deep feeling of safety about himself and where he is now. ARGO protects Pam from lowered or erratic vibrations. It may be appropriate to directly channel Pete later, but not now. Pete's vibration now might drain her some. ARGO then said:

> *The deeds Peter did were chosen over a lifetime. He negated much of the good that may have come to him. He has been taken now to a resting post by a legion of angels to dissipate his weariness, so he can come to understand that he does have endurance. His aloneness was most painful to him.*
>
> *He wants to contact you, Joe. He wants to plant seeds in your mind. He wants to work hard with you to effect some changes. He will be on the observation plane for a while. Maintain a very high, light energy level. He will observe the high vibration of your examples. A while from now, his own light will glow more magnificently and can reach your light more easily, after his vibrations smooth and raise up. Communication can occur more easily later, in a more relaxed manner later, after he has rested.*

[I asked if there was anything we could do to help him now].

> *Send thoughts of celebration at the new birthing of Peter. Send thoughts of death as warmth. Both these thoughts will add warmth*

to his resting sleep. Also, live your own life in a way that reflects "coming into your own light and power." This will help teach him how things can go. Delay strong attempts at two-way communication a few months—he is a weary man. It will be much easier to hear him later. Look for him on the observation plane. This is above the astral plane. They show him later with a notebook, taking notes and learning rapidly, learning by observing things on the physical plane: For example, "Oh, when a person does this, that is the result."

It is significant that I felt so alone and lost, even with these early feelings of contact in myself, in my family, and through Pam. These things were a paltry substitute for having Pete right next to me alive, visible, and tangible.

ECHOES

By the early fall of the year, three months after Pete died, our daily weeping had stopped, except for my mother's. And by then, even she had good moments during her days. For each member of my family, some semblance of normality returned. As Charleene and I harvested grapes and made a rich, clear juice that captured sunshine for the winter, we could smile and feel our link with the Earth. Yet much grief work continued.

Thank God, my daughter could now be caught singing and skipping once again. She was still anxious about separation in the mornings before school and in the evenings at bedtime, but her questions were now fewer. And I could respond to her with less distress.

Her queries usually came while we were driving in the car or working in the garden. One short question, then on to something else, usually after the statement, "I miss Pete," and my resonance, "I know honey, so do I."

She remained interested in the mechanics and technology of death: How hot was a cremation fire? Did I want to be cremated? Her questions concerning how someone is chosen for death contained a singular tension: When would I die? When would she die? As she picked up the understanding that the best predictor was age, it became "How old is" every pet and person she knew. She would comment on how hard it would be if they died and how much she would miss them. She figured that her great-grandma was next in line, and she was right—but not for a while yet.

My daughter was adopted at birth. Now her questions turned to how choices are made that result in separations—choices to die, to separate at college, and to give a child up for adoption were absorbing issues. Around this time, she began asking many questions about her birth mother and whether this woman were still living. I think she wanted a back-up. She insisted she did not have a birth father.

Children often work through trauma by focusing on their issues with animals rather than people. It can be less threatening this way. My daughter at this time claimed rights to all the family pets, a Border collie named Blackie and two cats, Coco and Thunder. These animals had learned to dodge her when she was a toddler. They were more tolerant of her than affectionate, but cooperated with being dressed in doll outfits and wheeled around in carriages—when she could catch them. They were older and could die anytime. I think she felt anyone or anything older than she could die at anytime.[20]

The only pet that was totally her own was a cream-colored rabbit named Cloudy. She played with death through Cloudy. She gave him away to a neighbor who kept a dozen or so rabbits, "because Cloudy would be happier with other rabbits." Then she visited Cloudy almost every day, keeping careful track of the multitudinous births, deaths, and giveaways of that rabbit family.

As fall came, I was still sad much of the time and wanted to bring new life into the house. As an attempt to do so, we attended our first party since Pete's death. It took place at a summer house deep in the woods. Walking up the long dirt drive, we could hear the laughter and see the lights piercing the forest. Nice, lively people spilled over the porches and crammed around tables scattered throughout the cottage, drawn inside by delicious smells. I found navigating through that sea of good cheer to be almost unbearable.

I ended up leaving the party at eleven in the evening and impulsively driving 200 miles through the quiet night to a distant town, glad to be alone. The next morning, I purchased identical twin white Manx kitten brothers and drove home. Each had one blue and one copper-colored eye. These two white tornadoes were presented to my daughter as her own. It was a great idea, helping us see that the future contained new life as well as death. Right now we needed our new life to be tender and vulnerable, like ourselves. We were not ready for a raucous party. Maybe that shouldn't have been a surprise, but it was.

During this time, family visiting was frequent. Although my family is scattered across the Northeast, Midwest, and South, someone was at my folks' house at least every other weekend. Brothers and sisters visited each other.

Pete's son came to see me. In the dark, cool basement of my office we sorted through his father's few things. There was clothing mostly and reams of yellowing paper records. We were surprised by the occasional modest memento that Pete had treasured. There was so little. We worked mostly silently, choked by tears. We shipped something of Pete's to each family member.

Since Pete was indigent, his estate was comparatively simple. I was executor; this meant writing letters to get junk mail to stop and creditors to desist. It continued to be hard to get unexpected mail in his name. Pete was able to leave a nice nest egg of life insurance to his son. I know this, at least, must have given my brother satisfaction. The lawyer handled the estate, which although simple took over a year to settle, basically for free. And all the business people, bureaucrats, and clerks involved were sensitive and kind. Telling these strangers a bit of Pete's story and hearing their compassionate responses helped with my healing.

Several casual acquaintances of Pete's in Las Vegas (a bank teller, a grocery store clerk, and his landlord) tracked us down and expressed their admiration for Pete, particularly his friendliness and warmth to the working person. These letters meant a lot.

The Las Vegas police called to ask if one of their officers could purchase the gun Pete used in his dying. We had previously indicated that we wanted the gun destroyed, but Pete's son now gave permission for them to buy it. Their request disturbed me. It is unsettling that something that has caused such sorrow is still on the loose. I held my silence about my concerns.

At the time of his death, Pete wrote notes to his son, parents, girlfriend, and each of his siblings. His letters while he was alive were usually two sentences long; these suicide letters were about a page long. We studied every word. I suppose suicide notes never convey enough information. Pete's note to me stated how he wished to dispose of his goods and directed me how to activate his life insurance. He thanked me and Charleene for our friendship. There was no explanation—none would have been sufficient. There was no "I will always love you"—that would have helped, I think.

The early stages of grief often block out much of the sense of the loved one's existence. Those left behind strive to maintain the sense of connection. They try to burn into their memory all that they know about the departed. It is unbearable to think that the deceased may simply not exist anymore, or even that they are now in an afterlife and becoming interested in other things, moving on from interest in us.

I had a recurring crazy concern. If Pete was on the other side, could he see all my faults which I usually consider hidden? And knowing me as I really am, did he still love me and want to see me again? Or was he disgusted by my imperfection? I knew that he had always had very black-and-white, perfectionist standards. This worry may seem a strange preoccupation, but it was important to me. My logic was that if there is an afterlife, then I would meet him again. I could endure this temporary separation and relish our ecstatic reunion. But if he no longer sought to be my friend and brother, then I had lost him forever. That possibility brought with it a crushing sorrow.

While I knew it is healthy and normal to feel anger at the deceased, particularly in suicide, I wasn't aware of very much anger. I couldn't bear it—I loved him in many ways like a father loves his son. Blended with this was the love I had for him as a brother, as father and mother to me early in my life, and as my teacher and mentor later on. I did have anger at him for not getting his ass back to school earlier in his life when he had the option. So he found school horribly boring; many of us have knuckled under to that!

I experienced another anger immediately after his death. The day after his death, I felt a sharp sense of his cheating me out of being able to take the suicide option myself at some time in the future. I knew the family could never get over two suicides. It was like he had let go of his end of the rope suddenly in tug-of-war, and that was grossly unfair. He broke free and I was stuck here no matter what happened. This anger was drowned within days by my own sadness as we went through the funeral process.

This feeling of being stuck here was an important emotion to notice. It came from my own experience with severe depression, starting when I was ten and continuing through my early thirties. Over that long span there were many times when suicide looked attractive as a way to get the hurting to stop. It was most tempting when it seemed a way to end the tiredness that such a long struggle involves.

Therapy, meditation, loving relationships, and hope that my mood would change all helped keep me here. Yet the most important reasons for me to keep living during those decades of despair were threefold: my sense of meaning, my curiosity, and my appreciation for beauty. I have always been blessed with the knowledge that my actions often helped others and found this a very meaningful reason to stay alive. Secondly, I have always had a driving desire to know and understand more. And thirdly, I have the capacity to be deeply transported by the beauty of nature and music. These three attributes never vanished for more than weeks at a time during all those years.

I suspect most people have considered suicide occasionally—some mildly, many seriously. There is such shame felt at having the thought and such panic at hearing it expressed that these deliberations are almost always kept private, deep within our hearts. I have had a great number of clients say, "If I were suicidal, I wouldn't tell my therapist or anyone because I would be afraid that they would commit me to a mental hospital." Underlying that thought, I suspect, is a more threatening fear that having these thoughts makes me so different from the rest of the human community (except for its failures) that it means I am not fit to be loved and respected.

As a society, we need to change this silence, one person at a time. Because the very act of sharing such thoughts allows healing to start. Through talking we can vent the emotional pressure cooker, be reminded of our value, be helped to see options, and, most importantly, be understood and accepted. Until we can freely talk about it, children, teenagers, the elderly, the alone, and all those who are depressed have to carry the burden of suicidal thoughts by themselves. And many will not be strong enough. To help the people who are hurting to talk, we must listen (defined as: to hear oneself or another with thoughtful, non-judging attention). And we must have the courage to accept that for some, as for Pete, this will not be enough.

While there was little anger consciously directed at Pete, in those first few months there was plenty of anger in me about almost everything else! I was glad to see my anger softening by the end of the summer. My remaining anger seemed to surface spontaneously from deep in my psyche at unexpected times.

Anger turned inward is a cause of depression. So, I guess directing my anger outward was good. But it was very uncomfortable. Growing up in our family, politeness and respect were emphasized. My parents never seemed to argue. As a therapist, I was trained to hold back my own feelings while encouraging others to express themselves. Now my own fury demanded to be felt and voiced.

Some feel that much of the pain of grieving is not from the loss of the loved one. Pain comes also from trying to harden one's heart against current feelings and future losses. I tend to agree. After all, the first three months of agony occurred before we could really miss Pete; if he were still alive, three months could have gone by between visits without distress.

It is a strange concept. Much of the emotional torment immediately after death is based on anticipation of the future. If the person had gone away for a long trip around the world, we would miss him but not be devastated. It is amazing to me, how much our idea of what will happen often colors how we feel today.

In my desire to find out how Pete was doing, I scheduled another channeling at this time. It was astonishing how well the session spoke to my concerns of whether Pete would still want to associate with me on the other side. It also gives a glimpse of what existence for the departed may be like in the Earth-weeks after death, at least when one leaves the Earth via suicide. Excerpts from the session follow.

November 1991

[This session occurred three months after Pete's death. I indicated a desire to connect with Pete if possible. Also, I asked for comments on what was happening within me. I received quite a lot of information about Pete and also got a therapeutic talking to!]

At this time, Pete is very willing to detach from what is here and from what was his darkness. It is very much a not wanting to be attached at this point to the physical plane, so that he doesn't have to be reminded … they still show the pull and weeping of the physical.

He is not, Joe, longing to see anyone particularly but you. He has some unresolved issues about his problems. He feels still less of a man. He feels most embittered, as if God had let him down.

Now as we are carrying him beyond this current state of powerlessness, he wishes to carry male to the light. You, Joe, need to see how your current feelings of powerlessness are reactionary to his, for there is still a heart-link between you. And in this linking, my child, there is a draining of self, as you feel somewhat castrated yourself and fear that you and God may have let everyone down.

Now you, Joe, do stand as a giant of light. You have been the emotional carrier for your entire extended family and the weightiness of it has carried you to where it was not personally safe for yourself. You were always willing to go way out on the limb for another.

Joe, the more you bend over to emotionally receive a spanking for not being the performer of all of God's acts, the more humbling the darkness would become for you. We would suggest that you would instead experience the light through the physical now. And it would be through manhood, and the pleasures that the physical can bring that God would like to heal you at this time. Release the fear that you have missed the mark and there will be instantly a new day dawning. It will come to you, my beloved, as a knowing and there will be gentle peace within your heart once more.

They are showing me that love of the heart is the answer. In peaceful situations, you can feel the light working on your heart. We would suggest, my child, that the more peaceful you become, the more the spirit will be felt by you. And it is through the feeling center that your bleeding heart will be healed.

My child, Pete is finished with the idea that he deserved sadness. He won't be looking for the darkness anymore, for he has come to believe his darkness was cleansed by his suffering in the physical. So he has seen within himself a certain amount of debt paid back. This does clear the way for easier learning. And for a reincarnation next time with gifts to give others. This is what the plan looks like that is unfolding now. He will come back to give back the generosities he had received.

My beloved Joe, do you see how your healing has aided him? For as he does remember you nourishing him, this allows him to remember what kindness light gives. So, memories of your kindness do remain behind with him as the darkness shifts to light.

It is your strong desire to do God's work but we would remind you that sometimes God's work goes way beyond your understanding. And your brother chose to join Him before he felt it was too late. Pete did feel that if he were to remain karmically bound too long, his bitterness would have grown so strong that he may have lost a sense of the light altogether. And as God would call him home in love, he felt that he must scurry to get there. We would suggest that you do adjust your perception to knowing that, as love is everlasting and as God is all-knowing, that there are always periods of transition, not death.

Now, there is another person here who is saying that the shock to your system, Joe, was great. You felt that Pete's struggle was going to be guided or governed by the light.

They are saying that you could not come totally to terms with the shock of it—of what he has chosen. And this has caused a numbing of parts around your heart and brain.

Letting go of the need to be the one who makes everybody okay will let you spend more time realizing the heaviness of the responsibility that you carried in your heart for Pete. You need to understand how powerful the guilt and concern was, even when he was alive. And once you see how loaded down you were emotionally by that, they said almost to the point, Joe, of being bankrupt emotionally, you will understand more clearly your feelings of powerlessness that have got a grip on you now.

Do you know what they are showing a picture of now? They show gunshot holes in you, in your heart and in your power center— and if you could see the picture of it, you would say, "Oh God," and you would stop it. Because that puts together your body again and allows you to rebuild all of your energy which you use in tremendously light ways!

They would rather see you quite angry. And to release a lot of your grieving through that. And this is where they are showing the chopping wood and a lot of physical activity to burn some of this off. It is okay to say "I am angry" and not try to have a spiritual view for now.

What Pete still treasures is what you taught him about giving and receiving. Something very good happened there. And it is that which he plans to re-live in his next incarnation. So it is the gift that you gave him, Joe.

Now, when he was here, he saw you as both the savior and a demon. As a savior you were absolutely fabulous, you were like an angel there. And then in a sense you would become a demon to him because he would say, "No, I can't really receive all of this goodness." What he sees on the other side is that your strong savior qualities were the most stabilizing influence he had toward the end. His decision to die would have been made earlier, Joe, except for you. Your intervention helped him grow a little bit more before his death.

So, he got a perspective that he would not have had the chance to get. He would have died totally embittered with all shadows, and with no sense of what light is about. And so from his perspective, he sees you as a stabilizing force for him. He sees you now meandering a bit in trying to find a safe connection for yourself in the physical.

I think I might be getting Pete directly here. Pete says that pride in yourself, Joe, is very important. He says that it is important for you to move on. This is not a family trait to have a lot of pride. If he could have allowed himself a sense of pride about his humanity, about his sensitivity, about his softness, about the good of him—that would have saved him. But he never really allowed himself to do anything that he could be proud of. You need to claim back pride, not just in yourself as a man, but also in what you have been able to create in your life.

You prolonged his life. You kept him on a life-support system. You weren't fully aware of it at the time, but he was nearly brain-dead and you kept pumping in and keeping everything going so he could get more information. He knew ultimately that he could not physically and emotionally be responsible for his actions. He knew that eventually he was going to lose it. It was just a matter of timing. But you gave him a lot of powerful information and you came in and filled in like a father, where he couldn't have gotten that from anyone.

He says that performance is part of your struggle, Joe. That first piece is about performance and the feeling of failure because that feeds into your worrying about whether he will be happy to see you again—that you have failed him.

You would be the first man he gave his Christmas package to, for in this package would be pride in yourself. Because the man of light that is you has surfaced. And now he would be knowing the Christ because he met him through you, Joe.

This man Pete wants no remorse over his passing, for he does not want more guilt showered on his life. He feels more remorse than anything and does not dare to judge you or another, for he feels at times himself so incomplete that he cannot make appropriate judgments. This is the dark shadow we are now removing from him. The only bag of gold he carries now is the love you gave him. He shudders to think that one would judge another, as he knows now that God has not judged him.

And as he removes himself from the blanket of darkness, he would rush back to you, the only man that stood as light in the desert, and hand you his package of serenity. He is letting his guilt go. What he is amazed by is that nobody is judging him. He takes the word "judgment" and has a huge line through it—"no judging." No judgment because his message to you is, his life was all about judging himself unfairly.

He knows that the way to light now is through the heart and he knows that he got caught in defeat and could not allow himself the way home to his heart. He is saying that wherever the wind blows and wherever your seed lands in your quest for the heart—that is fertile ground.

It is the feelings that are going to bring you to peace. Where you are is you have got to allow the anger. You have got to face the fact about how much it has taken from you. There is going to be a lot of anger, there is going to be a lot of weeping, and there is going to be "What is the use anyway." You gave love—but it is God and that individual that makes something happen. And so it is going to help you with a whole lot of detachment.

The message from Pete is real clear about taking pride in what you do. Claim it. And that there was no way that he could understand that. But that everything that you did made a difference right before his death to bring him to the point where he could start to learn love a bit. And there is a real strong need for him to be released, because he doesn't want any more guilt or pain in the physical, even around his name.

So that is what the channeled source said of Pete's status and my condition three months after his death. This message helped me gradually see the possibility that his suicide was not a great defeat for Pete, but rather a way for him to grow past issues that haunted him for lifetimes. The possibility that I had helped him see the reality of love soothed much of my own agony about having failed him. The channeled comments about my own condition and what needed to be done rang true in my heart.

SPRING IS RETURNING
SEPTEMBER 20, 1991
MY MOTHER'S BIRTHDAY

Spring is returning in the fall.
Some peace is returning to us all.

This spring fights with hard winter,
Erratic in its victories.

The sky blues after midsummer dullness.
And leaves turn slowly to splendor.

We've had our first birthday
After brother's death day.
Mother smiles in eighty candle light.

Beauty calls softly, again we can hear it.
We are sensitive to each other
And softer with self.

Rage is waning this Sunday night.

SEARCHING

S ix months after my brother's death, we had made it through the major holidays and his birthday. It was not an easy period. Thanksgiving surprised me with its difficulty. That day was usually not a big deal most years. I don't know if it was hard because it was the first big family holiday after his death, or because one was supposed to be thankful on that day.

At least by then my family knew when sadness was descending. And we had developed ways to function as a unit to deal with it. By now we had given up fighting so hard to resist grief's presence. That freed up a lot of energy for more constructive purposes. We could go with the flow when anguish appeared. By now we were confident that each particular period of sadness would end. Yet sorrow continued to interrupt our lives. It appeared as an unwelcome guest, particularly when we let our guard down, as one must often do when trying to relax or to celebrate something. I wanted grief to just completely and finally go away. And I hoped that whenever I would think of my brother in the future, it could be with a smile of delight at knowing him and a sense of peace.

Talking about hope brings up the issue of fear. I think my biggest fear during this time was that someone else really close, such as one of my parents, would die. The advantage of sudden death of a loved one is that you enter into the loss with an average amount of energy and are protected by shock for a while. The mind lets it sink in at a protectively slow pace. Now, the fear was that I would have to face another death with defenses torn and little energy left to deal with it.

I was struggling to understand death and how I felt about it. Much of my thinking was muddled and brooding. I was taking it personally, resenting death, and rebelling against its inevitability. So I decided to sit down and take a full look at my attitudes toward death without censoring myself as to good, bad, silly, or brilliant. Six months after my brother's death, here's what I wrote in a brainstorming fashion. Later that same night I went back and italicized the parts of my answer that seemed most powerful or central to me. The questions asked were suggested by the book *Rituals for Living and Dying* by David Feinstein and Peg Elliot Mayo.[21]

How do I feel deep down about my own death?

I think it stinks! I want to know more about what happens and to have an easy dying at a time of my own choosing. *I think we should all get a choice* and be informed of what comes after death. Why not? It would probably make us live life better. I hate not having any control over something that will affect me so deeply. I cannot even promise my own daughter that I will be here while she grows up.

Why do we die?

Our bodies break down—entropy up close and personal! Sometimes people withdraw their own life force. Nature seems to want change. Change equals life, so older organisms are obsolete, *new models are valued over old.* I would like to believe that *we live to learn and die to remember,* as a fifteen-year-old boy once told me.

What is death?

End, beginning? *unfulfilled* goals and unexperienced experiences, black, silence, fearsome, *lack of control,* sorrow for others, emptiness, missing the Spring, rest, welcome relief from pain, unfair trickery, plentiful, disease, fear, weakness, surrender, *unwanted*, unnecessary? gateway, eclipse, *mysterious,* sweet, peaceful.

I fear that it will be nonexistence more than I fear a hell, though I am uneasy about hell too. I don't like the loss of ego. *How much sense of self do you keep anyway—better be a lot!*

Different rules, possible traps, death may call on skills of an unknown nature. I feel it is an advantage to be intelligent, which I am, and trusting which I may or may not be. I'd like to believe that you are conscious throughout the whole process, peaceful and loving—and have a chance to rest on the other side as long as you want. I want no struggle, great wisdom, *all my questions answered*, then be free to decide whether to live again and have the choice between Earth existence and continuing some other way (angel?).

The veil—I'd like to be able to see my loved ones remaining here and let them know that I am okay and that I love them. *I fear aloneness during dying and after death.* Hope the next existence isn't so hard but just as real and filled with as much beauty. The robber, the thief, the enemy, failure. Could be an ecstatic experience. I have seven more tough deaths to go through, if the people I love die in order of age. I think it gets easier after you have experienced your first significant grief. When you are older, do you yield to death with greater acceptance?

What happens when we die?
I am not sure. I think it is most likely and most desirable that we are greeted by loved ones, feel peaceful, have a rest period, and decide on what we want to do next. But do we forget how difficult it is down here on Earth in our euphoria and sign up for another challenging life too eagerly? Perhaps we get in touch with other-life memories. Can there be love without judgment? Most come back to Earth for another round based on what experience they want, or to be with a person that they are still attached to. Some come back mainly to be

of service to others here. But I fear that *there is a danger of forgetting what you have learned previously* and having a terrible life after a good one. Can you slip back in your progress? Progress to what? I don't know. But I feel that *one's life continues forever* in some form, with or without a physical body.

If some of what I want to be true is true, then death can be a beautiful thing. We would get to start over, deep inside knowing what we have learned from the past, yet able to start again with a freshness and an innocence. From what I've gathered, the majority of the world's people, now and in the past, believe in life after death. And most, including a majority of Christians, unofficially consider some form of reincarnation to be the most likely possibility. Brain Weiss's book *Many Lives, Many Masters*[22] is a good introduction to the idea of reincarnation. But majority rule is an uncomfortable way to decide such a question. There is so little hard data, and it is of such importance to us all. Hopefully we have a collective wisdom.

In two decades of working as a psychotherapist, I have listened to many reports from clients about their connections and "conversations" with loved ones who have died. And now my family's own experiences at Christmas and many other times since my brother's death suggest to me an afterlife. Most experiences are subtle. Taken singly, they are easily dismissed as coincidences or random anomalies. Taken together, they have great power.

My family members felt strong feelings of Pete's presence at odd times—usually when they were not thinking about him but were involved in something that Pete was highly interested in when he was alive. For example, months after Pete's death, I sat down with my daughter to teach her for the first time the game of poker. We sat cross-legged in the living room on a beautiful blue silk carpet. Sunlight warmed and brightened our square of rug. We both were relaxed and playful. Beaming delight, she won every single hand from start to finish for more than a one-hour period. This is highly unusual in poker. About halfway through, I felt a strong sense of Pete, an excellent poker player, helping her. It felt like he was making a big affectionate joke. I could almost hear him laughing.

When I would think of Pete as sad and defeated, I didn't feel any connection with him. But I did feel a strong presence occasionally when I would imagine him as transformed into a light and free being, but still Pete. Often my sense of him in these "encounters" was that he was happy and playful. But even using all my meditation and Lifeline techniques, these encounters were disappointingly fragmentary. There were no long conversations, no robust exchange of ideas. I think that I was still too emotionally hot to get into the receptive state needed. Frustrating!

After the holidays, it was time to stop trying to live in two worlds at once. Wondering about Pete and where he might be produced a disconnection from the physical. My body was restless from so much thinking. I shifted to a simpler mode. As part of my grieving process, I started to chop wood, take long walks—anything physical. My body sang back its gratitude to me through the joy of muscle and sinew, and fresh air pulled deep into the lungs.

My emphasis shifted from caring for others to taking care of myself. I began to understand more deeply what had happened to me and how I was being changed by this experience.

By the end of January, two things were clear. The first was that suicide was going to be totally and forever unacceptable as an option for me because I now understood the pain it caused others. Also, I had decided that, whatever happened, I would stay around for the ride. I would learn to flow better with pain if I must, but I would be here for the duration. Given the permanency of death at least in this physical body, we die soon enough.

This new clarity represented the end of a way out that I had always kept in the back of my mind somewhere. It was replaced with a sense of obligation to myself to live fully. It was no longer acceptable to put off current experience, in hopes of future reward, or to live through a persona, the mask of what I believe others expect of me.

The second thing that became clear in the gut was that no matter how much I examined them, death and life were going to essentially remain puzzles. I gradually moved from resenting the lack of verifiable information, to an acceptance of mystery, and on to a celebration of mystery. We often pretend to understand, but can only understand from certain specific levels such as the scientific, and this does not fully capture the entire reality of even the simplest organism on this planet. On my good days, I was grateful and thrilled that we are blessed with the ineffable, the unspeakable, the unknown.

Desire to experience life remained, but the compulsion to understand vanished. I am going to rely on curiosity to get me through whatever comes along. Regardless of what pain or fear I might be in, I can be curious about the experience and relish staying in the experience because of that fact. For example, in Aruba my wife wanted to go on a tiny submarine to see the coral reefs. I went and saw the amazing undersea world there, using curiosity to balance my considerable motion sickness and claustrophobia that the small space, the state of being underwater, and the lack of sweet air produced. I am glad I went.

I continue to be eager for the next "went" that will come along. Since my brother's death, I more directly face my fears and explore life versus analyze it. This is a great victory for me.

So the three main reasons that kept me alive during my own decades of depression were each changed substantially by Pete's death. My sense of meaning was no longer tied so tightly to helping others. While helping is still a pleasure, now fulfilling my *self* is a greater priority. I have found that these two things conflict much less often than I would have anticipated. Also, my sense of curiosity ceased to be a drive to understand everything. Now it is more focused upon discovering and celebrating mystery. Finally, my appreciation of beauty deepened in intensity and widened to include the more humble things, such as the architecture of a simple kitchen chair.

By six months after Pete's death, I was just beginning to realize the value of these gifts that grief had brought to me.

LOST

While Pete was living at our office, in a funny way he and I danced a struggle around dress. He was impeccable in this area, and I was oblivious. Several times while I was at work, supposedly looking professional, he caught me with two different-colored socks on, dark black and dark blue. Twice he was distressed to find me, ready to see clients, in two different-colored shoes, dark brown and cordovan. All I could do was smile sheepishly and plead a dark morning bedroom and too little sleep. Then we would both laugh. At other times I would kid him by trying to mess up his hair.

Now, in the February after his death, I was all excited about going on television as a guest speaker for the first time. Very nervous about how I would look, I stood in my closet, reaching to pick out my tie. Some of the ties I had to choose from were Pete's. A great wave of grief hit me. Pete would have loved helping me select what to wear for this event, and I would have felt confident wearing his choices. More importantly, we would have shared all the aliveness of my TV debut.

In the grey of a seemingly always cold and rainy winter, I really missed my brother in the sense that it had been a long time since I had seen him.

Our society doesn't really focus much on brother-to-brother relations. Or, for that matter, sister-sister and sister-brother pairs. Movies, plays, and books seem to focus more on parent-child and spousal relationships. Odd, when you think about it, since sibling relationships are important.

The dynamics of parent-child relations are beautiful and essential to the continuation and progress of humankind, but the richness of intimacy that is experienced in these relations is often limited. The influence and support of your parents— highly important when you are young—often fade, and you may find yourself spending at least half of your life without them. Likewise, kids are parents' most intense focus for two decades, but then they hopefully leave home and create their own lives. Limiting the parent-child relationship also is the divisiveness of generational differences in values and experiences and an inequality of authority and power. There tends to be a one-sidedness to parent-child relations. Parents give to the needy child; then, after perhaps a period of some form of equality, later the adult-child often gives to a needy parent. Yet, despite these limitations, the parent-child relationship, in our culture, is the most sanctified.

Spousal relations, of course, are also essential to the continuation of humankind, and between spouses more intimacy is possible. Spouses usually select each other, are of the same generation, share the bond of sexual union, create and sustain a home, and parent together. These are very deep bonds indeed, often lasting throughout adulthood. There are also a few obvious challenges to intimacy here, however. Spouses do not bond from birth as parent-child pairs do. Moreover, spouses are often selected to be complementary to us (if we are quiet, we tend to marry someone outgoing), yet the complementary easily becomes the conflictual. Spouses are also often selected unconsciously to complete unfinished issues in the parent-child relationship, creating ongoing struggles between partners. Furthermore, spouses are sometimes selected for evanescent reasons, such as a desire to escape the parental home.

A relationship between brothers—between any siblings—has the potential for far fewer limitations and obstacles. Of course not all, and perhaps not many, brother relationships realize their potential; many relationships start out weakly and need blessed conditions initially to grow strong and resilient—much like the path of acorn to the oak. The fulfilling sibling relationship requires the consistent consent and desire of both parties and the encouragement of the surrounding community.

Given the proper environment, being brothers can be a deeply intimate and enriching experience. The bonding starts at birth for one brother and usually very young for the other. Unless adopted or step-children, they are united by the closest possible genetics, closer even than parent-child. They are further united by generational closeness and common teaching of culture and values by their parents. They share a common joy and sometimes a common enemy on a daily basis, as they react to their parenting situation. Their relationship extends from birth to death—frequently many more years longer than paren-tal or spousal relationships. By adulthood, authority and rivalry issues have usually softened, allowing a true friendship where physical affec-tion is possible without the complications of overt sexuality.

Brothers can easily become best of friends, confidantes, mutual mentors, a place of refuge from the struggles with parents and spouses, helpers with decision-making and supporters of those decisions. They can keep their family and individual histories alive for each other. A brother is someone with whom you can be fully honest about defeats, fears, imperfections. You can ask without shame for a loan—of money, car, time, or energy. Brothers are usually good repositories of secrets, particularly about deep feelings concerning the parent or spouse. Brothers usually have a code of silence allowing trust that, whatever tender issue is expressed, it will be kept private. Trust is fur-ther encouraged by the absence of the threat of retaliation that exists in the power dynamics of parent-child and spousal relationships.

While we have Mother's Day, Father's Day, and wedding anniver-saries, we do not celebrate a Brother's Day or a Sister's Day. Why do we not more vigorously acknowledge, encourage, and celebrate siblings?

On the one hand, perhaps it is best. The fact that I have celebrated my siblings with something more akin to internal prayer than to public celebration has kept rituals from trivializing feelings from the heart. On the other hand, rituals allow us to acknowledge perceptions that are more than facts and memories, perceptions that are facets of myth and imagination. And a myth of brotherhood may be important personally and culturally.

Myths color our perception of reality and allow us space for creativity and problem solving. Our myths become models for our behavior. Because we emphasize the parent myth so intensively, we confine ourselves to approaching all relationships from this perspective. God becomes God the father; bosses become fathers and employees become children. We look for mothering and fathering from our spouses. We look to government to be the good mother (nurturing and undemanding of us) and the good father (protective and enabling). We fear our government is becoming the bad mother (intrusive, controlling, and draining) and the bad father (self-absorbed, punitive, arbitrary, and violent). We feel as helpless and pessimistic as little children to change our government-parent. We feel no sense of control over our government and therefore have none. In our relationship with the Earth, too, we can see the effects of the parent model. When we view the Earth as mother, there is a danger of taking too much from her and returning too little, as children do.

If we expanded, celebrated, and applied the myth of brotherhood, many more options would open to us. What changes would happen in business if boss and employee, businessperson and customer related to each other as brothers? What changes in government would occur if bureaucrat and taxpayer were brothers? What if we viewed the Earth as brother as well as mother? What would it be like to relate to God as brother or sister? Bringing brotherhood into these relationships may help us remain sensitive to dimensions of fairness, balance, reciprocity, kindness, cooperation, and mutual power. We may see options where it appeared before there were none.

Since my brother's death, I am sensitized to the dimensions of brotherhood playing out in all aspects of life. It is in our power to enhance our appreciation of brotherhood in our relations with siblings, spouses, and friends. We can then extend this outward to change the impasse we feel with our institutions and to deepen our relationship with our Earth and our God. The brotherhood myth truly may have the potential to guide us from childhood into fully mature human adulthood.

All this musing is terribly abstract—in this February, seven months after his death, I miss Pete deeply. Part of my soul is torn and my heart is broken. I have other brothers and a sister whom I value highly, but Pete is gone and he is irreplaceable. I miss his smell, hands, smile, advice, humor, and interest in my life; I miss his help, and I miss helping him. I feel incomplete at my core. I long for him at a place deep inside where I have never longed for a lover.

The yearning hit at odd times. Shock had given way to fatigue. Nothing had ever before produced such a tiredness of spirit in me—not mononucleosis, not 130-hour weeks in graduate school, not waking up several times a night for months with a sick child. At that moment, deep in winter, it felt as though relief and rest would never come. Warmth and life seemed to have permanently died much of the time. There was a sense of being out of control and unable to change the scenario of grief, loss, and lack.

I felt a sense of community with the many that I have never met who are struggling in the absence of a spouse, child, or best friend—all players in the symphony of grief. And I knew I was in the percussion section, which speaks loudly but not often of the grief of a lost brother. My heart beat with the rhythm of these drums. The closest rhythm to this I had felt before was the drums pounding in muted profundity during President Kennedy's funeral procession. They accurately captured the sadness and the length of the march. They echoed the loss of hope.

At that point I'd have been grateful for any after-life that provides rest and reunion with all those I have come to love. But that was for later. For my daughter's sake and for my own, I needed to struggle back to life on the surface again. I would take as much rest as I could find, when I could find it. But I had to keep marching forward.

Here's what Pam's channelings were saying during this period of my grieving:

> *You respond sometimes to Pete's old self, and when you do that, you reconnect with the darker side of yourself which is always located in the heart near Pete and Pete's death. So in a lot of ways what you are going through is the birthing of a new man, and the death of the old. That is why there is so much sense of the loss—the emotions get mixed up with the loss of your old self but also the significant loss of Pete.*
>
> *And whenever you have a problem with that, it is like your energy connects with old energy patterns of Pete's. Not Pete as spirit now, but the remnants of Pete's energies, which still hang around a bit, because the whole grieving process is not completed. And they want you (this is a very clear picture) to see that they are separate things—that Pete's soul energy is way beyond the physical. Pete's soul energy is way beyond the ideas of loss.*
>
> *As a matter of fact, they show him in a marching band. He is having the time of his life, Okay? But his ego remnants are still clinging in the physical and they tend to cling where the loss is felt the most and really, outside of his mother, it is you. So you need to disconnect from any idea, from any stress related to Pete's disease. And Pete's disease was refusal to allow himself success.*
>
> *And so the focus is on yourself right now and on letting go of the whole idea that there should be limitation around success. They are saying that as you do this, you will find yourself going through some*

grieving about Pete's old ways of being. And they are saying that you need to allow pieces of this grieving, but they are saying it is the remnants, all right?

[At this point I asked if this energy remnant had an intelligence to it, like a ghost, or was it just the memory of Pete?]

Ah, it is like a ghost. That energy is very thick. It is not formed like a ghost, but if I were going to say that it is one or the other, I would say it is a ghost, not a memory. So we are talking about a literal energy that hangs around. So see, the minute you start to slip into the shades of you that are a bit like the old Pete, you hook right into it. And Pete's energy is connected to your home. Yes, your home is where you tried to heal him and so that was really his last home.

They show you pulling forth friends and relations who are willing to support this. And they show you building a huge bonfire on your farm. They show you standing around in a circle, hands held, and they show you singing your last farewells to him. You are to show Pete through song that your hearts wish to be free of him now, as you see him in a glorious estate of love.

In other words, he is in another home and in the state of love. And you and your friends on Earth share with each other. There is food. It is like a feast. And they show you shaking hands, communicating, holding one another and talking about your lives and your future. You leave no room for sadness in this new energy field that you are planting. And this bonfire dissolves the ghost-like mist that hangs there. They are showing this energy of Pete's is so thick around there, that when this is gone, a lot of the pressure you are under will ease.

The power of the ego is most strong right before death. It attaches to those who are strongly involved with the dying person. It is these attachments on the passing of another that cause great distress for the survivors and the terrible sense of loss.

Be not sad at your brother's death now, but happy at the letting go of the form of his life. This is a great celebration to be had, for it is the dissolving of the energies of his personality which refused to let him alter his life plan. So the form of his unhappiness must and can be dissipated, as each person is willing to release him.

We pass no judgment on the suicidal notion of your brother Pete. But we must make it very clear that the horror of one's life is bound to energies, and unless they are forgiven and let go of, they travel wherever you are. This is the human term of hell. The passing of your brother from the physical was a blessing for him in that he could not escape from the harsh karma of his lifetime.

That bonfire, I have never been so sure of anything, it is so clear it is like my eyes are blazing with it. And that fire does consume the mist. You are talking about a real thing. You can't see it. If you saw a mist over the mountains you'd say, Oh well, the sun just has to burn it off. This fire is going to do the same thing to dissipate old Pete energies.

Feeling a little silly, my wife and I gathered friends and had the recommended bonfire and fellowship. A friend of mine blew notes of sorrow on a conch that echoed through the mountains. I read some of my poetry and found myself weeping. We danced, sang, and said goodbye once again to Pete. I could feel the strong loving as good friends each in turn held me, as the fire died down and the night got cold. Strangely, our house and our moods seemed much lighter after this ritual and that peculiar heaviness never returned. It was a significant step in our moving on.

TIRED AND TENDER
JANUARY 20, 1992

Death leaves the living tired and tender.
Twilight time often catches you.
But bright sunlight too, is suspect.
Sweet-ache longing returns again and again.
Even to the strongest of men.

You swim through your sea, rounding to places
Before you shared with the now dead.

The restaurant at the far edge of town,
The closet where clothes were hung.

Tired and tender—those places
Produce a swell of sweet suffering.

You want to remember all you can.
Try to recapture the essence of man.

Each memory, opens the sad scar
Yet gives you him back—he can't be far.

You go through this, there is no choice.
Hoping uncertainly, fearing defeat.

The after-life becomes paramount.
It is the place of reunion
And a rest from so much tiredness.

FULL STOP

About ten months after my brother died, things had quieted down considerably inside of me. But somehow it felt that I hadn't completely said goodbye to Pete. I had not yet let the experience fully penetrate to the center of my being.

I also hadn't been alone for an extended period of time. I am a private person, in the sense of doing my best "getting in touch" when alone, and then, after this solitary encounter, sharing my perceptions with others. But I had been avoiding solitude, over-scheduling activities to keep Pete's death from penetrating too deeply.

There was some part of me that was waiting to see his corpse to believe that it actually had happened. Pete's body had been quickly cremated and shipped back East in a six-by-six-inch plain cardboard box, the kind that could have contained mail order vitamins or new parts for a shaver. This box bore no relationship to the brother I knew. My sister shared my discomfort about this aspect to the degree that she wondered if Pete had faked his death to escape creditors and was now living in some foreign land. She reasoned that perhaps my older brother, in collusion with this plan, had lied about identifying Pete's body. Hope does not die easily.

I realized that it was time for me to face reality more deeply. And I needed something to help me do this. I decided to go to the place where Pete had died. I scheduled a five-day trip to Las Vegas for July, on the one-year anniversary of his death. There, alone and with total anonymity, I could sleep, eat, and cry when I wanted and nobody would really get excited given the daily strange goings-on in that city. I figured any emotional outburst would just look like I had been unlucky at the tables.

It seemed like a good idea at the time.

About two weeks before the trip, anxiety began rising. Two days before I was to head out on my quest, I became clearly afraid. Ahead of me was the unknown. I could not predict what would be experienced, felt, and expressed. Suddenly I did not trust myself to maintain control.

Usually I feel a wonderful excitement at the thought of going someplace alone. For this trip, I had arranged to take good care of myself. First-class airplane reservations were booked for the first time in my life and a nice hotel suite was reserved. Yet now, with the trip imminent, I felt more than alone; I felt lonely.

Anger, disgust, and fear about Las Vegas surfaced. This was a city that I had previously loved for its freedom, friendliness, variety, and excitement. Could I really blame a whole city for somehow not welcoming and saving my brother? Evidently a part of me could. It felt as though Vegas did not care about my brother and would not care about me. It became a place where one could get lost and never return. Las Vegas pulled at me like a black hole.

The morning after arriving in the city, I asked a cabby to drive me to the mortuary that handled my brother's remains. I found myself telling the cabby what was going on; he was quietly sympathetic. The mortuary was round and modern. I entered, palms sweaty, and there was nothing to see but a small reception desk behind a glass window. Its feel was more of a bank than of sacred space. I turned around without saying anything and got back into the cab. My strongest emotion was, "He is not here."

I asked the cabby to drive to Pete's old apartment. The last time I had been there, we sat in his apartment and by the pool, enjoying a relaxed intimacy. Now, in mid-morning, in the eerie silence of a community where all residents had gone to work, I walked up to his door, then to the pool, and left within five minutes of arriving—not having seen a soul. Again I had a strong sense of, "He is not here."

It was bittersweet, remembering the times we had shared together there. I had planned to walk the neighborhood as we had done together before. Now it felt fruitless.

The cabby took me back to the hotel. The whole trip had taken less than thirty minutes. I had planned on it taking hours, and now I realized that my trip was as much an attempt to find him as to let go of him. I went up to my hotel room and decided to try to get angry or something—to get out what was inside of me. Nothing came.

I felt spent and very tired of focusing on death. I went down to the hotel pool, sat in the shade to avoid the worst of the pounding heat, and wrote the poem that appears at the end of this chapter. It really was time to move on.

The rest of the time in Vegas, at every opportunity I willed myself to let go of this sticky grief. As the elevator rose, I imagined leaving the grief behind on the ground. As I walked down the long hall from the hotel to the casino, I imagined dropping a dull grey cloak of grief behind me, and walked faster—never looking back. I repeated these images often over the days to come. Finally, I began to feel lighter.

I purposefully threw myself into the excitement of the casino, letting the din of coins and flashing lights enfold me. I expansively started conversations with strangers and was extra nice to the casino personnel. They responded warmly. When I got tired I would go up to my bed, enter a relaxed state, and imagine myself floating high above the desert—free of all the responsibility that I had carried toward Pete, free of being responsible for my family's feelings. I took an oath to now live fully, freely, and joyously, even if I forgot Pete totally in the process and lost him forever.

As my stay continued, I did exactly what I felt like doing in each moment, allowing myself to change my mind instantly. Sometimes I slept for thirty minutes, stayed up for twenty minutes, and went back to sleep. Sometimes I stayed up for thirty hours and then slept for ten. I would begin a meal, change my mind, and walk out. For a few days I stopped all the "shoulds"—from showering, shaving, and brushing teeth to any "should" about grieving, caring, or calling home.

This "vacation" was one of the best gifts I had ever given myself. My recommitment to myself and to what life can bestow charged me with great energy. Part of the freedom was fueled by anger. "Well, Pete. You decided to check out, so Fuck You!" Part of the freedom was fueled by love. For both of us, our relationship needed to close. It was the only way that the good in the relationship could continue to outweigh the bad. Our relationship was too fabulously beautiful, too sacred, to tarnish it with more regrets, guilt, and sorrow.

Here's what Pam's channelings said about Pete's progress on the other side after I had returned from Vegas:

> Let's see... now, Pete's energy is watchful of you. He is still... it is like he is still in town, he just isn't in your house. And he has a wistful energy about him when he watches you. It is not jealous, it is wistful in the sense that he wishes that he could have gotten himself together but it doesn't come across as a jealousy of what you are doing. It is more his sense of loss.
>
> If you get hooked into that... it looks pretty far away from you, but if you find yourself connecting with sort of a wistful "Gee, things just really don't work just the way you want them to," then cleanse yourself. Because he is growing and is freed up considerably to get more light. He is in a weakened state in that he doesn't have as much energy. And this has opened him so that the light can get in. It is like when you are the most vulnerable, when after a good cry someone can really come in and talk to you. That is where he is. So actually in

freeing yourself from him and insisting on the distance, he is suddenly being surrounded by more light as he too lets go a little.

[I mentioned writing this book and asked if I should continue because writing it was making me sad.]

When you can laugh out loud at Pete's predicament, you can pull this from the shelf. Until then, the timing would be poor as it would create an open doorway for his re-entry. His energy would seek the book to help redefine himself, and you would be left writing the tears of his life.

So, as you would remove self a bit from this and become very drawn into the physical world... They want you to enjoy the physical world, Joe. As you do this, you will find yourself solidified and then able to look back with a luxurious laugh at Peter's predicament and his means of resolving it. They are saying the more grounded you are in the sense of pleasure in the physical, the less Pete's energies can inhibit you. Okay? He really doesn't mean to, he is just enormously sad! Your farm home feels freer.

[I asked how at one time they could report he was "playing-in-the-band" happy and at another time report that he was sad.]

I think that they go back and forth in emotions like we do, only it is in another dimension. It is interesting, they are saying that the dead can get greedy for more physical experiences through those who are mourning, as a way to gather more information for themselves to improve their situation—to further their understanding or just to be a part of physical life again. They may not want to let go of physical attachments because, in their sudden deaths, they have lost their means of grounding and of learning. And they are saying that these visitations are not always necessarily good for the mourner. All souls are seeking peace and enlightenment on various dimensions and so, in many ways, life does go on the way it was here.

As you feel the closeness of Pete's old energy, you do have the right to create a free zone for self—and they are showing a huge bubble of light, so that, in Earth terms, the passage of time allows a general healing. Right now, Pete just wishes like crazy that he had been able to pull it off.

This channeling was, of course, encouraging. I put the writing of this book aside, figuring to pick it up in a few months, after I was feeling more solid. It would be two more years before it felt safe to write again. When I finally began again, I was delighted to find that I could write about Pete without sadness.

MAPPING THE TERRITORY

By the time I was completing this book, three years after Pete's passing, I was feeling almost fully healed and excited to be growing in many new dimensions. What about Pete? What might his existence be like at this point in time? Of course we cannot know for certain, but this chapter will conclude with the final channeling about him received three years after his death. Some of it suggests what the afterlife might contain for us.

From my loss of Pete, experience with clients, work in meditation, meeting with participants at The Monroe Institute and hearing their experiences, and from reading what seems like countless books over the years, here is my clearest sense of what may actually happen after we die. What I will say occurs in the context of knowing that humans have traditionally believed that there is an afterlife. Egyptian, Tibetan, Hindu, Buddhist, Moslem, Mesoamerican traditions and religions, as well as Judaism and Christianity, all accept life after death.

First, the Near-Death Experience literature appears to be accurate as to what happens during dying. My only personal taste of this was the out-of-body that I experienced during my motorcycle accident. I felt many of the things described in near-death experiences. This experience went a long way in convincing me that the experiences reported are real. Raymond Moody's books[23] and others[24] describe this phenomenon in detail.

These reports of near-death experiences cannot be dismissed as hallucinations caused by neurochemical changes at the time of death. The reports are very different in content and coherence from hallucinations caused by a disturbed brain. The reports often contain information that the unconscious, dying person could not possibly know through ordinary perceptual means, such as which tools the doctors used and what people were doing in adjacent rooms. Commonalities across reported experiences from diverse cultures suggest that we may encounter the following events in any order:

1. We may hear or feel a buzzing sensation.

2. We may find that we exist as energy or in an energy body while still being able to hear and see into the physical world.

3. We may experience an awesome sense or vision of light.

4. We may have feelings of great love, deep peace, and of coming home.

5. We may encounter spiritual beings and perhaps loved ones who have previously died.

6. We may experience a review of our significant life events.

Reports of these near-death experiences are not all positive, but negative experiences seem extremely rare. As we move further in time from the act of dying, there is naturally nothing written from the first-person perspective. Organized religions all have their traditions. Many traditions speak of an initial period spent in cleansing or purification, followed by a period of rest. Many feel that prayers for the dead are helpful and contact between the living and the dead is possible. The Tibetans believed that it was critical to pray for the person for the first month to guide the person to God. A modern book of interest on this subject is the *American Book of the Dead* by E.J. Gold.[25] Most traditions involve the idea that the soul's final destiny is eventual full union with God.

The Monroe Institute offers a series of tapes developed by the expert in death and dying, Elisabeth Kubler-Ross, M.D., by the expert in consciousness Charles Tart, Ph.D., and by the out-of-body expert Robert Monroe. This tape series, called *Going Home*, is designed to help a terminally ill person feel more comfortable and, when the time comes for death, make his transition a loving, peaceful, fearless, and conscious process regardless of his religious orientation. It also provides tapes to assist the loved ones left behind to understand the process more fully and to let go with less pain.

Many traditions allow for reincarnation. In his book *Journey of Souls*, Michael Newton, Ph.D., uses the hypnotic sessions of many subjects to map out a detailed description of the between-lives state.[26] I am personally aware of a few of my past lives. Through my direct experience with the concept, reincarnation has gained credibility for me.

My belief in reincarnation was confirmed because in these memories I knew I was "me" but the quality of my thoughts and emotions had a completely different imprint than what I know as twentieth-century Joe Gallenberger. I felt that I could not be making it up as I went along. One of my memories was unearthed during a session in which my wife gave me a simple instruction, to remember a past life. I relaxed and went through a tunnel. On the other side I looked down at my feet, and then gradually looked up and saw where I was.

I found myself in ancient Egypt, a slave pulling a rope with many other men. The heat and dryness were palpable. I felt a pride in being part of a big project. Charleene asked me what were the names of the men next to me. I didn't know, and it seemed completely unimportant. She asked me how I got there, and I was immediately filled with a deep sadness as the memory of being torn from my tribe overtook me.

While this was going on, I was struck with how simple and uncomplicated my consciousness was, compared to now. The primitiveness was startling and more than a little bit refreshing.

I told Charleene that this was too intense; I wanted to come back. She suggested instead that I go to when I was younger and immediately I was about five years old, with my tribe. The consciousness shift was again amazing. The tribe was linked telepathically as one unit in thought, and its mood alternated dramatically, depending on how close to an oasis it was. I was aware of a very strong imprinting, somewhat similar to modern children knowing to look both ways before crossing a street. The imprint here was, "Always know where your water is." I began to feel indescribably tired, and Charleene brought me back to present time.

Another of my past-life memories illustrates how we may be influenced by strong thought-forms or addictions and how they may lead to less comfortable incarnations. This one occurred spontaneously during meditation. I suddenly found myself experiencing a rest period between lives. It was dark, and I was deeply sleeping yet aware of being surrounding by many others doing the same thing. A great peace came from the full knowledge that we are not alone. I decided to go back and see what the previous life had been like.

I was surprised to find myself a few-days-old infant, thrown away on a desert trail as my family kept walking. I was disturbed to experience my own death by exposure. I tried to figure what was going on. The mother loved the child but the father said "too many" and dropped me there. Why would I let myself get in that mess? I discovered that, in the life before that one, I had been addicted to a woman. When I died I immediately willed to be with her, not looking at anything else, and dove back into a physical life to follow her. She was an older sister in the family which threw me away, and I got to experience losing her all over again, hopefully by this lesson, learning some of the difference between addiction and love.

The Monroe Institute has recently established a new program, called Exploration 27. I had the good fortune to be a co-trainer for the program's maiden voyage. Exploration 27 takes up where Lifeline leaves off. It facilitates participants going into deep meditation and exploring what goes on in the afterlife space called the Park.

From data gathered by these meditators, it seems that when we die there is indeed a period of reunion with loved ones, then a period of rest and rejuvenation. It seems that there are other functions within this consciousness space such as education via simulated experiences, direct knowledge, and observation. Also, there appears to be a planning function where one is helped to design further experiences for one's development, including perhaps another Earth lifetime.

Reports from Lifeline, psychics, channelers, and clients all suggest that some people after passing remain attached to or concerned with the physical for at least a while. A good example is from one of my clients after the sudden death of a mother of young children. The client reported seeing the mother nightly in the house where her children were sleeping, until it was decided who would continue the care for her children.

It appears that, during the period of rest and rejuvenation contact with loved ones on Earth is least likely or most difficult. When contact is initiated by those they knew on Earth, some of the deceased seem to discourage contact, at least for a while. Many meditators report a first contact with a deceased love one as a joyous reunion; but then, if they pursue frequent contacts, the deceased appears less pleased, as if to say, "Nice to see you but your energy is better spent living than visiting with me."

There are many exceptions to this generality, particularly the frequent reports of a vivid sense of the deceased's consoling presence that seems to occur spontaneously in dreams. During the waking life of the loved one on Earth, contacts come most commonly at stressful times but also occur at happy times. Contacts of this type may continue for decades. But they tend to be very infrequent for most people.

Information from the sources also suggests that the afterlife is filled with the essential quality of all life—change and growth. It appears that in the afterlife experience, one still has the opportunity for varieties of emotion. And changes in plans and thoughts may occur, at least in the short term (however that may be defined in a place where time does not appear to exist as we know it).

These sources suggest that we humans are much more than our physical bodies and our conscious minds—that after death, once we break free of any restrictive thought-forms, we become significantly more aware of the fullness of our being which some call our Greater Self or Higher Self. It seems that, because we are aware of the larger picture of our own nature and also the love and connection between all consciousness, even while there is change, we have a greater awareness of being essentially safe and loved, and we cease to worry about being judged. This liberating freedom from judgment is explored in detail in an interesting book, *Conversations with God*.[27] Robert Monroe's book, *Ultimate Journey*, published the year before he died, provides his perceptions of what we may find after we finish Earth existence.[28] Most of these sources agree with religious thought that says that the eventual path is to become one with God or realize that the kingdom of heaven is within, that we are already an intimate part of God-source.

My own experiences suggest to me now that dying can be a struggle, but that it doesn't need to be if we are prepared and supported. Then death can be peaceful and natural. I feel that during death we do see the light, meet with someone with whom we feel loved, rest deeply, receive guidance, then usually reincarnate to continue our growth. In exceptional situations, we may go straight to union with God if we are ready, or fairly quickly back to Earth if we are addicted to a particular person or experience. We can be kept stuck by strong thought forms, such as the idea of Judgment Day or karma (as you sow, ye shall reap). But eventually we all merge with God.

I have grown and learned incredible lessons on this journey of grief and discovery following Pete's death. Even with all my religious, clinical, and scientific preparation, my brother's death by suicide still hit me like a ton of bricks. I had to go through the human stages of sorrow, anger, and eventually acceptance. I am now convinced that an afterlife exists and that contact with loved ones who have died is possible. And if accomplished, such contact is a poor substitute for having them alive but will bring the peace of knowing that they are okay.

I know now that the stages of human grief can be used, with grace and support, to bring about tremendous positive changes in one's life. And finally, I know that mystery abounds—we might as well celebrate the fact, rather than living under the delusion that someday some authority will explain everything for us.

The following channeling session occurred three years after Pete's death and is the latest channeled information that I have about him. It occurred during my final re-write of the original *Brothers Forever* book.

October 1994

The soul of Pete is more buoyant. It has been freed up. It has a much more angelic quality, which is actually the quality that you related to when you remember him in terms of love and sweetness.

Now he is feeling more free to communicate with you. He has a new kind of consciousness. He is laughing. Now that you are more free of guilt and sadness, he can communicate directly with you. As a matter of fact, he will be a facilitator of a lot of the ideas for moving things around within your book. He is certainly out of sleeping.

And that is the part that I am seeing of Pete that is surviving. He is just getting out of his shell. He is staying very close to the third dimension. I think he will reincarnate. But this is the first taste of free-

dom that I have ever seen with him. He is totally enjoying. He looks almost cherubic.

He is around you . . . there is a great releasing and what he is showing me is freedom for you. It is like taking your hands off of a plow. He is showing me pictures. The plow is a symbol of work. He is taking your hands off the plow. Higher consciousness does not get involved in work as he did. And it removes itself from the plow. Fundamentally what he is saying is that things don't need to be so hard. Things just aren't that hard. It was just his Earth consciousness that made him believe that it was.

When you have a consciousness of work, then you will, no matter how good a soul you are, have the experience of toil and the disappointment and all the limits that come with work. His kind of suffering does not have anything to do with the goodness of the soul. It has to do with the consciousness around work and the valuing of yourself. He shows you breaking the mold. He has broken the mold in his own way by leaving that behind, by shedding that skin.

Now, don't relate success to goodness of soul. This needs to be a theme in your book. Now, he is showing me a picture, he is going into the well with tears filling up. I think it is related to grief. Yes, there is some grief left back there, more in terms of regret. He is showing grief and it weighs him down. Now he turns into a firefly and the grief puts water in the light, and the little fireflies can't light.

He is going to hang around you, Joe. And he can do that as long as you feel safe with it. There is no heaviness around him at all. The firefly thing seems to be significant. I do not know why. It is sort of an odd image to show me.

He is also saying that he had a real chemical imbalance. So that many of his mood shifts and just his whole psyche were unavoidable. A lot of his pain was just not being able to control that. And it was chemical.

Now, in talking about while he was here, he is saying that he could not forgive himself to experience his passion. Now, he gets back out of that energy to continue to talk to you. He does not like to get into that energy even to mention it. When he gets even close to the energy of that life, it is like getting short of breath. That is how important it is to really release any connection to guilt and judgment.

It is interesting, he feels very free now. I don't suppose that he will create anything like that again. He seems very clear about not drawing up another bad plan for a hard life. He sees it was really a bad plan and from his point of view he also knows that he does not have to draw up the same plan. He is starting to understand choice. He flies like an angel. He is funny. He is enjoying the lightness, the freedom of non-physical.

I CAN NOW GO LIGHTLY

I have had one more significant release on my journey. Near the second Christmas to follow Pete's death, while I was teaching at The Monroe Institute, a woman offered to perform an ancient American Indian ceremony, called smudging, to help me release my grief. I said, "Sure." A few other women were standing around, heard our plans, and asked to watch. To this I also said, "Sure." We went outside at dusk. The splendid mountain view was fading. The wind sharpened at the top of the hill as we began.

The ceremony is a blur. But at some point these six women formed a circle around me. I have never felt a more powerful, more positive, and safer energy than I did within this circle. Within this energy, without intending to, I began to weep deeply. I had a clear vision of the dance of responsibility and failure that my brother and I had been doing through what felt like eons of time and hundreds of lives. I screamed and I let this all go. It was finished.

The women then moved in close, supporting my body with their warmth as I collapsed on that cold winter night. They held me upright, swaying and singing gently. I will always remember their loving support. I thank them again here for expanding my knowledge of positive female power and helping me release what may have been a pattern held for a millennium.

Time passed, into another winter. I realized that the past six months had been much better for me. A number of projects had been completed and some new exciting ones were begun. My family was well. The holidays were better this year. But I had become subtly impenetrable in some hard-to-explain way. I was friendly enough and still cared about people, but part of me had hardened so that no one would hurt me so deeply again. And there was some sense of feeling that in situations of deep pain, it was "every man for himself," because no one else could really help.

I liked this new freedom from responsibility for everyone else's feelings. My wife was the only one who commented on my hardness. She didn't like it. I interpreted her comments as meaning that I was more difficult to manipulate and less easy to predict. I was very engaged in my work and that felt good.

I came to know of my closed-offness in a strange way. It happened in March. I was passionately wrapped up in negotiating for a project that promised to make me happy for decades to come. If it came about, I would be living with a community of friends whom I loved and would be doing work that was perfect for me. Everything seemed to be going well and I was celebrating a done deal. Suddenly I was cut off at the knees; the project fell through. I was devastated. Within minutes, I understood that after my brother's death, I had arranged myself inside to never be ravaged again. But I had thought that death was the only way I could be devastated at such a deep level. I was wrong—here was another way.

Seconds after I realized this, I let myself open wide to this new hurt. For hours I let it flow through me, keeping my defenses down. It felt good, even with all the pain, to not resist, to not struggle to control and contain. I realized that I could stop the loss and save the project by "kissing ass" and compromising a few important values. I didn't. I understood then that I was fully committed to living my own life, not someone else's idea of it. After this all had calmed down, I took a look at what I had discovered about myself and my stance toward letting people hurt me.

I had thought that the key was to learn nonattachment, and I had thought I had mastered this. What I had really done was close off to people and become attached to not feeling any more deep pain. This fear of the agony of loss, if left unchecked, could destroy intimacy and genuineness for the rest of my life.

Yet it was not acceptable to go back to the old position of vulnerability with which I had lived life before my brother's suicide. Very likely, it was not possible. If you have ever lived through an earthquake, the solidity of the ground cannot be taken for granted again, not all the way, deep down. Inside yourself, you know that the solid can liquefy and change.

I searched fatalistically for a good while for an answer to the question of how to be open and fully engaged with people, and yet not be vulnerable to full devastation once again. It seemed that there was no way out of this dilemma. Then, in a moment of grace, I was surprised to find an answer that had hope of working for me. I trust that the answer will also be useful to others.

It had to do with the idea of completeness and perfection that I feel must be the true reality of things here on Earth. For nearly forty years, I had been perplexed and deeply disturbed by the presence of so much pain in our world. How could a loving God allow it?

Logic dictated that there was a God. I could not see a way for inanimate matter to create mind and spirit. The big bang, evolutionary theory and natural selection all could be true, and yet for me could not account for the original something from nothing. Nor could blind random physical events account for the formation of the beauty and complexity of life on this planet.

So for me, there was a God, and often I was awed by the love and intelligence of the Creator. But I feared that He was either dead or cruel to allow so much suffering to proceed unabated in the world.

Sometimes, when I was confronted with how much pain exists, religion and faith seemed like just so much whistling in the dark.

I was walking along a country road at The Monroe Institute that spring enjoying birdsongs and roadside flowers that glowed a most vibrant blue in the fresh sunshine. Feeling relaxed and happy, suddenly I glimpsed a newborn fawn bounding through the field on my left. The fawn had been roused by a tractor slowly moving through the field, filling the air with new-mown smells. Thrilled, I moved quietly closer on an intersecting path. As the deer approached, horror filled me. The newborn innocent had been hit by the tractor. It paused on the road, looking for its mother, and ran into the woods with its leg broken and bleeding. I tried to follow but couldn't keep up with it.

Feeling terrible about the fawn, I returned to the Institute for help. They sent an expert tracker to find her. I lay down to rest and to meditate, but I couldn't get the fawn out of my mind. Remember, I had broken my own leg years earlier and knew what it felt like.

I then decided to face a fearful old enemy of mine—pain. I went into deep meditation and made pain the focus with my full consciousness. I let myself feel my own pain. Opening wider, I felt the pain of my family, friends, and twenty years of clients. Feeling as if I would be crushed under the weight of all this pain, yet somewhere realizing that I was surviving this experience, I willed myself to go into the nature of pain even more deeply and felt what seemed to be the pain of the whole world. Tears puddling in my ears and overflowing to soak the bed, mouth wide open to breathe under the annihilating weight, forcing myself defiantly to stay with the experience, with great rage I yelled out at the universe, "Why is there so much pain?"

Immediately I felt an indescribably powerful presence. It was filled with compassion and eclipsed my own sorrow at pain with its own. I got back an answer in an inaudible but strong and loving voice: "Freedom—Beauty." I gradually came out of my meditation, shaken but victorious. There was no feeling of being humbled by the presence; rather, it conveyed a great empowering respect for humans, including me.

I could buy the answer that I had received to my question about pain. It was the first answer that made sense to me. If God grants us freedom, we are allowed to drive tired and have an accident, or allowed to let our hate build until it is discharged against someone else. We are either free or we are not. Even God cannot create a square circle. Freedom is freedom. And it results in great pain as well as pleasure.

The beauty part also made sense. For there to be the magnificent abundance of resplendent diversity on this planet, everything has to eat something else and push against everything else for living space. Pain thus is intrinsic to both freedom and beauty. God, therefore, has to allow pain for both freedom and beauty to flourish.

Still, a compassionate intelligence could not bear this without there being a greater reality, a context in the infinity of time, or free of time, where a full peace and a dynamic harmony exists. It had always seemed to me that it was inelegant and insufficient that these two realities (one pain-filled and the other blissful) proceed one after another like acts in a play—Earth and then Heaven. For me the blissful reality has to be the greater eternal reality that is always present and always available to be perceived. In some way, physical matter and its suffering has to be as a dream in relation to fully awake, pure consciousness.

It is fine in dreams or in play to pretend to kill or be killed. In some way this physical existence is just a very serious game of pretend, through which consciousness can learn things that there is no other way to learn. Hence we live to learn about limits, and then die to remember our true nature.

The possibility may exist that we can remember while still immersed in physical reality—as in lucid dreaming[29], where the dreamer wakes up enough to know that he is dreaming but remains asleep enough to continue the dream. God is always aware that this physical life is just a dream or a play. We can seek to be aware as well.

I am reminded of the time I went to my daughter's first play. She was in kindergarten. Her wise old teacher set up a simple play, *The Pied Piper of Hamlin*. The most advanced child got to be the piper. The other children got to be mice. All they had to do was follow the piper around and go "Squeak, squeak." What could go wrong?

A pounding scrambling could be heard behind the curtain, echoing through the silent cinderblock auditorium. The lights dimmed and the curtain rose, revealing twenty mice-children, staring straight ahead as if they were about to be shot. The kids were dead serious about how they looked and nervous they would forget their lines. As the play proceeded, bedlam began. Mice ran into each other from all directions, whiskers and tails akimbo. The young actors looked surprised, offended, and distressed yet proceeded through the play as each defined it. The play met all definitions of disaster.

The audience, however, comprised of parents, was overwhelmed with love and delight at their children's efforts. Tears of pride and love glistened on the faces of these moms and dads. Crying too, I thought, "This is how God must look at us in our struggles and errors." This play was perfect imperfection. If we could always look at ourselves with a love as pure as these parents had for their children, we would always feel safe and valued.

The preface of *A Course in Miracles* states: "Nothing real can be threatened. Nothing unreal exists. Herein lies the peace of God." I hope and feel that the deepest level of truth about reality is that this Earth existence is child's play, overseen by a loving God who invites us to awaken to the perfect imperfection of it all.

Something within Pete's death catalyzed my ability to finally sever the indoctrination of my parents, culture, religion, and twenty-two years of schooling. There was plenty of wisdom within all the information society had imparted to me, and I am grateful for all the love and energy that went into this education. It formed a platform from which to look far and wide. Yet, to fully live my life, I had to think for myself.

My thinking coalesced into my philosophy—what is true for me. I choose to believe it until strong data to the contrary appears. In some ways I don't care whether my version of reality is truer than anyone else's. I simply need a positive and constructive model, in order for me to even want to go on with the game.

My model is that at the deepest level of reality there exists a completeness and a perfection. From this model, an image emerged that saved me from bitterness and fear. The image came in that second winter after Pete's death, while I was struggling with my own hardness and broken heart.

The image was of water. That liquid was the answer to my dilemma about openness and protection. If I viewed my heart, my feeling center, as a container filled with water—always complete in itself, yielding easily, full alone, full when embracing some object, full again when the object was removed—if I could do this, then I would indeed be open and non-resisting, yet unable to be devastated by the leaving of a love. I would still be full and complete whether I was embracing my beloved or separated from my beloved.

Again, myths are powerful influences on our perception and experience. Our myth of a broken heart, while speaking accurately of our pain, may do a great disservice to our true nature and underestimate the resilience of the human spirit. My myth of a water-like heart, as vast as the ocean—strong and complete, yet yielding and embracing—reflects our ever-renewing nature.

I have had a chance to live my myth for a while now. Immediately after discovering my ocean heart image, I became more open, welcoming, and responsive toward people. Instantly my fear of hurt and feelings of lack decreased. And when my wife's grandmother, a woman I dearly loved, died, there was some sadness but little pain. I seemed to be able to see beyond the drama of loss and see the beauty of her life and death. I could appreciate the beauty and dignity of myself and the loved ones around me, be fully involved in her dying, and yet at peace, even celebrating the process that was unfolding.

I can sense much more easily now when I shut down and go back to some fear form. I think I am beginning to learn the art of lucid-dreaming the dream we call life. My best indication that I am on the right path, for now, is the abundance of energy and love that I feel even when sad things happen—part of me being fully compassionate, part of me fully sorrowful, but a core within me singing sweet celebration and gratitude at the perfect imperfection of it all.

By now I have connected with Pete in several of my own meditations. My sense also is that he is now playful, lighthearted, friendly, and loving.

I have heard that in certain tribes, when a woman wants to have a child, she quiets herself and listens carefully until she hears the song of her child. She mates and when first aware that she is pregnant, teaches the unborn child's song to the whole village. Her husband and everyone else in her life then sing the song during her pregnancy and at the birth of her child. They continue to sing the song to the infant, baby, and child as that child grows. It is sung then at important transitions, such as marriage, and finally at death of the body.

I think I have found my song. It is a song of deep joy and hope. I trust that my brother, freed now from all his distractions and drama, is singing his own eternal song. I have written this book from my heart to your heart. I hope that you, who have shared my journey through grief, find your own beautiful song that will sustain you through your own dark woundings and bright victories. Thank you for listening to mine.

Part Two

TWENTY YEARS LATER

TWO DECADES PASS

Since the time that I completed my book *Brothers Forever* in 1996, a lot has happened to me in my life, and to Pete on the other side. I would like to give a brief overview of some of the events on my journey and my contacts with Pete from 1996 until present day 2016, where we will then pick up the story in detail.

In 1998 my wife Charleene and I found that it was best to end our marriage. It was an agonizing decision but the parting was done as friends. We both still live in the same town and have been involved in raising my daughter Sarah together. Sarah is now thirty-two years old. Charleene and I have both remarried other people and yet enjoy occasionally working as trainers together at The Monroe Institute.

Proving that you never know what life has in store for you, I met my wife Elena and married her in June of 2001. At the time we met, both of us were in grief. Elena had lost her daughter Erica to brain cancer when she was six years old, about the same time that I lost Pete. The first time Elena and I hugged, something happened that neither of us had experienced before. During the hug we both had an immediate sense of ancient love and spending many lifetimes together with some scenes from those lives flashing by too rapidly to now recall. But the feel of that hug we will never forget. There was an instant and powerful joy, and feeling of coming home with peace and wonderment at finding each other again. Our relationship since that hug has been one of soul-mates.

At the beginning of our relationship one of the first things that happened was that we shared each other's grief so strongly and cleanly that the sharing became a resurrection out of a deadness that neither of us knew we were carrying. We both had been plugging along in our roles in our families, yet had not felt fully alive for a long time, until we helped each other out of the pit. Faint smiles at highly humorous situations again became belly laughs. I think that we could do this because we instantly felt so safe with each other.

Elena brought two beautiful daughters with her into our marriage and we became a family. We stayed on our mountain farm haven mentioned in *Brothers Forever*, where I have now lived for over thirty-five years. I planted two-inch tall pine slips there when I first arrived in order to someday be able to hear the wind in the pines. Now there is small forest where the wind sings to me there as I head down the driveway to get the mail. Both of these daughters are now happily married and the youngest gifted us with our first granddaughter about a year ago. To make things even better, both daughters live close by so that we get to see them and our granddaughter as often as we would like. We went to see her this morning, and today she walked for the very first time.

Twelve years ago, in 2004, I quit my private psychotherapy practice after more than thirty years of seeing clients. I began to teach how to create what we would like to experience in our lives. This was a direct result of my interactions with Pete and we will explore this more thoroughly later. I happily continue to teach at The Monroe Institute about ten weeks a year and have now been a trainer there for more than twenty-five years.

My mother died in 1999 and I have been blessed with feeling her presence quite often since her passing. My father died in 2002. We had celebrated his ninetieth birthday with a big party where he was on his feet for hours being the perfect guest of honor. When he passed of a heart attack, his comments from the other side were that it was as easy as passing from one room to another and then he joked, "Death agrees with me; I should have done it sooner!" My dear brother John passed away in 2014 from an ALS-type illness. He went through his illness and dying with true nobility. My wife, his wife, and I held him in great love as he drew his last breath. The message from the other side shortly after his death was that he had experienced such love and light from us at the end that he was months ahead in his settling in to his new life in spirit.

I am mentioning these changes along life's journey because after Pete's suicide and in the first two years of grieving, it felt that time had stood still and that things were cycling over and over. So if a person is reading this book soon after a significant loss, please know that if you hang in there, time will resume its more rapid course and many good and unexpected things may well happen that will bring you joy.

My periods of grief gradually became less frequent, shorter, and less intense. After a few years, they were mostly centered around holidays where there would be a focus not so much on how or why this happened but just missing him. About five years after his death I realized that finally when I thought of Pete, 95 percent of the time it was with fondness and joy and not sadness. At that point I considered myself fully recovered. I mention the loss of my parents and brother John because after Pete died I feared the possibility that I could not survive, at least psychologically, the death of anyone else close to me. These deaths of deeply loved family have been a hundred times easier than Pete's death was for me. The circumstances of death were different and my perspectives had changed so much that these transitions were soul enhancing rather than soul tearing experiences.

My contacts with Pete over these two decades have been sporadic and often spontaneous. I continued to have sessions on roughly a yearly basis with Pam Hogan, the channeler extensively presented in Part One. During these sessions we often spend some time "with Pete."

He at first wanted to help ameliorate as much as possible the chaos of emotions that his passing caused in those that he loved. Although wistful, he seemed quite peaceful and wasn't agonizing over what had happened. Knowing what he did from the perspective of the other side, he could now see how many things would have gone differently in his life with different choices and attitudes.

He initially seemed quite eager to return to the physical to try again. His counsel of helpers advised that he sit on the sidelines for a while and observe how other people, particularly his family and me, dealt with life challenges and what attitudes were helpful to get through life more comfortably. He seemed good with doing this. And he felt that he could influence and be of assistance to those who remained in the physical. In sessions with Pam, he would often come through with a bit of advice for me on something that I was dealing with. The advice was uplifting, compassionate, and often very practical. At times his comments would be about the rhythm of things: when to push toward a goal and when to take it easy. On other occasions he would share insights into what others around me were thinking and feeling and how I could be of help to them. He seemed particularly protective and interested in my daughter Sarah's progress through life, which made sense since they were very close when he was alive and she was having her own struggles. I enjoyed these "talks" very much and felt his support.

As time passed, the sense of his personality changed from very much like I knew him on earth to more of his higher self, if you will, which often was felt by me as a pulsing heart of love. He seemed very present when our parents each passed and also our brother, John: being there to greet and guide them in their adjustment to the other side. In one channeling there was an extensive description of a process after both my parents had died where they got together with him and replayed some critical years from his life when he was deciding whether to attend college or start a business. It seems to me that they were free to play out several scenarios to see the consequences of each.

It appeared over these years that he was also in a kind of school where he was learning about how love works, the nature of masculine and feminine energy, and how each of these energies was important to master to do well in physical existence. Each time we would touch in with Pete, Pam reported that he seemed quite peaceful and happy and definitely retained his sense of humor.

Every few months during this span of years I would have direct experiences with Pete myself. Often this would occur when I was walking in the woods, my thoughts quieted by the beauty of nature. Occasionally there would be vivid dreams where I strongly felt his presence and intense feelings of love were exchanged. He also would often show up before some meaningful event in my life, such as going on TV for the first time (helping me pick out the right tie), or when I finished a book or CD project. As we will see later, I often connect with him when I am in a casino and enjoy a very loving and playful exchange with him there, almost as if we are buddies playing together. When our energies are together we often win and I get to keep all the money!

Other people have occasionally reported to me contact with Pete even though they had never met or heard of him before the contact. What follows here is an edited report from the journal of a women named Andrea from when she took her Gateway Voyage with me as her trainer at The Monroe Institute in September of 2003. The encounters she reports occurred during the Hemi-Sync meditation experiences during her Gateway. She has given me permission to share her experiences with you. She did not know of Pete before the initial contact.

- In a Focus 12 Exercise: *see doors, tunnels and a park.*

- *I smell cigarette smoke in my check unit (a booth where people recline and meditate). I am pretty alert, though my body is still asleep. I see a flash of a face. It looks like Joe Gallenberger, but slightly younger/different. The name "Peter" comes through, also in a flash. At the moment, I believe it's Joe, checking on me. I don't feel scared, but highly curious and excited. He looks happy and slightly shy (get the sense he doesn't want to inconvenience me or impose on me). I feel love and peace.*

Note: I later ask Joe if he "visited" me about five minutes before the tape was over and he says "no." He checked on me at the beginning. I ask him if the name "Peter" tells him anything. He says it's his brother, who died years ago of suicide.

In a Focus 15 Exercise:

- *I know that Peter will be taking me somewhere to show me something, even before the tape starts. Because I need to know what my connection with Peter is? I'm not scared and I trust him.*

- *Peter takes me into a dark cave. I see Jesus and some of his followers.*

- *Next, I find myself on a mountaintop with Jesus and Peter. I'm overwhelmed with love and emotion and I sob uncontrollably (also my physical body is crying). I feel my right arm twitch several times (that's my "YES"), so I know it's real. I hadn't planned to go visit Jesus—Peter took me there to my utmost surprise and joy!!*

- *It's so beautiful. I feel so much love. I sense that Peter is part of Jesus. I'm part of Jesus too. I feel a strong connection to him (though I'm not religious).*

- *There are only two or three of us with Jesus. He loves us so much! He died for our sins and took on so much burden from us. I sense that Peter's death was also needed to take away some burdens from us.*

In the Five Messages Exercise:

- *Peter is attending this training with me (through me). Apparently we committed to do this together.*

Last Night of the program:

> • *I feel Peter's presence. I "saw" a misty white form near my bed.*
> *Out of the right side, I see thin smoke (like cigarette) rising up.*
> *Smoke is his trademark signal … He came to say good-bye … …*
> *He's been so considerate and gentle, never intruding on my space.*
> *I love him dearly!*

Andrea's story moved me deeply. It was very confirming. Andrea's over-all impression was that Pete wanted to experience the Gateway Voyage program because The Monroe Institute was so important to me and he had a curiosity to see what it was about. I particularly liked that Pete could experience the Gateway program from the other side. In life I had strongly urged him to take Gateway, as it is such a transformational learning opportunity and I felt at the time it might shift things for him. But he resisted this idea of taking Gateway when he was alive. It was inspiring to receive confirmation that Pete was around and interested in my life. The story created a special bond between Andrea and me, as she is now a trainer at The Monroe Institute, and we enjoy training together when we have the opportunity. Lastly I would mention that Andrea worked as a successful high-level executive in a major corporation, so is a well grounded and discerning individual and not taken to flights of fancy.

Just as I was preparing to write this book (a fact that I kept private from everyone except my wife) we had a new person come stay at our house to care for our animals while we were away training an Inner Vegas Adventure™ workshop. This woman was just starting to open up to the spiritual and psychic part of life. She was referred by someone we knew well, but she did not know us. While resting in our home, alone with the animals, she felt a presence. I had never talked to her about Pete. She was kind enough to let me share her experience with you.

I am not sure of the exact date on the first visitation from Peter but as I sat in your chair reading Liquid Luck, *I felt his presence to the left of me. I knew it was him and so I said, "Hello, Peter" and he said hello back to me. I asked him how he was doing and he asked me to tell you (Joe) that he loved you. I asked him if he loved himself and he said that he was learning to love himself. I told him I would relay the message and his energy faded away as quickly as it appeared. I had been studying about these kinds of energy encounters under Charles Marshall [Electrical Theorist] and I had experienced only one other episode before this one in which my father came through and we were able to exchange information with one another. I felt a little juvenile about sharing this experience with you, Joe, yet I knew it was very important to Peter and I gave him my word.*

The second encounter happened the last time I stayed in your home when you and Elena went to Las Vegas. Once again, I was sitting in your chair (by the way, it's quite comfy) and I was reading a magazine. I was distracted by a slight change in temperature and I put the magazine down and sensed Peter's presence. I greeted him but he did not greet me back. I had a vision in my mind of a medieval looking wooden cart with large wooden wheels going by me on a dirt road and inside the cart was a hand-painted wooden sign with the word SHAME painted on it. Peter's presence was around this cart but I did not actually see him and no audible words were spoken. My hunch was that he was pulling the cart but I am not sure about this.

On a different note, Peter made an appearance during my meditation time this morning when I was working with raising the soul frequencies of some of my ancestors and departed friends and loved ones so I included him in with what I was practicing and sent him Divine healing energy, Divine love, and Divine light. I sent little cleaners to his soul transmitter and receiver to be cleaned so that he would be able to receive and absorb what was being sent to him. He thanked me.

There you have it Joe. I hope this helps. K.S.

This report by K.S. also touched me. It feels compatible with what I know of Pete. Of particular interest is the medieval cart pulling "Shame." After this time in a session with Pam I would end up talking to Pete about shame in the sense of not fully allowing himself to feel his own grandeur as a being and a spirit.

NO LIFE IS WASTED

As the impulse to write *Heaven is for Healing* began to strengthen, there were four ideas that were clear to me from the start.

1. People devastated by the suicide of someone close to them need understanding and hope beyond what is usually available through friends, churches, and cultural beliefs.

2. If communities expanded their beliefs about what might happen to the person after death by suicide, they could be more supportive of loved ones who were grieving after suicide.

3. Non-judgmental compassion needs to be applied to this "problem" that was usually swept under a rug woven from shame, denial, and anguish.

4. While my writing might alleviate the fear of eternal damnation or heavy karmic retribution as inevitable results of suicide, I wanted to be clear that suicide is usually a terrible choice.

With these four ideas in mind, I prayed about whether I was up to writing such a book and came to the conclusion that the only way I would know for certain was to begin the project and see how it developed. Besides my desire to help others struggling with some aspect of the suicide experience, I was intensely curious about whether I could discover more about what happens to us after death and particularly after a death by suicide. The perfect way to jump start this project was to once again contact Pam Hogan, the channeler who had helped me connect with Pete so extensively and clearly in the past. I explained the project to her to see if she, ARGO (the intelligence that she communicates with), and Pete thought that the project was worth doing and if they would be willing to participate in it. The answer through Pam was an enthusiastic, "Yes." So we scheduled four sessions to begin in the late fall of 2015. I will present transcripts of these sessions here with minor editing for clarity and then comment after each session to expand upon the material delivered. I will put my comments in plain type and Pam's and ARGO's comments in italics.

ARGO session 11/23/15

Joe: It's been over twenty years since Pete died and I wrote *Brothers Forever.* His suicide stimulated much of my focus for the past twenty years on learning why good people sometimes struggle with repeated destructive and limiting patterns in their lives. In my explorations, I discovered that one needs to feel deserving to manifest a good life. And that there are ways of working with energy and clearing limiting emotions and beliefs that are powerful aids in creating a life of meaning, joy, and abundance.

I am planning a book which again presents the grieving response and initial experience of Pete right after his death, which was in *Brothers Forever.* This new book will also look at what Pete has been doing on the other side during the two decades after his death. I want to explore what his life is like over there, so we can have a more realistic view of the consequences of suicide for the soul who takes that action. I hope to produce a book that will be very healing for people who have experienced a suicide in their lives while not promoting suicide. I think it would be interesting over the next four sessions if Pete could come in and talk about things from his point of view: What it's like for him now? What were the stages he went through? Is there a variety of experience people go through on the other side after suicide? My wish is to help people understand what happens in a more accurate and enlightened way, rather than just what has been taught by religion and culture.

Pam: *Wow, that can help a lot of people. You are right that part of the challenge is to write the book in a way so as not to give people permission to commit suicide.*

Joe: The original *Brothers Forever* showed anyone considering suicide how hard it is on the family remaining, so this book would include that as Part One and then move into Part Two, which would cover what happens to people after death if they have committed suicide and what has happened to Pete since his death.

Pam: *We will have to see what he has . . . I have been thinking this morning about people who have died who were really not nice people and how content and released they are on the other side. To me that is proof that there is no hell and how whole, and even kind of humorous they are after their transition. Yes, different point of view. Yea, that proves there is not hell when they are just walking around having a great time. We'll see what the process is. How do we want to start this?*

Joe: Pete did say he was willing to be part of this project. Perhaps we could see if this offer still extends and perhaps have him speak to wherever he was at the start of his experience on the other side and then now, with the perspective of twenty years of earth time, how he views his experience over there and what is he doing now? Any other way is fine with me, too; any way keeps us in the energy of love.

Pam: *Yes, exactly, and we will really turn it over to them (ARGO) and let them organize this. Here we go. ARGO, Joe is starting out on this new project and would like to write the sequel to* Brothers Forever *that talks about the process of healing from suicide on the other side and also to talk to Pete about his process. He is willing to do that. We ask for the highest message and we ask for the light to come through, so the messages can heal those who need to understand how their relatives who committed suicide are doing and to heal the wound of that, to take the fear and condemnation out of it. And these things and anything else you want to do, we are open to it. I ask to be used as a clear and loving channel of light and to get these things with clarity and accuracy. Thank you, ARGO.*

ARGO: Dear children, there are many parameters around the mind as it undergoes mental anguish. It pulls those who endure this from the center focus of their own creative light and pulls them towards the dismal shadow of early death. The parameters of mental anguish will vary in that the person who undergoes such torment cannot really manage a return to light without some help. Suicidal people typically do not ask for help or show signs that they are enduring such mental pain/emotional pain. Those who love them can fear for their safety but not realize the impending sense of doom that begins to permeate the cerebral cortex of the brain. In going through this anguish alone, these people often are accusatory towards others, typically in the family realm. They tend to blame parents, siblings, marital partners for their anguish. It is the only way they can endure being themselves, as to look at the question deep within themselves about what moves them to such mental anguish causes such devastation to the ego that they remove the guilt of association with failure as a human by pointing fingers at others. Usually sweet souls are crushed this way in those surrounding the mentally ill [Pam: they are showing the family members]. So as they seek to find a haven within themselves, the family members feel the self-hatred of the mentally ill and experience a similar . . .

Pam: *So they are showing the image of the crushing of the souls of the family members who don't really understand what is going on and how the family members start to take within themselves what is actually the self-hatred of the person who is in so much anguish and take it on as their own.*

ARGO: Now . . . the healing of the heart begins almost at the point of death for the soul who has committed suicide, for the freedom from the ego is immediate. However, because it is an unnatural death, an element of ego pain remains like rain clouds around the physical dimension. The pain can be so palatable that others can absorb this without their own consciousness realizing it.

Now, to move into the spiritual realm with a sense of feeling guilt-free one must feel that one has completed one's assignment on earth. That one has brought their chosen life to a mortal conclusion and that the way home is offered to them, as all stages of their life are complete. Therefore, one who has taken an early leave of their life experience does lift some of the grueling pain that they have endured, however, in general, they do move into another realm in a more unnatural or let's call it uncomfortable position [Pam: they are showing someone cramped and trying to get themselves comfortable in small quarters, boxed in.] and must be moved safely to a place where other spirits of great heart and love can comfort and soothe them, as well as help them maintain a better sense of balance in their spirit.

There are various methods in which this is handled. The most popular method is to sit closely with the soul who still has some dementia of spirit entangled in its spiritual core and allow them to drift in and out of consciousness where they understand more of, shall we say, the rules of the game of life. Where they see, much like watching a video, different opportunities that have been shown to them in their life process and also to view where they started this conception of self-hatred in their lives. Then they are taken through their minds on the journey of their life, how it would have been if they had they not killed themselves. They begin to experience, while their hands are held by great generous spirits of light, the way forward, had they moved through the natural process to die. They see the bumps on the road and they are shown the emotional entanglement that comes with projecting self-hatred to themselves as well as to others and are shown the whole consciousness of victimization.

Sometimes these souls do quake with shame or fear at seeing the result of living in such a dense energy of lack of self-love. We hold them tight to our light and we help them through the shuddering reality of the conscious awareness of where such dark travels have taken them. They are also given energy much like a human hug which allows them to begin the process of true self-forgiveness, of love on an existential plane as well as on a human psychological dimension. This kind of self-forgiveness catapults them out of much remaining sorrow and they are encouraged then to help with some of the cleanup of the residue that still lives closer to the physical as the rain cloud.

They can at times visit family members or others who are open to them in the form of dreams and they can help alleviate some of the sorrow by making suggestions for healing, much as our beloved Pete did with you, Joe. Seeking to help harmonize what had been disturbed by his actions. When we first introduced ourselves to you through Pam, we showed that your beloved brother was on a trajectory for this dark death. It was such a challenge for him to find this love, a love that cannot be given to him by brother, mother, or friend. It is a love of self from consciousness. So, now your beautiful brother resides in light and love and does recognize and experience the pure joy of self-love. He vibrates at greater rate today than he ever has and is also in a position to help others and is happy to have the opportunity to share such light when in the past he had created such pain.

But now let us go back to the other challenges of healing those who have killed themselves. The second of three proposals for helping a suicidal victim is to take them to a place of study. As their beloved beings of light follow them around this higher university, they study first the principles of light as if they were in a university classroom. It is taught through remnants of intellect so that there is a bypass of the hurting heart. It is our opinion that for someone who is a tougher case, that the first introduction to this great change in their energy should be fed to the intellect as one can study something in a detached way. Studying how light and love are energies and work in a more biochemical way in the physical helps to relax this sort of soul personality so that they can begin to eventually trust enough their surroundings to allow the feeling memories to emerge.

Again we sit tight with them in a movie theatre and watch a very similar scenario as our first approach described. As they view the potential of their lives, they see from a more removed state. They do feel these emotions again but they are helped through them to a conclusion of complete understanding of their life purpose, even if it was filled with suffering. We hold hands with them and embrace them as a mother who loves her child and eventually they come to understand that love does exist on all levels of this plane as well as on the earth plane: that all attempts that are made to remove blocks of love on the earth plane build positive reinforcement for future good in a life.

Now Joe, we move to your heart and we send you our love wrapped like a great present. We are deeply appreciative to you for your willingness to scour the depths of pain that a heart can bring and to seek the joy that it also offers. We sing now in our choir of light to you a song of great love and we hold you close to us, child, as we will look forward to our next conversation. Please child, live and breathe through your beautiful heart. This self-love, which is the elixir for all sadness, give to yourself as you offer to others the true route to heaven on earth, the embracing of light as it exists in spirit within you. We love you so and will stay with you always. With love and blessings and kisses blown to your beautiful Elena, we do say goodbye for now.

Pam: *Wow, Joe. Thank you. That was very moving and very interesting. I got such a rush of emotion just as they were showing me the mentally ill person and the dementia and the suffering of it. It is terrible and then how the family members sort of sponge it in, not knowing that that is what is happening and how that illness is just so painful for everyone. I mean really, I am crying now, it is just terrible. But I guess the answer is self-love, huh?*

And the images too, while they are still in my mind, it's like going to the movie theatre and holding hands with the soul and saying, "Well if you hadn't ended it, this is sort of the point of things, this is how it would have come out, this is the plan of this. And they still do experience these feelings, but their hands are being held and they are sort of living it on the other side with a <u>lot</u> of loving assistance, so that they can understand where they took a detour or why they came with such pain to experience in a life and to also realize that in an unnatural end of a life, there is still a real sense of completion of that lesson and that learning. But also seeing it not so much with their nose in it, like when in the physical, but being able to be more of an observer of it, like watching a movie and being attached emotionally to the excitement of what is going on but you know it's a movie.

The love that they (ARGO and the helpers on the other side) feel for these people who have committed suicide is tremendous with tremendous nurturing, compassion, and sympathy. I don't know what the third way of helping is. I guess we'll find out next session. The third approach to how they can bring them to a place where they can then proceed more naturally on the other side in the process of enlightenment. So those are the images and sense that was coming and was what was bringing tears to my eyes. It was the intensity of the love they feel: it is just amazing. I mean it's just amazing, and you know, there is no hell, and there is an "Okay, let's face it together" kind of energy. "You're okay, but let's face it and let's find a way to feel that love again within you." It's amazing!

Joe: The amount of feeling during our session moved me very much!

Pam: *Yeah, I mean I thought I was going to cry too hard to get the words.*

Joe: And while it's fresh in your mind . . . in the movie theatre scenario too, it sounds as if they get to see, if they did not commit suicide, what their life would be like and actually in some way live the lesson of that life.

Pam: *Exactly!*

Joe: But they do it from more of an observation and perhaps learn what they would have learned here but with more support.

Pam: *Yes, to feel support, but also to feel some of the emotion because apparently without that they can't relate to the lack of love, so by feeling the pain of the lack of feeling self-love they can see the distance between how they were living and what really exists. So like the movie theatre scenario that we get caught up in the story we get caught up in the emotions of what's going on: it's like that, but yes, with more distance and incredible beings holding their hands.*

Joe: What that says to me is that even if you terminate early, you still basically complete the goodness of what you would have learned in that life.

Pam: *Yes. There is so much compassion, God, there is just so much compassion. Yes, no life is wasted and no matter how painful it appears for some people, no life is without purpose despite what seems so purposeless or might seem so random: that it all counts and* *everyone grows and everyone is loved, absolutely without exception. So, no lives are lost or thrown away ever.*

I guess we'll see what the third way of helping is. It looks like for those who commit suicide: usually a large number of them seem to work well with the first approach of soothing, and the second approach would be for someone who would be a harder nut to crack. And I think this was interesting too how an intellectual person sometimes can be very disconnected from their feelings and they were feeding these strong intellects with all the information that they could relate to about love as an energy, as a mystic chemistry, of how it works, and watching it, kind of how you learn about chemistry, and watching it, and getting to a place where it is not so threatening or dangerous. So they would first fill the intellect with this, then go down into the heart and allow the heart to have the courage to experience these things again so that then they could look at the movie of their life.

I was thinking while they were showing me that, that someone who was very caught in the mind and disconnected from the heart on earth, when they study any of this, it is really such an important first step: the intellect actually is a doorway in. It is learning how to approach someone who has a different doorway open—yes, approach them through logic, but patiently. It looks like it's tougher and they have to get a sense of connection to safety. It has to feel safe, then they will download it more into the emotional body, the heart.

Joe: Did you get a sense in earth time how long that project might take, like a hundred years, or three months?

Pam: *I didn't get a sense of time. We will have to ask them for that. Just me watching, it didn't look like a long time, but that's on the other side where time doesn't exist. I really didn't get a strong sense.*

What did really hit me though was the raincloud left behind, the energetic of all that pain that soaks into the family and friends.

And what they are saying now is that family and friends would feel that person was still suffering nearby, but they have been lifted out of it, removed from the ego. The raincloud is like an ego fragment of all their experiences that hang around. When someone feels that their loved one is not alright, that is just that cloud. They are showing me how, when the person who commits suicide gets healed, they would come in and try to clean up the cloud and help those left behind.

Joe: I guess you are implying that if this takes say, six months, they could come back and help those in acute grief.

Pam: *It doesn't sound like a hundred-year process but not thirty days either. Some cases are tougher than others and it would take longer—just the personality of the soul.*

Joe: Like murder suicide, there is a lot of guilt and karma around that.

Pam: *We can ask them, but they would probably be in very different places, the murdered one and the suicide one. What really got me was how they were removing the shame and pointing to: if self-love existed here, none of this would be happening. And how hard it is for our psychology to really get that: how self-love can feel narcissistic or self-centered and how hard it is to actually make that connection to the divine and feel the divine love in this life. There seems to be varying degrees of success with that, but when it gets really extreme, the separation from that, the source and the light, the self-hatred becomes so palatable that you get all this other stuff.*

Joe: I really found today important and hope you did too.

Pam: *Yes, it really was for me too, with a mentally ill son, as a family member to get that. In many ways it was really wonderful. I wonder what they will have for us next time.*

Joe: I hope you have a wonderful Thanksgiving, thanks, I love you Pam.

Pam: *I love you too Joe.*

End Session

I have included the content of the channeling sessions verbatim so that the reader can get the sense of flow and how the content is delivered directly. Yet the speech patterns during channelings can seem a bit foreign and the information quite dense and complex. Therefore I will summarize what I understood from each session. First, I want to be clear that most of the information in this session applies to a person who cuts their life short when other options are more elegant. In later sessions ARGO covers persons who are terminally ill. It seems that they have a much easier time, requiring just a dusting off and they are ready to soar.

ARGO starts his message by extending great compassion toward the family members of one who commits suicide. I would extend that compassion to close friends and even the entire community, as all who hear of suicide are affected and particularly those who knew the person well. There is an almost inescapable loop of, "Would have, could have, should have," agonizing in the survivors. And ARGO clearly makes an important point that because of the depth of mental and emotional distortion occurring in the person as they contemplate suicide, that they often become unreachable. Earlier in the process, a kind word, psychotherapy, medication, and help with reducing stress are all very viable ways to help but at some point the person seems to block all attempts at help and often feels absolutely too tired and despondent to go on.

ARGO is also highlighting that for a suicidal person the defense of projection (blaming others and feeling a victim) makes it harder and harder to take responsibility, which includes the ability to respond and change things for the better. Yet for them to feel responsible for all the pain and failure in their lives is too great for the ego to handle, resulting in feeling crushed and worthless. In my experience, suicidal people often vacillate between blaming the world and mercilessly taking all the blame upon themselves, which indeed is felt as a crushing blow and sets up the thinking that, "The world will be much better off without me." This distortion can happen even when they are leaving behind young children who need them. The community response of, "How could they be so selfish?" ignores that the person is not able to comprehend their own value and may see themselves as so toxic that it is better that they disappear. It is truly not a case of "taking the easy way out," rather they feel it's the only way out. ARGO also explains that often the suicidal person's sense of hopelessness is so strong that it is subconsciously transmitted to those around them in a way that can paralyze their creativity and ability to help.

Next ARGO talks about what condition the suicide person tends to be in when they arrive on the other side and how help is delivered to them. I was impressed at how methodical and planned out this response tends to be. It seems help is immediate and ARGO describes it is as being offered under essentially three main methods. The first and second methods are covered in this first session. This first method appears to be used for many who arrive who are fairly amenable to help right off. The other methods are reserved for people who are more challenging in terms of the depths of their blockage from self-love and understanding.

It seems that upon arriving on the other side, most people who have taken their own lives feel an immediate lifting of much of the psychological and physical pain they may have been experiencing prior to the act. ARGO's words here are full of hope and love: *"The healing of the heart begins almost at the point of death for the soul who has committed suicide."* Yet there is some confinement or stifling of their energy compared to those who die a natural death. And there seems to been a fragment of self tied to ego that often can hang around the earth space as if it were a "rain cloud" of guilt and sadness. Loved ones in earth embodiment can pick up this in a way that weighs them down and causes them to have concern that the person who has passed on may be suffering still.

It appears that the soul is allowed to rest, and within that rest images and thoughts are introduced that allow them to begin to reach greater understanding. They may see how they got off track, the consequences of self-hatred, and what their lives would have been like if they were able to respond with self-love and chose differently. Within this life review that is taking place described much like watching a movie, the soul's consciousness is held with the greatest of compassion. There is no external harsh judgment of their actions and they are given much energy to withstand any feelings of regret or shame. This is done through an open transfer of highest love from their guides and helpers. I remember one of my first messages that I received from Pete immediately after his death was a feeling of great relief and amazement that there was no judgment of his actions and instead unconditional love being radiated toward him. At that time Pete kept flashing what looked like a circular road sign which depicted a judge's gavel with a slash across it, as on a "no smoking" sign, meaning no judgment. One can easily imagine how powerfully healing this experience would be, if the person were open to it.

Next ARGO mentions that the newly deceased can at times come back into the consciousness of those loved ones remaining on earth, often in dreams, to help them heal from the trauma of the death. In my experience personally and as a therapist, this happens quite often. Many people report a sense of their loved ones who have passed and also dreams or appearances at the end of their bed, where the loved one usually conveys two important things: that they are doing well and that they love the person very much. If those in grief are too upset and agitated to receive these messages, it seems very common that someone close to the deceased but a bit further removed from the trauma, will be the one to receive the message and then convey it to the grieving person. Over the years I have heard many stories of the grieving person receiving a message about something such as the location of an object, that there would be no way of them knowing, as a form of verification that the message was coming from the person who has died.

ARGO then discussed the second method of helping, when the recently deceased person needs more extensive "rehabilitation." Here ARGO speaks of souls finding themselves in a more academic university-type setting, where they can intellectually learn the principles of love and how life works, while their hearts are protected from much of the strong emotional impact of their actions. Only after there is a good comprehension of the "rules of the game" and principles of love are they moved into observing the life they have just completed and the consequences of their actions. Again this occurs while surrounded all the while by the most powerful and enveloping energies of love, so that they can begin to see themselves with great compassion and greater perspective.

Finally ARGO in this session delivered the message, "*So, now your beautiful brother resides in light and love and does recognize and experience the pure joy of self-love.*" It impressed me that the high energies of ARGO seem to realize that these sessions are not just an intellectual curiosity exercise for me, but do reopen some of my own grief. I want to emphasize the amazing energy I felt all around me during this session. I could not sit still and had to walk around as the energy was so great. I did indeed cry but rather than tears of grief, they were tears of being moved so deeply at the amount of compassion that I could feel coming through so clearly. There was not a hint of sadness or pity, rather a peaceful, joyful compassion. I have heard many near-death experiencers report this joyful compassion as one of the most profound and transformative parts of their experience. To deeply understand, to know, not just intellectually but in the core of our heart that we are loved and all our experiences treasured is an amazing insight. It removes all doubt in the goodness of the universe and any sense that we are in some way alone. And it is so good to know that, despite appearances, no life or life experience is wasted.

LEARNING THROUGH EXPERIENCE

About two weeks later, after my family had a wonderful Thanksgiving with our new granddaughter being the star entertainment, I had my second session with Pam. Before officially starting, Pam shared some of her continued impressions from the last session.

ARGO session—December 2, 2015

Pam: *I was really aware, when they were showing me Peter observing, how these people were really being helped through the emotions, and watching from the other side watching what their lives were like, that their important lessons were being learned. Once they really were pulled through it and experienced the emotion with the angelic support, they then got that lesson.*

Joe: They do not have to repeat the lesson in the physical?

Pam: *Yea, rather than, "Now since you have committed suicide you have to go back and it's going to be worse this time." No, it's really all about getting the lesson any way it works. Certainly the person reviewing their life has a lot of support but they really do feel the emotions that were part of the life experience. That was an important point, they couldn't escape those feelings. Part of why they kill them-*

selves is that they don't want to feel bad. So, it is walking through the emotional responses with a lot of support and so it really was re-experiencing the same circumstances but with the great support from their helpers to be able to have greater perspective and in a way where they could handle the emotions better. Anyway, I'm just report-ing back to how it felt when I saw that. Okay, are you ready?

Joe: I am.

Pam: *Okay, ARGO, Joe is here for continued conversation about suicide and what happens on the other side. He is interested in know-ing about the third method of helping someone on the other side. Joe is also wondering in earth time how long this process takes: years, days, months, in our concept of time. Then he is really wondering about the concept of hell and asking for a confirmed statement of the existence of hell and is despair an unforgivable sin? So we turn all this over to you. I ask to be used as a clear and loving channel of light for clearest message.*

ARGO: Blessings given to you dear children as you continue to make wondrous progress in defining the meaning of the death passage whether through natural means or suicide. It is our privilege to work with you this day and to bring more good news your way. In the event of a premature death by suicide, one who maintains such a dark consciousness through lack of love and who does remain bitter in inner realms of both psyche and soul passage needs a variety of messages from various guides whose specialties are just this kind of support for "lost souls."

Persons in the inner darkest realm of despair are those who encounter the third method of retrieval. They are first placed into a semi-conscious state much like you would

Matt & Laurie, here's my gift as I partner with you and TBN to send the Gospel around the world through Christian television.

Enclosed is my gift of $_____

In thanks for my gift, please send me:

- *Drive Thru History: The Gospels* 18-part DVD series.

- The above, plus the *Where Jesus Walked* photography book, with my gift of $168 or more.

- All of the above, plus *Jesus, I Trust You* 16" x 20" framed art, with my gift of $1,680 or more.

Trinity Broadcasting Network
PO Box A
Santa Ana, CA 92711-2101

0024869930MBAAN   11092017

For credit/debit card gifts, please complete other side.

Please make checks payable to:
Trinity Broadcasting Network
PO Box A, Santa Ana, CA 92711-2101
Prayer line: 1-888-731-1000
Donor Services: 1-877-731-1000
TBN.org/giving

TBN
NETWORKS

☐ VISA ☐ MasterCard ☐ American Express ☐ Discover

Card # ☐☐☐☐☐☐☐☐☐☐☐☐☐☐☐☐

TBN

NETWORKS

If more funds are received by TBN for a designated project than are needed, the excess funds will be used by TBN for other tax-exempt ministry purposes.

Expiration Date: ☐☐ / ☐☐ (mm/yy)

Please charge / debit my card:

☐ This <u>one time</u> OR ☐ monthly on this day ____.

Signature: _____ Amount: $ _____

Name on card: _____

Phone: (_____

Email: _____

experience a coma in physical reality. The soul is maintained, but the deep desperation and lack of confidence in love as a vehicle for salvation starts to be removed from their energy field, so that when they wake up they do not believe they are in hell. For if one was to reawaken after a death passage into such a deepened despair and dislike for love and for self, it would hold in their disturbed psyche a vision of hell.

This is where many religions interpret the existence of hell. It is however but a memory of the inner distaste for the self that gives this poor soul a belief in eternal suffering, despair, and disjointed understanding of their own soul. So as we would help remove such noxious energy from around this soul, deepening their own coma like state, we can begin to infuse in through the mortal consciousness of ideas that still remain stuck in their personal vision and enter into the vault of their core souls. In there, in that soul, each guide who holds a specific specialty will attempt to redesign a capacity for understanding the truth about love. It would be like you in your physical plane having a decorator come to redo your home. In this particular activity there is much going on like polishing mirrors, where a soul can awaken to a vision of themselves as pure energy and not that mortal being (how they experienced themselves in their incarnation).

It is most important that they do not have a vision of themselves in physicality for this brings back such negative energetic reminders of who they are without spirit that they can relapse into despair. So we are there to light up the halls of their darkened memory and to set the stage for their reawakening. As they start to move into a divine energy of support around them, slowly they move to an awakened state. There they will see what might look like fog to them but it is really an energy of healing love attempting to soothe that soul's "nervous system." This brings them back to a state of feeling safer and removed from any sense of hell.

In this place we begin to tend to them rapidly much as a physician in an emergency room would tend to a car crash victim. In our coordinated manner, we slowly advise this soul that they are indeed removed from a physical embodiment and are safe in a place of love. In this place of love they are taught that they do not have to earn this love, that this love is given to them without regard to their past history, that love is the nature of this universe and that even a despairing or darkened soul can be retrieved through this love. So as we move to give them this feeling of love and a deeper understanding of the consciousness of divinity in the universe, they begin to wake up.

Oh, alleluia! It is such a beautiful sight to see the birthing of a soul's awakening. As they blink at first at the brilliance of the light and love around them, they are warmed up and given soul food. They are shown with great love and attention how they had made some dangerous errors in judgment during their physical existences that had caused this terrible removal from the power and beauty of light. As they are directed to see how this has caused such a derailment of pleasure for them, they are comforted, as it is true that the soul at times wants to weep both for what may have been done to them but also for the pain they may have caused others.

In seeing how dark and devastating these behaviors are, they eagerly move to a room of instruction. In this classroom we gain their attention through soft, nurturing reinforcement of their own light. They are shown this light frequently, almost as if they are gazing at it for the first moment in their entire spiritual existence. In this way they can refocus their energy on embracing the fundamentals of how love works in all lives and in all dimensions. This can be shown as a chemistry equation. This can be given as visuals such as a mother nursing her baby. This can be offered through philosophically credentialed individuals who teach how the laws of love through history have actually reclaimed many who have lived in dark times. It varies according to how their personality makeup as a soul is organized.

Then after graduation from these classes, they are then turned over to guides who will help them further define how they may want to rest before recycling into another life experience or they can watch the show from a very distant energy field just to see how others are experiencing life in process. They are kept at quite a distance, safe and tucked away in an energy field of these loving guides so they do not relapse into old reactions regarding life experiences, nor will their own lowered energy negatively affect the people on the physical plane that they are observing. What these poor souls generally do not realize is how potent their energies are, how powerful they are as beings, because they had come to believe through loss of love that their souls had no power. So, that takes training and that takes miles and miles of inner work.

In the case that someone at this point may still want to reject their own power and beauty, their own divinity as a soul, they are then moved to a place where the reclaiming of that energy is possible. By this we mean that their soul energy may join a vast pool of energies of souls who cannot find and hold this love. In this place of amazing love, this soul then is transferred into another dimension where there is a new soul born. It is an extension of their original soul but it is vastly different and like a new baby, many options are open to it for learning, through many lives yet to discover. This is always an option but it is one that is really exercised only when it is impossible for that soul to hold and ingest even a thimbleful of light. One need not maintain mastery on this side of the force field from your planet earth, but a soul must be held accountable to hold at least a thimbleful of loving energy. So no matter where you turn, in physical reality or non-physical reality, there is always a happy ending possible in that the love that is given will always transform into greater light in one manner or another.

It is only the human psyche that believes that there would be eternal punishment since the human psyche is full with evil thoughts about itself. So the concept of heaven versus hell is truly the imagination of humanity. In the ego resides a conscious judgment of how one feels one must behave in order to be rewarded by love. It does not really hold a concept of unconditional love. So yes, my dear son Joe, it is true that hell resides only in the mind of humanity and if they allow their imaginations to grow so powerful through ego, that this hell can exist in a realm of imagined reality, so in that sense in their minds it is real and in this realm of imagined realities it is also real. So, hell can rain fire and damnation on those souls who truly believe it exists. It is like calling a raincloud to oneself and going outside on a regular basis without an umbrella.

The human psyche then says, Oh, God will not give me more than I can bear, or it can say I that am being punished for this or that, but it is truly self-flagellation and always on the other side of this storm cloud resides a host of loving beings ready to help that spirit find eternal salvation. When one does commit to loving on a higher level through the consciousness of Christ, through the consciousness of Buddha, through the consciousness of all those who ask all humans to love and to share in forgiveness, one then chooses to move away from the raincloud. But in reality many people still believe that the raincloud will find them one day if they do not perform perfectly, for they do not truly understand the concept of unconditional love and the idea of rising above this pain in a physical existence.

The term of life for many beings on this planet is planned before birth. So there is a map by which a soul will experience life, leading it eventually to the end of life. It is like finishing up the last chapter of a book. This is normal and if a consciousness decides to ride the beam of death through a devastating disease to be removed from the physical there is much goodness in that decision. And so it is that they are not failing to find the light if they die from a tragedy of some form. In the purest of ideals as you will find in the yogis of India, a transformation from the physical to non-physical can be made more easily without any trauma associated. It is merely a transfer of energy and a removal of spirit from physicality.

So, dear one, please do always remember in all events in your physical lives, in all ways of passing through the door of physical to non-physical, you are regarded with the highest esteem and loved with great intensity. There is no energy in this greater love that would ever seek vengeance. Please do remember this in your human consciousness so that when you do hold hurt in your hearts from unfair acts, do not seek vengeance. We would say to you with great love that this becomes your own hell on earth. It is a dis-eased heart, a diseased mind overwhelmed with rage, with intense anger, that creates this horror for themselves and others in the physical.

We do love you so. We do hold you in our hearts at all times. We do hold always an energy of hope for mankind and we do ask you, beloved children, to hold open your arms to reach out your hands to us and sit with great receptivity to receive the radiating love from our dimension of great light to you, so that you may be removed from the concepts of devastation of hell, of terrorizing despair. Please come eagerly to our arms, beloved children, and let us hold you while your physical dimension now does struggle with the heavy aftermath of so many wars of vengeance, of so many fears of hell, of so much negative intervention by religion into a lighted consciousness. We do seek to remind that you are indeed, when in human earth life, experiencing a difficult dimension dense in its energies and seemingly lost from the light. The light does exist eternally for you and while you watch many transformations in physical, some of them being quite difficult for to you observe, please do stand in the power of love and light and please do call to us always, for we gain great heart by watching your under-standing that love is greater than tragedy.

(Pause)

Joe: There is a program at The Monroe Institute called Life-line where we do soul retrieval or soul rescue work. I was a participant in the first Lifeline ever taught and it was coin-cidentally one week before Pete's death. I've trained many Lifeline programs since. The idea is that those of us still in physical human existence can go into deep meditation and connect with folks who don't know they've passed over and bring them into greater light, usually with a reunion with guides and family. I have curiosity whether ARGO sees Lifeline as a valid program: that we aren't just making it up, if you will, and that this is another type of help available to people on the other side. I know there are other traditions such as shamanism and other people on earth who work with people who are dead. ARGO may want to go in a different direction and that is fine.

Pam: *So, ARGO can you respond to Joe about the work on Lifeline and shamanism?*

ARGO: Yes, it does help. We do appreciate your loving.

Pam: *They are showing someone giving someone a nudge, a gentle push toward the light.*

ARGO: For if they are awakened [Pam: they are talking about someone in the third category] before they can be placed into a sleep, it is as we said before, often a version of hell and they feel lost, desperately unloved, and alone. When anyone prays or meditates to search out that specific energy that has passed on, it does offer them a boost from behind to move towards greater redemption. This energy is also helpful in that it does set up a barrier between the individual human life and their new life in light. It also does help shave off some of the darkened memories and energies that linger behind after their passing, so those on the earth plane are released from the passionate pain these individuals have felt.

It is important to note however, that all souls are retrieved through the light and the energies of our great beings of light in the non-physical. Sometimes it take a bit more encouragement to gather someone into our gentle embrace but no one should feel that someone is eternally bound to a haunting or to a version of their own inner hell. There are beings on this side that work tirelessly to make certain that each soul is found and brought back to light.

Now in cases such as the dramatic loss of life at 9/11, some of these souls are so shocked that they are indeed disoriented and although their souls are almost immediately retrieved onto the other side, there is still great ego attachment to their lives lost. And in that, it feels as though they are in great pain and are haunting the premises or the lives of those who miss them so. But this is their ego fragment and those who have lost people through such tragedy should not fear that their souls are wandering aimlessly. They are cradled in the arms of love and they are carefully removed from the scene. Any energetic work through meditation, prayer, cleansing of energies on the site of such a tragedy does help to remove these energy fragments and to give peace to all who are experiencing the pain of loss and shock on earth.

So we do greatly appreciate and highly recommend that you take advantage of those souls in physical who are willing to look for and shift the consciousness that remains hanging like a teardrop above the physical plane after such wars or other such physical happenings. This is a time of great intervention in the lives of humanity on the physical plane, for so much hangs in the balance as we seek to move consciousness to a higher love. As you dear children would hold and counsel together a vision of an earth healed with all souls happy and confidently cradled in love, this will be of enormous help to us as we seek to remove the lack of consciousness in physical reality.

Pam: *They just stopped, do you have another question?*

Joe: Again, maybe concerning the methods of helping those who have committed suicide: one, two, and three, is there a general average of time in earth years that it might take? I'm hearing in some ways that the soul transition is quite instant but that the family might feel the suffering of the fragments of energy left behind? I'm also wondering which of the three methods Pete experienced and now that it's been twenty years for him, what goes on beyond the immediate help that is given such as counseling for another life, etc.?

Pam: *Okay, ARGO, Joe has asked the questions ... particularly the time element, if you can translate that?*

ARGO: The time varies. For example, someone who uses euthanasia to remove self from physical when there is the presence of a painful fatal disease moves through at remarkable speed. Let's say they are gathered in a day in the arms of love, are shown the brief moments of life left, if they had not used such a method to depart the physical. They are hurried off to other dimensions of light to rest for a time before meeting with guides for planning their next experience, so they would have just a brief stopover and then move quickly into the embrace of love.

There are others though, who are strong souls who have suffered much and who are defiant in that they cannot believe in the goodness of love. These men and women could take several years more time to revolutionize their beliefs and make themselves eligible to be moved to other dimensions for further study and enlightenment. There are those who have caused great harm to physical [Pam: they are showing me like mass murderers, they are showing me Hitler, who killed himself.] who may sleep for a century before being pulled into light for further discussion and understanding. These poor souls who have experienced such dementia of spirit in physical, that have caused such terrible harm to the consciousness of others, frequently cannot find a reasonable belief in love or light and may find themselves being remade in a vision of light by being put into the pool of new souls. So as you ask for time element we can only say it varies according to the heart of the spirit involved. There is always enough time in our dimension of light to wait with love for these spirits to grasp the concept of self-acceptance of eternal love and light.

Your brother Pete is more of an average Joe [Pam: they are laughing . . . that was a joke, Joe]. He moved through various stages of his own return to light . . . let's put it like a staircase to heaven. Let's say he made the first landing in four or five months which is, "Oh, hello there, I am Pete. I have died and I have some time on my hands now to learn more about love and light."

Then as he was instructed and given great love both from your dimension and ours, he moved up the steps to another landing where his consciousness began to under-stand the importance of helping others, of sharing love with all who can receive it, of finding a place in his own heart to share from his dimension to yours the love that he believed that was unrequited to him in physical because of such dif-ficult karma. In this place of understanding he stayed for quite a while, thinking of oh so many plans as to how he could help others be retrieved from the dungeon of grief and guilt and find their way home to truly trusting all forms of love whether in masculine or feminine form. We would call this Pete's dreaming phase, like California Dreaming and in it we saw that he was quite happy and content listing in his soul's mind a variety of methods to generate and share love with others.

Now we are moving Pete to a more practical phase. This is coming up shortly for him where he will be planning on how to market himself in physical reality. [Pam: laughs, it looks like he's coming to a place where he is going to think about reincarnation]. As he would discuss this there are still so many options available to him.

Now we will tell you about a dimension of light where Pete could choose to go, where he would have an inter-dimensional experience of life without being born in a human body. It would be like practicing a play or being a stand-in in a play and having many lessons understood and integrated in the soul's reality without ever stepping a foot onto the earth planet. This is always an option and many different styles of plays and roles are offered to him as he works through his own personal issues and some trepidation about working through issues in life in the physical.

It is most normal for many souls who have worked through such difficult karma to have a case of nervous jitters in considering a return to the planet, for they do hold deep in their memory and have observed from our dimension of light that it is common for humans to suffer great pain both emotionally and physically. Who would want to leave such beauty in the presence of such pain? We do then sit with Pete to show how a plan in a physical reality could suit a lifestyle where he would have many doors open to him, so that he could move through the difficult tasks of physical reality, and learning through belief systems without so much sense of pain or hopelessness. Many options are shown to him and he is also shown how other people of great consciousness could move into his life to help him find safety, security, and love in a physical reality.

Many times human beings may re-experience a catastrophic life because they feel that maybe a repeat of the old show would help really drive the point home. So if it is decided that this would be a good idea, he could come back home to the physical and replay the same story. However there is always another option. We do note that humans seem to respond to pain unfortunately as a motivation to learn.

However it is also possible that Pete, if he decides to reclaim a human form, could decide to come back as a female. He did not fully understand the feminine in the physical reality of his last life and Pete could live a life free from harm and experience the pleasures of being a feminine power. This would shake his being to the core because it is so different from his old belief. But if it is deemed possible for him to learn how to embrace the power of the feminine through pleasure, this is always an option.

Oh, dear children, how we do seek to open your hearts to the possibility of learning through pleasure and delight, to removing yourself from the horror chamber, and to come home to a pleasure-full field of light, to smell the flowers, the roses of joy and to learn how to increase your capacity for love and joy in this manner. We would suggest to all of you now to please make this delightful prayer of light to the universe that you be taught through love and joy, that you find great happiness and passion always in life and that you remember then to return that love and that light to your fellow humans so that it may return with great joy. It is not to be grabbed as in greed for fear that it is of limited supply, but to really learn that there is really a limitless supply of love and it is to be shared with those who fear that it does not exist.

So yes, dear child, we have caught you by surprise somewhat in suggesting that Pete may return to physical reality soon. He does hope to see you move forward with this writing and would desire to help you put words of light to the page. He is at this time considering how to proceed for himself. Whether to live in the "movie reality" in nonphysical to see how it feels to be full of love and joy in a feminine form, how it feels to have enough love to share easily with others, to see others heal from pain through this love. There are, however, so many stories open to Pete at this time, so many options of love, one of them is the potential for Pete to come into physical reality as a human and born into a feminine body with some physical deformity. In that place of physical deformity there will be some limitation or suffering and not being like others or feeling powerless. But as he would grow, he would find that in his heart and in his mind was great power of light and in the long run he could turn into a magnificent healer of others. So that the crippled [Pam: bones?] would indeed catapult him into the experience of being a glorious bringer of light to many others, so they can relieve themselves of emotional suffering and even at times physical pain. Pete seems to like this plan a lot although he still is not sure about physical deformity as he considers this a personal form of hell in the physical. [Note by Joe: Pete was crippled by a bad car accident in the life in which I knew him].

There are other options that we are in the discussion about with him. One is to be born into a family with three brothers, with one who is physically ill and possibly may not live a full life. He will see his own early death in this dilemma and he will hold great love and compassion for that child who is designed to die early. In so doing he would relive moments of his own life where he also received great love and compassion from you and he would remember always to be forgiving of the crippled child, of the child with vast limitations. It would bring full circle much of the love that was missing within him towards himself in his past life. He would live with a heart open to compassion and unafraid of grief. He would come to an altered reality for his soul where he would then feel a compulsion to help others whose children are destined to die young. It could be an amazing experience for him and it is a popular story around these parts now, we believe, for him to take part in. It is important always to remember that these are Pete's choices and in our next hour spent with you he would like to discuss with you these options and what he thinks about them, telling you more and more about his time in healing from physical reality.

Joe: Terrific!

Pam: *Wow. What time is it?*

Joe: About twelve minutes after.

Pam: *Oh, they've stopped. Yeah, I guess next time it will be really Peter.*

Joe: It was a really wonderful session today, thank you and ARGO both.

Pam: *Yes, really wonderful how they explained despair. Even if someone would in a sense lose their soul, meaning going to this great vat of love where souls are regenerated where the consciousness as they know of themselves as a soul is removed, their energy is revital-ized into something else, so no one is ever lost. And to also remark on the tremendous amount of love and compassion, and how present they are to give help to those of us that still are in body on earth, if people in the physical can look past their pain and their anger and reach out for it. How present they are! Also it felt very hopeful to me that if these times on earth now look very desperate, there is a return to light. Which is very helpful—I got a definite sense that eventually the light wins out over the shadow and it happens in all our lives. It's just a matter of time. Other than that, I think that they were really clear and it was just again the deep sense of love, presence, and avail-ability that is always present for these souls. I think that's it.*

End Session

ARGO begins this second session with a clear statement that there is no objective hell, meaning a place where one is consigned to eternal damnation and suffers eternally. However, if a person has strong belief in such a concept and dies feeling deserving of such punishment, then in that person's mind such a place can appear, at least for a while, real. Therefore people who are the most severely enmeshed in the bitter-ness and despair that often accompanies suicide are quickly placed in a coma-like rest state upon dropping the physical body.

This allows helpers and guides to work with them on what sounds to me like an unconscious level, removing blocks to being able to per-ceive love and themselves in their true nature as shining beings of love.

Only after this work is done are they slowly brought back into a more conscious state. And their re-wakening is greeted with great joy by the helpers as a true resurrection. In this method too, there is a life review, now that the soul is more balanced. The soul is shown the events of their lives and their effect on others while their whole being is held in great comfort and light. ARGO reports that they then are usually eager to learn more about how things really work and are instructed in this in a setting the makes sense for them. They then have the option of beginning to plan for another life but are often encouraged for a good while to just observe how others live their lives. While this is occurring, it sounds like the helpers are very careful to keep the soul removed from direct earth contact, to protect them from falling back into more limited thinking and also to protect those on earth from their energy until they are cleaner and clearer.

ARGO then talks about what sounds like very rare cases where the soul "cannot contain even a thimbleful of light" even after all their attempts to heal that soul's attitudes and experience. Here there is an option of returning the soul's basic energy back into a more general pool of soul energy from which new souls can be born. This perhaps is the most difficult concept to understand in what ARGO is presenting, but it sounds to me that the continuous flow of learning and building identity through many incarnations is broken or interrupted, and that particular consciousness now projects a new soul fragment that is akin to a relative of the first soul and gets to start from a much fresher perspective. In any event, it sounds to me as if ARGO is saying that life patterns are not allowed to continue unless they can hold at least some light. And it sounds to me as if, just as there is no everlasting hell, there is never complete annihilation of a soul. We in our essence go on forever.

Another very important point ARGO is making in this session, for example when he is countering our concepts of hell, is that there is only unconditional love and that we here on earth have such a limited understanding of this reality. Within unconditional love there is no room for and cannot be, by definition, harsh judgment and vengeance even under the illusion of justice. He states clearly that here on earth we are suffering with the hellish results of so many wars of vengeance. He strongly entreats us still on earth not to slip into thoughts of vengeance when we perceive wrongdoing, but rather, as much as possible he encourages us to resonate with the reality that is true here and throughout the physical and non-physical universe: unconditional love. He is clear that we do not have to be perfect but as much as we can, to live within the comfort of unconditional love towards ourselves and all others. So it seems to me that unconditional love becomes the way to rise above hellish energy, both here and when on the other side. This energy may be challenging to access when we are surrounded here by so many fears that activate our physical survival program. But we will truly create more safety through love than through war, both within ourselves and within our world community.

Next within this session I asked about The Monroe Institute program called Lifeline, which engages in soul rescue work. ARGO responded that activities such as in the Lifeline program and prayers for the dead in general serve an important function to raise the newly deceased's energy, separate them from the density of the physical, and help protect and heal them on the other side. In my research for *Brothers Forever*, I did find that every major religion I researched has a process of praying for the dead that they feel is helpful. ARGO's words seem to verify that this tradition of praying for the dead is a very helpful one. Interestingly, the Lifeline program just a few years ago was the subject of a two-part documentary on television in a program called, *The Unexplained*. The film crew was able to verify, using historical records, some of the reports of contact with the other side that were reported by the Lifeline participants, even concerning people who had died as far back as the Civil War.

The other aspect of praying for the dead that ARGO mentions is that, after sudden death and particularly massive death, such as terrorist events that at times the newly departed are in a type of shock and, while immediately comforted, leave an ego remnant behind, if you will, that hangs on near the site of the event, and that we can be helpful in clearing this energy. We do find much of this in the Lifeline program around events such as 9/11. Most times it is a question of getting that "person's" attention, helping them understand that they have died and then immediately they are able to perceive guides and loved ones who have passed before them, and who are there to help them onward and upward. These loving reunions are amazing to experience because there is such love and light present there.

Next I asked about time-frames for the soul recovering from suicide in this session. ARGO described a continuum of time that may span from hours to a century or more. He was clear that in cases of euthanasia the person progresses at lightning speed through the orientation process immediately after death and then into a period of rest. My sense was this was true for suicides when there is terminal illness and for assisted suicides.

He said that Pete was an "average Joe" in this case and took about four months to reach the first plateau where he was ready to receive instruction. Then Pete advanced to what they called his "California Dreaming" phase where, having learned the principles of love and light, he explored all the ways that he could help shed light back upon those he left in the physical and also help in general with the spreading of love and light. Now they are saying that he is in a practical or planning phase where he is deciding upon his next life experience. Given the time when this book is being written compared to when he died we could say that it took him about twenty-five years to get to this planning stage from the time of his death. And again they are calling this average after a suicide.

ARGO then describes souls who are very embedded in the distrust in the possibility of love, who may take years just to reach the first plateau of being ready to receive instruction and insight. And finally ARGO describes the extremes of where there has been mass murder and suicide, such as Hitler, where a hundred years may pass and then if love cannot be held in the soul's consciousness, that the soul is recycled into a pool of soul energy, as we mentioned above.

Hitler, for most of us, is a great example of applying the principles of no judgment and vengeance, given his horrific acts. It can seem that everlasting hell is needed for justice there. We must be humble in knowing that we never know the whole story, yet repudiate with all your strength the deeds that occurred and put our efforts into making sure that they are not repeated. Lives such as his and all the people who cooperated, or at least did not risk everything to stop him, are beacons showing us the horrible power of fear. As we look around today we can again see fear and desire for vengeance poisoning our world in ways that result in much appalling behavior towards our fellow man, fellow creatures, and the planet. Now we have suicide bombers who we may believe are consummate evil and who deserve hell for engaging in murder-suicide. Indeed they may be among those needing a hundred years of healing, or in the end not able to hold a thimbleful of light and need to be recycled. But it is really not up to us to judge their souls, even as we repudiate their acts. It can help us to remain non-vengeful if we understand that from the perspective of the innocent people who die when we bomb villages from high above with our advanced war machinery, that we are the terrorists in their view. I think that ARGO is pointing out here the futility of trying to create peace by meeting vengeance with vengeance. Great wisdom is needed to separate out legitimate self-defense, deterrence, and justice from vengeance. Contrasting with this, of course, are also clear signs of progress in terms of love and tolerance, and more consciousness about our effect on others and the world.

In this second session, ARGO then began to outline some of what Pete was encountering in his planning phase that he is currently experiencing. Many options for different physical lives were being considered. But perhaps more surprising was the option of having "lives" that would take place in another non-physical dimension, where it is less challenging and there is more awareness of support. ARGO mentions that many beings who have experienced the difficulty and density of life on earth are naturally reluctant to come back, feeling a lack of confidence that they can handle the challenges here. This surely is understandable. So it is wonderful to hear there are other options in which to learn and grow.

This planning period for the soul seems to unfold with great care, with the assistance of many wise ones to guide the soul and always with respect for the soul as having the final determination about which path to follow next in their journey of evolution toward greater light and awareness. It seems that major life events for the anticipated life are scripted in advance on the other side, as well as selection of the parents and other important figures for that life. ARGO mentions that humans seem to often learn through pain, that they pay attention more carefully when they are in pain. He invites us to powerfully affirm that we are eager to learn through love and joy. I hear in this that it is a free choice universe and that we are free to choose more gentle, loving, and abundant ways to progress and learn. That is good news, the power of which I will explore later in this book because it has largely been my focus for the last twenty years.

It is interesting to me that in all these sessions ARGO does not reference any materialistic benchmarks, such as how much money we have been able to accumulate in a life, as any criterion for success. Rather it is all about how much love we can receive and express and how we handle fear. This perception is exactly what people who have had a serious heart attack, a pitched battle with cancer, or a near-death experience tend to report: that what is important in life has shifted for them away from the mundane and toward experiencing love and beauty. And they no longer sweat the small stuff!

There was surely a lot of information conveyed in this hour-long session. I have now reviewed the content many times and each time reach deeper insights into the impact and implications of what was being said. I looked forward to the next session eagerly but with some trepidation, as Pete had said that he would like my help in deciding what type of live experience he would chose next. I feel quite unqualified to council him from my limited earth perspective on such an important issue, but commit to do my best in love and light.

MANY CHOICES

ARGO Session December 18, 2015

Pam: *Okay, ARGO, This is for Joe. He is here to talk further about the book, about suicide, the after-effects for those who commit it and their families. In our last conversation it looks like Pete may discuss things about reincarnational possibilities, but Joe absolutely leaves it up to you and your wisdom of guiding this information. So I ask to be used as a clear and loving channel of light to get this information with clarity and accuracy, thank you ARGO.*

Joe: Yes, thank you, ARGO.

Pam: *I am certainly moving into Pete's energy and he is taking me through the emotions he was experiencing shortly before his suicide up to this point. He's talking about emotion to me and saying that now from his perspective he sees how fleeting yet impactful emotions are, and in the greater scheme of things time-wise, how momentary they are. So he is showing it to me as if he can see the entire scope of emotions in a second's time, he is saying "in the blink of an eye." And that when someone is caught in a dark emotional state, there is this psychological sense of a deep well of pain and grief and that one is incapable of moving beyond it, and in the case of the suicidal person,* *without ending their lives. It seems so "rich in pain" but it is fleeting in reality.*

And emotions can be moved from one state to another by mental power. So someone can start to remember happier times or become aware that yes, emotions are fleeting and the things will start to lighten up. Now he saying that in his life, with his issues with the feminine, he did not really believe that emotions, even though they may be passing, would be absolutely pleasurable for the long term: that pleasure was more fleeting than pain. Pain was the more emotional enduring state in life. And although this is not true, it was his mental fixation and this belief that caused him to end his life. It is also why no one could really help him or talk him out of this strong mental belief.

So now on the other side, really having in so many ways the big picture about emotional states from looking at his own life as well as observing family members' lives as they move through what seems to be slow-moving anxieties or questioning about the value of life, that these are actually so inconsequential to the big picture. Now in planning his next experience and he is saying life experience but he is putting quotation marks around "life" and what that says to me, Joe, is that it is not necessarily going to be a physical incarnation but it is going to be a strong experience. That he will set up scenarios where he has strong impactful challenges that will impact him emotionally like the loss of a sibling, the death of a child early in life, so that when that experience overwhelms him, he will have to learn how to endure. He will set it up so that if he does not endure, others around him would suffer terribly. And that he would see the selfishness in leaving, so everything is set up for him to learn emotional endurance.

This is being prepared as an option for him either in a physical reality or in a sort of movie scene dimension where that reality is lived but is not fully experienced in a physical way. He's leaning toward the non-physical experience because when in a physical body, when inhabiting a physical body, the emotional impact of family sto-ries, genetics, trauma experiences, memories are all encoded in the physical form which makes it more difficult to endure if there is ter-rible trauma. This takes a tremendous amount of courage to march through, to move through. So it is felt not just emotionally but physi-cally, tangibly.

Joe: I do not know if now is a good time but one of my questions would be with physical life being so painful for even an average life: why do it?

Pam: *(laughs heartily) That's a good question!*

Joe: It is a question of what, especially since we forget every-thing when we come back again, what is the value?

Pam: *ARGO is right here: greater growth. Okay, Pete is here, but ARGO is saying that one can move through a variety of scenarios in a non-physical form and be led along by guides without the deep intention of physical and not make as much progress as quickly. It is more of a study. It is like somebody you know is reading about something and thinking that you actually know it; it is almost an intellectual study, a process. Whereas when one comes into a physical embodiment, and again he shows great courage, that the courage to forget in a conscious way what true reality exists for you, and endur-ing the physical impact of a body and a deterioration of a body in a normal death process, just springboards you forward into much faster evolution and moves you more quickly into a healing place where those reincarnations are not needed or required.*
It is really up to the soul, so that when someone in the physical reality looks around and says, you know, "Was I crazy?" This is a dreadful experience in so many ways. ARGO says, grinning, that they have

only themselves to blame but they will find on the other side that the expansion of the soul, the heart, sort of the spiritual mind, that connection to things greater and the impact on the universe is greater. They are … oh, for lack of another word, Joe, I think he is trying to say that they are more important players in universal processing of light.

Joe: I imagine the goal is to just become more and more loving?

Pam: *Yes.*

Joe: And less responsive to fear?

Pam: *Yes.*

Joe: Somehow I am hearing that the physical is a very important classroom for that?

Pam: *Yes, the intensity of it. They are saying as well as the intensity of the pleasure made available. You know, there is a sensuality, a sort of a physicality, if someone can open to it and the sense of physical beauty, of cosmic beauty in the body. It is amazing and they can transform that body into greater light so that, yes, it also seems to have a great symbiotic effect for the universe in general. So if you are going to try to support a greater expansion of light and love, this is one way to do it and the other alternatives are felt but not with such impact, so that there is less impact.*

Joe: And I can understand why Pete might want to take it a little slowly.

Pam: *That is my sense, yes, to take it slower because he is showing how in this life when we knew him, how deeply entrenched was his belief, you know that pleasure is fleeting and pain is everlasting.*

Joe: So even with the perspective that he would have now, if he came back into physical, it sounds like there would almost be a physical program, genetically, if you will, and family circumstance to still have that as an issue?

Pam: *Yes, that would still be an issue. He would have a chance to apply what he knows. His chances of success in a physical life are good. It is like coming back and saying, okay, you have spiritually now an understanding of these other lives, so you are going to come in and you're going to have this really difficult emotional experience very early on for you to use what you know, the value of living through and growing, so that you have completely conquered it. When he looks at it, he just does not know if he is up for it. I can appreciate it too, how … He is saying, you know gradually getting there, but you still get there.*

Joe: Yes.

Pam: *It is like the tortoise and the hare; he doesn't mind being the tortoise.*

Joe: I can respect that.

Pam: *I can too.*

Joe (laughs): So it sounds like, you would have new perspective coming in, but then you forget everything anyway and so when this terrible event happens . . .

Pam: *Well, I think the forgetting is where ARGO is stepping in a bit to correct. You might forget the other side but that, through the development and learning on the other side, there is a part of the consciousness that does know better, so it is like the difference between an older soul and a younger soul in terms of the experience and having certain information to apply to certain life events.*

Joe: So in the dark night of the soul here, as you cry out, your own soul can somehow convey that it is okay?

Pam: *Exactly, a part of you would know that if you just hang on and white-knuckle through this, there will be a clearing. And ARGO says, for example, in this situation he would come back, that there would be people around, as you tried to do with him, who would encourage the more positive approach. In other words there would be people on board trying to help but that his own soul would not be as defeated by lack of knowledge, so the soul does influence choice in a lifetime. This is what they are saying.*

Joe: Before this life Pete just experienced here, he probably also had perspective, but he was carrying in to this particular life here in which I knew him as Pete, ah, a pessimism if you will, about the feminine, let's call it that.

Pam: *Yes, a deep, deep pessimism that actually was his undoing, you know, because the feminine holds emotion, intuition, the whole feeling world, playfulness: yes, it was his undoing. And where he is now, the way he shows himself, he feels pretty good, he doesn't … you know he does not feel like a failed soul for what has happened, he is calling it, "for his divorce from the physical" but he also notes the nature of his soul, and it's cute, he is sort of laughing, he says he is a bit of a slow learner, Joe. (Pam laughs)*

That his soul wants a lot of experience, impactful experience, to change its beliefs, whereas you are an older soul. You certainly should question things and you do, but you can arrive at conclusions a little more easily. You think things through more than he could. So souls are not generically the same when it comes to their age, or really in comparison to one another. They are as unique as the personalities that we are walking around with in the physical.

Pete's soul . . . he feels that he needs some experience, more experiential, not just understanding under his belt without something being so devastating, before he would be ready to come into the physical and try to do it in 3-D. And his guides are around him supporting those choices, and certainly it is a sense of, "Let's do the best for you and certainly let's not be reckless with you." It looks to me that they would not allow him to take on something so extraordinary that the chances of him moving through it would be negligible. They would want to do everything that they could to set him up for the best success.

And ARGO is showing me an example. It is like you see some souls can come in and have a lot of loss and turn it around and help others through their losses, turn it into compassion. Other souls are not able to do this. They can become embittered and a lot of that has to do with . . . it is sort of the persona of the soul, but really it is also the soul age and the amount of experience that it has already had with loss. So ARGO is showing it is sort of like when we look around our world at people responding so differently to experiences—they are showing the immigration crisis, where some people want to throw them out and other people want to help them. ARGO is saying that it is the difference in the level of compassion that has a lot to do with the level of the soul's experience.

Joe: So in this life for me, the loss of Pete was very devastating. And I have struggled from a place where I have changed from having a broken heart to having a heart like an ocean: that you could put your hand in water and if you remove your hand it goes back to complete, losing only a drop. Since then I have had other losses and they have not affected me nearly like the loss of Pete did.

Pam: *Exactly*

Joe: Would that be an example of this?

Pam: *That would be a perfect example. You are a living example of that.*

Joe: So I could trust that next time, I do not have to go through this again, maybe because I have conquered it a bit?

Pam: *Absolutely! And ARGO is saying that eventually souls get to the point when they become so good at this that they simply don't bother with a physical incarnation: it's done. That they can live on as guides to people who are working with that, there are just all kinds of wonderful things that they can do to expand light. But yes, your healing through this, and healing others and helping them understand these tragedies is a perfect example of success with this. And not being as impacted when life's (ARGO is calling them misadventures) occur.*

Joe: If Pete were to select an incarnation physically (and or in the non-physical idea, too) does he get to choose the time-frame, the country, the parents: is the scenario pretty detailed or . . .

Pam: *Pretty much. They are saying that they would help him with this. He is not evolved enough to be able to coordinate all of it so well. So this is where there is like a board that is set up that says, "This* *culture will be really deeply ingrained and here are a couple people who have good hearts but they are a bit troubled: they would be great parents, but here is a child that just isn't intended to live long," that sort of thing. They are saying that it is so complicated, mostly because everyone has free will in the mix. So it is not just living. Certain things are certainly set up with a sense of destiny to happen but in the mix of that, everyone is trying to evolve and as people evolve, circumstances change for them.*

So it is really complicated and they are saying it really takes high level guides and experienced teachers to get everything set up so that it is as well coordinated as possible for the desired outcome. And Pete is included in the planning and shown this, and things are discussed with him, so it is not as though it is an assignment that he is pointed to. They are also showing this other option of having sort of a milder form of the experience, where there is not such a physical impact, to get him to move forward a little bit. What ARGO is saying is that everyone wants for Pete the kinder, sort of softer approach, and the reason they are is that includes such a feminine energy for him, so that he has a softer experience. And the planning is to make it as least abusive as possible, so that he learns to trust those energies also. He is doing really well and he is really content and he really does see the big picture. He's not in a state where he is questioning different realities at all and he is very content to move forward in something where again, he is saying, "easy does it."

Joe: I am just curious, does he hang out much with my mother, father, and brother John at this point or is he kind of more engaged in a bigger world, less tied to the personality of Pete and more toward his core self? I do not know quite how to phrase this.

Pam: *Pete, do you hang out with family or are you in another frame of mind? At each person's passing, family members passing, he was present to reassure them of the love and the well being and to reassure them of their own goodness and their . . . it was some very happy times for reunion. And he had a lot of fun with John. Yes, but as far as studying to make future lives together, not particularly. And he is showing me that he would visit and it was just a beautiful reunion and then he would go back to his learning station to continue to expand and to grow in his heart the way he needs to. And he sees them to their own places of learning also, so that there is an awareness of the presence of all of them. So all of them are aware of the others and all of them are sort of putting their heads in the books of learning, their noses to the grind-stone to figure out next moves which may or may not include one another.*

When the family is in what Pete is calling the state of flux on the other side, it does not exclude the possibility that your parents would not be his parents again. It is offered frequently as an option, but it is not a necessity. Again, it all depends on the personal expansion of each soul and what that soul is trying to rediscover or learn or share or heal on the planet.

You know, Pete is looking at you and saying that you can teach others and he is saying that there is no one else who is doing that (Pam laughs) in the family. So that you hopped on board this family that was perfectly set up for all the psychological challenges and dimensions and even the spiritual upbringing, so that you would move through these really hard experiences but with the consciousness of a healer and a teacher. The rest of your family really was not set up for that: that was not the intention. In other words, he is showing that it is like you came into this incarnation from out of teacher's school on the other side and into this family, where the rest of your family were sort of students.

And they benefited and they still benefit greatly from your doing this and your presence in the family is really, Pete is sort of grinning, he is calling it a healing bonus. And again he is showing me how complicated it really is, I mean when I am looking at all of this, I say Wow! It really does take a wizardly mind to understand all of this and to put this together considering free will in the mix as well. So Pete is leaning towards the less painful, which he thinks is the more obvious choice for him in this other dimension.

Now what ARGO is saying is that in this other dimension, it is not like it will be easier to remember himself now, as he is now. But he will not be so challenged that his thinking will be as confused and there will be a lot of tutors available. The way they are showing it to me, when we look at time in our lives, it certainly seems that life seems to be a lot about time and certain expected number of years, let's say ninety years. Whereas in this experience he would be going through, it can be in terms of time as the blink of an eye because it is not a physical dimension. So he can have multiple experiences in a shorter period of time, if you are going to compare it to how we experience time on earth and having one life. He also sees this non-physical movie show life experience as more efficient, which is kind of cool.

Joe: He may not learn as much in one of those non-physical life experiences but he might have five or ten of them as opposed to the time and planning for one physical life?

Pam: *Exactly: kind of ingenious.*

Joe: There was discussion last session about his having other choices. For example to be a woman with a birth defect who would become a great healer. Has that now settled more to the ones we are discussing?

Pam: *Yes it has, because when he looks at that, it feels overwhelming to him (to reincarnate into a physical life at this point), that the possibilities of making it seem more limited . . . he does not really want to try something until he feels more assured of success. Which means these other things are more like training for the Olympics. He is extremely happy. Boy, he wants to communicate that, Joe! And one of the things that he wants to communicate, through you in this book is how fair and balanced everything really is. That is all basically regulated by the amount of light and energy you have, he is smiling, he is saying, "You know, the number of kilowatts that you have in your bulb," that kind of thing. That your experiences are related directly to your kilowattage and that the universe, in great kindness, tries to soften the blows as much as possible where it can, dependent on your kilowattage. If you in a lifetime want to move beyond some kind of repeated hurtful pattern, when you turn the kilowattage up, that pattern is less impacting and maybe not as frequent. Really, it isn't about victimization, it is about learning how to love and to turn on the light. He sees when he looks at his lifetime, he sees himself as a pretty stubborn person, actually. That what you were calling pessimism, he is calling stubbornness (Pam laughs)*

Joe: I hope he understands . . .

Pam: *Oh, he understands completely, you know he is in the state where we will all be eventually, of having complete clarity about how everything works and what went on without negative judgment around it.*

Joe: Good, because with all he did in this life, he generated a tremendous amount of love toward him from his spouse, to his siblings, to his parents.

Pam: *Absolutely and all of you loving him, you were part of the support system to help him turn around this pessimism, so you were all on board to offer that because you all had hearts with the capacity to do that. That was part of the plan as well and this is why he is saying that he sees himself sort of as a bratty stubborn kid from the other side but he is not judging himself negatively for it. I want to be really clear about that. So that all of the help that was offered is deeply, deeply appreciated by him. And it was his, he is saying refusal, I almost said inability, but he is saying refusal to make that change that brought around these circumstances that were so painful.*

But he is saying in the light of day, which is what he is showing me, that he is in now, he is showing me being in a very bright and sunny place, he understands it and he understands how foolish resistance is, how it brings such suffering and grief to everyone involved and that it isn't something that one should use to identify themselves. So he is showing someone who is resistant to the love around them or to making a change or to believing that they are lovable, anything like that: if they use their own negative psychology to sort of make an identity for themselves which could be like, "Well I'm a victim, these things aren't for me," or if the ego is allowed to over-identify with the victim and resist what is being offered, it truly is sort of the illness of the soul that leads one to do that. So when he looks at it, again it is with this understanding that as well. That he was offered love and help and guidance and he just was resistant.

So this plan (the new life experience he is planning) that he has going, it would be to sort of wear down the tendency to over-identify through an ego, the tendency to say, "No, I am a victim, I do not care what you are showing me, I see it another way." So the plan will wear that resistance down so that it shows that when he will sail into physical again, he will be more malleable. He loves you dearly, Joe.

Joe: I feel like I am lecturing but I feel moved to say this once more. I heard him acknowledge all the love and support that we gave him, but I want him to acknowledge how much he graced our lives. He provided us with delight and pleasure, even though his passing was painful. He was able to light up a light in my daughter Sarah's eyes that nobody else did, and in my heart, my whole definition of friendship and support that I felt in my family, where I felt quite bereft and misunderstood at times, I always felt support from him. I want him to know how much value he gave us and I am hoping that has also penetrated into his larger perspective.

Pam: *Pete, do you hear Joe? He wants you to acknowledge the gift you were unto your entire family and how important you were in their lives in spite of the difficult passing. Joe wants you to acknowledge it as part of your history in that lifetime. Pete, can you acknowledge this? Pete? [long pause] Do you see it? [long pause]*
    He is mulling it over, Joe. (Pam laughs) He is stubborn.

Joe: Well, please do mull that over.

Pam: *The image that he is giving me, and this is probably. . . . maybe he will be doing some of that learning the gift of who he is in those lifetimes because what he is showing me is that all of you were sunlight shining on him and it just bounced back at yourselves: he mirrored it back to you and you were really seeing your own beauty when he was around you; so he has a little ways to go with that self-love and acceptance.*

Joe: Yes, maybe he mirrored for us, but he has his own light and it is really beautiful.

Pam: *He has his own light and ARGO shows me this, it is like this beautiful bed they are making for him. It is like this wonderful soft inviting bed that they are making up for him in this next life, meaning okay, it is like a resting life, a nurturing resting life where one can start to see their own beauty. They show him looking in a mirror in that life and seeing his beauty and able to recognize what he brings to others.*

I will tell you one thing his soul is, he is very intelligent, Pete is. So they are going to move him into what they are calling heart resonance, Joe, through a nurturing, resting experience that will mimic a physical life. ARGO is saying it is like getting a massage before. . .

Joe: So he would have this nurturing experience you were just talking about before he would move into the life where the child dies?

Pam: *Yes, they would be filling him up. ARGO is saying it is not like the universe is willing to just throw him to the dogs and saying okay, remember you didn't do it so well last time, let's do it differently this time, it is not that. There would be more soul strength and experience in a positive way, before sending him back. He would be more prepared in that life: he would probably want you with him in that life, just in case, Joe. (Pam laughs)*

But for now it is this series of . . . ARGO is just showing it as a series of general feel good life experiences that have some loss, again it mimics life on the physical planet. But that is something that he has to get on board with is that self-love. And you know I think about it, in the very beginning that is what they were saying was lacking in people who suffer from mental illness, remember?

Joe: Yes.

Pam: *In the very beginning of these sessions I remember being hardly able to breathe looking at this deep lack of self-love that these people live with and they project these things out. It is just horrific and Pete is still trying to get a little more buff in that area, let's put it that way, strengthening self. They do show him in a place also where there is just a tremendous condensation of light all around him. I mean he is immersed in light and he is also being kept with a sense of identity of himself as a soul. He is not feeling at this stage so merged into light that he becomes one with the essence of all. He still feels identified with the soul, just sort of the stage that soul is in, as it's evolving.*

I am asking them if, when he is in these other states, if a part of his consciousness would still be aware of you, Elena, and the kids, or the rest of the family, Sarah: Is that okay to ask?

Joe: Yes, that would be good.

Pam: *So Pete, when you go into this will they feel you, will you be aware of them? Okay, the aspect of his soul that was incarnated as Pete will be immersed in the new story and not as available but the center foundation of the soul which manifested as Pete will still be aware of you. The soul is constant and in its purest essence is in constant love, it is the creation, then it splinters off aspects of itself to more greatly expand its light, so any soul in a reincarnational process is a splintering off of a foundation which remains constant in another dimension which is not attached so much to a sense of perception of a personality. It is much more involved than we think, Joe.*

Joe: Just to clarify, if I brought him into my consciousness as the Pete I knew while being aware that he is much more than that, but as a handy way for the human mind to get in touch with that energy, and I asked him to help me at a slot machine, or to think, when it is Christmas time, on his being at the dining table with us: in any way does that pull his energy away from what he needs to be doing right now?

Pam: *No. And what you might experience is the higher core of his being sending a shot of light toward you. ARGO is chiming in a bit also. Let's say that you were at a slot machine. Call to your higher consciousness to bring that in, let's say the core of you anchored on the other side to manifest what you want.*

Joe: It has been very useful this year while at the slot machines to be very loving, and to be thinking of my brother, John, my mother, and Pete and saying, "If you guys want to play with me, that is great." I am sitting there in a loving soul communication and I have been getting a lot of jackpots that way. But even without the jackpots it feels very nurturing.

Pam: *Yes, it is really lovely. And it is a way for you to expand that love which brings in that positive love. They are bringing up what they were saying earlier about the human mind getting through diffi-cult emotional times, that positive memories can pull you away from a dark emotional place of abandonment. When you take your heart and your mind and you use the love you remember with all of these people and pull them to you, that expands the light which brings good fortune, so it is: it is a healing psychologically but it can also manifest physically.*

I think what ARGO is showing is whatever works, Joe, as a way to get to greater love and light, and to dwell in it and to feel it. The more it can be felt, not just emotionally but in the body, allowing love to move through the body, the greater the healing for . . . really geneti-cally and for the whole family. When this light is invited in and moves through the body, the body starts to heal those patterns, ARGO is showing like the yogis could transmute their bodies, or just leave their bodies and move on. It is the same principle, they are saying but what is important is that you keep your love vibration at the highest point available and in communication with your soul as much as possible in a physical incarnation.

Joe: It may be off topic a bit but it has been generated by what we have been talking about. I am assuming that in this life in my incarnation that I am on track and that I have done well?

Pam: *Oh, my heaven's yes, Joe.*

Joe: And there is not any big thing that I am missing that when I get to the other side they say . . .

Pam: *[laughs] I tell you that they would tell you if there is, Joe.*

Joe: If I get to the other side and they say you forgot this whole segment you were going to work on and you didn't.

Pam: *Oh, no. Really what you are doing, going through now is primarily why you came and why you came as an assistant to Pete. Really it was symbiotic because the chances of his suicide were so strong. You were learning that you couldn't stop it no matter how much love you were feeling. You were trying to help and to teach, which is exactly what you are doing.*

ARGO is saying that the only thing that they would be suggesting to you, Joe, is just to continue the work. They are saying to harmonize self-love.

Joe: So I have not become world famous but I feel like in the smaller circle that I am dealing with, that I am having a great impact.

Pam: *You are having a great impact and you are not finished yet. And the thing about that is that there is a ripple effect. You can see a more immediate impact on the people surrounding you, but what you don't see is how that radiates out and alters all energies around you and beyond your knowledge. All of these teachings and this personal work, everything that you do has a global impact eventually. And their concern for you is to keep you and Elena, to keep you as comfortable as possible in that process, while you are living in the physical. I do not want to make promises here but I think that the real tragedies are behind you.*

Joe: That would be good!

Pam: *They are certainly not showing me… they are not saying warn him of this or that. They show you coming out of the ocean, someone who had to swim a very long, long, long way and coming out onto a sandy beach: it is a very positive image, okay?*

Joe: Well thank you again for today. I have not had time to transcribe the first sessions, yet, so in terms of more sessions needed for the book, I am not sure yet, but I am wondering if they have a feeling about it. ARGO or Pete, if there are some other critical things they would like to talk about before I write this book, so please schedule with Pam, or whether it is fine to have things on hold until I get rolling?

Pam: *What ARGO is saying is that you have been given plenty to assimilate and to work with right now. I am not the one doing the* *writing but they are also showing it being not so difficult for you. Guess what I am saying is that it is easy for me to say, but I think it flows more easily, that it does not look like it is booby trapped in any way. But they are just showing that you need to mull over what you have.*

And I think the point that was made today to remember that in the very beginning they do talk about, and that is my biggest emotional memory, about just how tragic it is that these people who have some form of mental illness, that deep sadness: how they just cannot attach to that self-love and to the divine love within them. They just can't and how tragic that is and to hear Pete on the other side still dancing around it a little bit. I think it is a very interesting connection to see that it really is a soul malfunction and that it takes a guided process to bring that soul to a place where it really cannot only just believe in love as a concept, but actually touch into it, tap into it within themselves.

Joe: Well, Pam we love you and sure appreciate all you have been in my life.

Pam: *We love you too, Joe. I hope you two have a wonderful Christmas. It is sort of interesting wondering about our souls coming in and making this kind of connection. The life designing is really fabulous and I when I look at the . . . when they are showing me what goes into that design: how brilliant the minds on the other side have to be, understanding the dynamic of the human personality as well as how universal energies work, and what the goals are, and everybody's goals. Oh my Lord! And it really looks as though they have being specializing just in that, that if we were left to choose on our own, I would just shudder to think what we would be doing. I guess it is just very hard to accept the tragedies in life. It is part of this earthly experience and it is temporary. It can be very painful and frightening but the rewards on the other side apparently are huge and it is not* *just ourselves that are affected by it; the universe in general grows, you know glows a little brighter for it. Okay, have a good afternoon, Joe.*

End Session

This third session starts with the energy of Pete coming in clearly and strongly. He explains that from his perspective now, he can see that emotional states are very fleeting but while on earth they can seem interminable. While in physical life his experiences led him to be convinced that pain was more enduring than pleasure and that this was a leading factor that led him to suicide. He can see now from the broader view of the other side that emotions can be changed through better attitudes and thoughts.

From my own experience with decades of depression, once a certain tipping point is reached, our biology and neurochemistry is so out of balance that it can be almost impossible to access those empowering thoughts and find the perspective that those things can change. All one is feeling is agonizing psychological (and sometimes physical) pain. There is no oasis of rest even during sleep when profoundly depressed. The nights become eight hours of restlessness to slog through alone while everyone else is sleeping. At some point one becomes so tired of the daily, and at times hourly, struggle just to have the will to go on, that one can finally just give up. I surely understand this and have great compassion for anyone who has had to suffer in this manner. Compared to a major depressive episode, my year's time in the body cast was a piece of cake.

Given Pete's recent life experience of earth, I can fully understand and respect that he is now reluctant to reincarnate on earth and according to this session is leaning towards a less intense non-physical life experience. Pam is saying here than it takes great courage to move into an earth life with a physical body, when there is this level of work being done, because the stress from past experience is encoded into our very

DNA and family tree. From this I asked the serious question, "Why do this? Why agree to take on a physical life on this planet in turmoil?"

When I asked this question, Pete's energy was present but ARGO also came right in with the short answer being that experiencing a physical life allows greater growth. The type of movie scene life that Pete is considering is more like reading a book, than directly experiencing it. Yes, there can be great understanding achieved, but still direct experience produces an even greater knowing, where greater soul evolution is possible. In a physical incarnation, one can experience the expansion of soul, heart, and knowledge that allows one to be, in ARGO's words "a more important player in the universal processing of light." Yet there is no hurry, as outside of the earth system time does not flow as it does here. So it is fine to proceed more patiently and cautiously by moving through experiences in a less challenging dimension than the physical.

The phrase "player in the universal processing of light" was unclear in meaning to me so I asked if the point of having a physical life was to become more loving and less fearful and received a clear confirmation that this was so. To this Pam added that there is also an exceptional opportunity here on this planet while in physical body to experience the amazing beauty of the physical world and all its sensations. I definitely agree with this. Even while in deepest grief about Pete, whenever my heart has been open, I have been moved to the depths of my being with the beauty that surrounds us, from the miracle of the human hand, through the beauty of nature and music, to the newborn's smile. To me this planet is a great place to learn how to love through limits and see through the bad to the magnificently good.

When I first put out my question as to why do a physical life, I added the phrase "because you forget everything you have learned in other lives when you reincarnate." Pam and ARGO clarified this a bit. They say that souls vary in experience level and personality. When you are more experienced or an older soul, if you will, when you are here in a physical life, some part of you retains your knowledge at an unconscious level, and at times when it is needed you can tap into this well of strength and perspective. And at some point you have learned what you need to learn for your development, and coming back into incarnation here becomes something that you may feel that you have graduated from. Then you go on to do other things and to be in other ways, perhaps as guides or helpers. I know that some who have looked at this also feel that there are other physical planets where one might incarnate, where the level of societal and individual evolution is on a higher level. These places may have different challenges and excitements to offer when the earth system game has been played well and it is time to move on.

In this session we then cycled back to Pete's plans for his next life experience. I asked whether he gets to choose important aspects such as time-frame, parents, and culture, etc. They said, "Yes indeed," but that there is much guidance in this because it is so complex it takes a great level of skill and foresight to anticipate what would be the next ideal setting for a life that will have great potential to expand the soul's growth and learning. They were very clear that it is not that you are given an assignment and charged with "Go do this now." Rather, there is extensive planning with utmost respect for the soul's own desires and choices.

It was interesting to me that just in the two weeks between the second and third session, many of the choices for lives mentioned in the second session for Pete had been narrowed down considerably and most attention was now being focused of the less intense non-physical life experience for him. This relieved me because I had been concerned about his request in the second session that I might help guide him. I did feel the beings on the other side were much better equipped to guide him in this process with their more expanded perspective than I currently enjoy. This progress in just two weeks also suggested to me that things were moving quickly on the other side for Pete at this time and that soon he would be engaged in his new experiences.

This brought up the feeling for me about the type of connections he might have. When asked about hanging out with others in my family who have also passed, they said that Pete meets and greets each one, that they have a meaningful and joyful reunion but then go each to their own path or classroom for their "studies," while also being aware of each other. I also asked about his connection with me, particularly as he engages in whatever new life he selects. The answer was that the part I knew as Pete in this life would be absorbed in his new experiences but that the core essence of Pete would be available to me and that I might experience that connection as a beam of light from him to me. This fits with my experience and others' reports of communication with those who have passed. There often is a strong first contact where the soul expresses his or her love for those remaining on earth and sends a message that they are happy and well. Then contact often fades as they seem busy on the other side with other things. If the person on earth continues to press for extensive contact they are often gently chided to let go of the deceased and to pay attention to their own path on earth.

Pete wanted to clearly convey for this book that from his perspective everything is elegant, fair, and balanced. He feels that our experiences are determined by our "wattage." This means to me the amount of love energy we can receive, feel, embody, and shine forth. He states that the universe in all kindness helps to gentle the effects of our less loving beliefs and actions and tries to support us in every way possible but that we are responsible for our own wattage and do get to experience the consequences of whatever wattage we carry. It sounds to me that each life we have is an opportunity to increase that wattage and that sooner or later we all will shine more brightly.

Robert Monroe in his second book, *Far Journeys*, from his decades of out-of-body (OBE) explorations summarizes his wisdom about the meaning of coming here to this planet. He calls this energy "Super Love" to distinguish it from more ego-involved types of love and states, "The major, if not the only, reasons for attending the human experience school are first, to learn to translate such energy (Super Love) into a discernible form, and second, to become a first-order generator thereof." This idea of the main reason to incarnate is to experience and generate love in a discernible form is a very appealing idea to me in that it is succinct and resonates as being full of profound truth.

As the session progressed and Pete repeatedly conveyed his appreciation of what I and other loved ones did on earth for him, I began to feel uneasy. I did not hear him claiming his own worth. I confronted him directly with this in the form of the question, "Could he acknowledge his own beauty, power, and how he graced us here on earth?" He had trouble seeing this. And I think this points strongly to why the energies on the other side are trying to arrange for him some life experiences where he can get in touch with his own beauty and value.

I know from my experiences as a therapist that one of the hardest things to get people to embrace is their own power and beauty. They may have been treated poorly by others and therefore feel they deserve little in the way of abundance and happiness, or they may have done things that they are not proud of and feel lack of deservingness from that. It may even be that they feel one has to be perfect to deserve good things and to have value in the world. THIS IS NOT TRUE! Most of us cannot comprehend the impact that we are having. Witness how after Pete's death even checkout clerks with whom he had just passing contact took the time to write to us, his family, to say what a positive impact Pete had in their lives.

I think that if Pete and many others contemplating taking their own lives could understand and feel just one thing: their intrinsic value and their importance to the paths of others, then the rate of suicide would plummet. It is so simple and yet at times so difficult a concept to grasp: our own magnificence. We really in the end have to give ourselves this gift of understanding. Others cannot provide it for us except on a very short-term basis. We have trouble acknowledging let alone celebrating our own beauty and worth on a consistent basis, even if we are not clinically depressed. We have been taught that to do so would be lacking in humility and that pride goes before the fall. But as we shall see, this genuine pride in ourselves and extension of this valuing to all other beings is necessary for us to create blessed experiences for ourselves and an abundant and safer world for all.

ALL DEATH LEADS TO LIGHT

I waited for four months before having another channeling session with Pam and ARGO to give myself time to integrate the richness of information that had been given so far. After I transcribed the previous sessions and studied them, I was surprised to find that they seemed quite complete and that I had only three remaining questions. These are answered in the last channeling obtained for this book and presented below.

ARGO Session May 23, 2016

Joe: These are my follow up questions to some of the things that ARGO said:

1. If Pete chooses a simulated life, when people do that, do they have to go through a simulated birth and infancy, or can they just start as adults?

2. In terms of another life, can people go back in time or do you always need to go forward in time, for example if this life ended in 2050, could you back to 1950 or do you have to go forwards?

3. I am wondering if there is equivalent beauty in the spirit world, such as my love of music and nature, or it

sounds like people may come back to earth because it is so beautiful here.

These are the questions that I have, not too many. And I am assuming Pete may be going into his next simulated life, so it might be that ARGO is only available or it might be that Pete might be available as well, I do not know.

Pam: *Well, let's see: Okay, ARGO this is for the book for Joe and also for Joe, as he wants to know. If Pete is going into a simulated life, does he have to go through the birth process, the way we have a physical birth here, or does he just step into adulthood or childhood, how does that work? And then he would like to know if you have to progress forward in linear time for your next life, or can you go backwards? And I forget the third question, Joe.*

Joe: it concerns the beauty that is here.

Pam: *Okay, yes. Because there is such a physical component to this life: sensual. So with the beauty and the music here, ARGO is there an equivalent on the other side? Because it sounds like people come to the physical to have that experience of the beauty … one of the reasons.*

So I asked to be used as a clear and loving channel of light and to get this information with clarity and accuracy and thank you ARGO for helping us today. Wow, in the simulated life, you are really talking about sort of a mental experience. So, you are not in a physical form but you can have a memory that feels as real as if you were being born. It is all taking place in the mind. They are showing me much like watching a movie on a screen. It's in the physical realm, where we are, we are having a physical experience that is being generated by oneness, you know, by the mind. So in other words, Pete is having an experience that is felt very intensely but is really mental.

So Pete would say, Yes, I was born. Yes, I moved through this scraped knee or this difficult time in a school or I lost my first love, she rejected me: all of this would feel genuine, but not as impacting as in the physical, because in physical there is a greater intensity. So from Pete's perspective, the answer is, why yes. From the guides and helper's experience or perspective, it is well yes and no (Pam laughs). But all of it is intended to move along really rather quickly, so that the impact can be felt and movement can be made forward.

That when you look at time on the earth plane in your mind, the time is linear, it takes years or months or days but actually in the simulation it is really in terms of cosmic time, an instant, you know? So in the physical realm it's…Okay, ARGO, give me a word that I can get. Okay, ARGO is showing me a clock, an old-fashioned clock and of course time moves forward and there is a death and rebirth and so it is linear; so in terms of earth memory, everything is linear time but in the eye of creation, or the eye of God, it is all happening at once.

So when you are talking about moving forward to the next life, in a sense it has already happened, you are just stepping into it. That the soul, as it is birthing, has a blueprint and it has expressed experiences it needs to have in order to return to the source. There is a greater plan and sort of a mini-plan, a smaller plan where the soul chooses and eventually comes back home. In the eye of God, this is all happening at once, so our future lives have already happened because it is all simultaneous. So to answer your question: yes, you move forward in the idea of linear time but in the cosmos, time is non-existent.

Joe: I understand. Say things are really lousy on this planet in twenty years but if a person wanted to reincarnate, could they decide to go back and have a life in the 1950s?

Pam: *In the 1950s instead of the year 2070: no.*

Joe: We go forward?

Pam: *Yes, we go forward. And the images I am getting, it is all in the flash of an eye! And in the blink of an eye, all these lifetimes take place in cosmic reality. It is just in our consciousness as humans that as we are in this dimension, we see things: it is slowed down in this dimension and so dense that we see it and experience it as linear. To answer our human brains about it, yes, we move forward but we have already experienced these others. Am I making sense? It is all at once, it is all happening at once.*

Joe: Yes, there is a bit of paradox but I understand.

Pam: *Okay, I was just making sure that I was clear. They have a little more to talk about. They are saying that when someone talks about time travel, say they want to go back to the 1850s, they really can do it, in the sense that they open that door psychically or mentally and they are in that time, but they are in a time that has already been lived by them.*

Joe: A past-life regression if you will?

Pam*: Yes, all of that.*

Okay, now let's ask about the beauty and the intensity of this plane versus the other side. (long pause) Well, it is complementary. That the intensity of the physical beauty that can come through the senses depends on the capacity of the viewer to perceive it but it holds a physical aspect and it elicits feelings of joy.

In the dimension beyond death there is ecstatic joy that is experienced in all things. There is music that does not come through sensually but is absorbed more, almost taking it in organically by a spirit, and which enhances a greater and greater sense of joy and wellbeing.

It is like one drum beat amplifies the next heart beat of love and light and on and on, and there is no end to the joy and the sense of ecstasy and beauty on the other side, as one finds themselves in a more exalted situation. And for those who are not quite to that place, there is a recalling that is allowed. Let's say someone really loved the 1960s, they could come back to, and it is all in the mind, where they could come back and experience the pleasures and the beauty of that, really at will. So they can bring back pleasant memories. They are saying just like we can remember the taste of fresh-squeezed orange juice in the morning or an orange dripping with juice and it can be so intense in our memory that we can taste it: it is like that on the other side.

Joe: Sometimes we could have a very vivid dream on this side, where it feels completely real?

Pam: *Yes, it is sort of like that. And it can be done at will. And the whole experience is really intended to enhance the pleasure and joy centers of the soul, so that they can release the grief and the sorrow, and move into sort of better circumstances and energy fields. They are teasing you: you can smoke cigarettes over there, Joe. (laughs)*

Joe: Well, I can smoke them over here too. (laughs)

Pam: *Well, you don't have to give them up on the other side!*

Joe: That's funny! Is there any particular message that they felt was incomplete that needs to go in this book?

Pam: *Okay, ARGO, is there anything he missed that you want in the book? (Pause) It looks complete. They have a feather quill pen and they are putting it down.*

ARGO: Free from the pain of death, all souls achieve a reclaiming of spiritual (life). They retrieve their souls regardless of the method of passing. Put to your publishers a note such as, "All death leads to light." Death in all its forms, transforms us to light. That it is the passage of greater good and harmony for all souls. It is the fear that creates the drama in man's mind. So do not fear death but show simply that how one leaves the planet is not a determiner of fate on the other side. It is a multitude of life decisions that brings a soul to a certain time where they choose a passage by their own hand, but all things in life revolve around the power of love and all things are forgiven. All creatures are raised in light to great good. All creation is nothing but love.

So go in peace my son and do not worry about your brother's wellbeing anymore. As you choose to move to great realms of understanding, your own capacity for joy will increase and your sense of wellbeing will be ever present. We go forth with you daily through your routine as well as your teaching schedule and are currently looking out for your own emotional state as you are quite traumatized in memories. Please be at peace at night and we will move to soothe a worried mind so that your days are filled with great higher energy.

Pam: *They just stopped.*

Joe: I thank ARGO very much for the messages and you as well.

Pam: *You are welcome, ARGO is nodding. Be at peace, Joe.*

End Session

In this channeling session I feel they answered my questions as clearly as possible, given that a full spiritual perspective is difficult for us to comprehend while in a time-space incarnation. As for Pete or anyone having what we are calling a simulated life on the other side, it appears that such an experience is designed to be very similar to having an earth life, where one experiences birth, progressing through linear time and eventual death. It is just done in the mental realm without need for an actual incarnation into earth space within a physical body.

From what is being said in the channelings, I gather that the process of having a life comprised of sequential experiences is a great way to learn, whether one has a body or not! And without a physical body it looks like the experience can proceed faster and with less intensity and more awareness of support from spiritual guides. So this type of "life" can allow learning without the density and consequences of problems being encoded in the genetic makeup, including ongoing issues that weight heavily in the family tree.

My question of whether one needs in their next incarnation to always move forward in terms of earth time generated some complex and paradoxical discussion about the nature of time and how it is really a local construct within the time-space earth perspective. This contrasts with what they called "The Eye of God" perspective, where there is only the one and only infinite now. This information seemed to me compatible with how I understand the issue of time from my own deep meditation experiences. I use the following model to get as close to my understanding as I can within the limits of language. For me, if one views time as a large and long ruler, one can view our experience while being time-bound on earth as having the experience of walking along the ruler, moving from inch one to inch two, etc., and being able to see only a little bit ahead and recall all the inches we have already walked that are now behind us. But if you then soar high above you can see the whole ruler as one. From that perspective it is all one "Now" occurring simultaneously. From above you could experience yourself at any and all points along the ruler in the same instant. Both perspectives are true.

The perplexities of time, not withstanding, it appears from a linear time perspective that one proceeds from one incarnation to another sequentially forward in time, one to the next, so if this incarnation ends in 2050, then the next would begin sometime after that. If true, this surely gives us incentive to fix the formidable social, ecological, and economic challenges that we currently face, not only for our children and grandchildren, but for ourselves if we are coming back in what we would call the future. This is in line with the concept of karma (cause and effect). It is important to remember that, "As you sow, you shall reap" does not only refer to negative consequences but also that if we invest in positive processes we can enjoy positive outcomes.

While we live sequential lives from earth perspective, ARGO did say that one could re-visit the past by tapping into that time-frame meditatively. This coincides with my own meditation experience and is also consistent with the Lifeline rescue work that we have referred to in this book. We did not cover this in the channeling questions, but other bodies of work suggest that we can also travel forward in time. Psychologists measure us reacting to events physiologically shortly before they happen, and the remote viewing science literature suggests that we can perceive without constraint across time both forward and backward. Stranger still, psychokinesis experiments suggest that we can influence events in the past from the present, as long as no human has yet observed the event.

ARGO's answer about beauty and pleasure in the afterlife was very consoling to me. Earlier in my life, descriptions of heaven as a place where there was constant harp music for eternity always sounded like it would be unbearably boring after a few years. I do not even like harp music all that much! ARGO's description that there was a type of music on the other side that refreshed and healed the soul and that also one is able to conjure up any pleasant experience from one's earth past to re-enjoy, for purposes of elevating the soul's energy, both sound good to me. ARGO mentioned that the earth system and the other side were complementary. This suggest to me that the richness of experience here feeds the richness of who we are and also that the richness of experience in spirit also enhances the fullness of our beings.

ARGO's final words in this channeling and for this book, to me, were very profound and comforting, including: "All death leads to light." "How one leaves the planet is not a determiner of fate on the other side." And, "All creation is nothing but love." ARGO instructed me to, "Go in peace my son and do not worry about your brother's wellbeing anymore." I feel the richness of compassion and information in these channelings, and the whole process of writing this work is allowing a deeper healing and letting go. Indeed I feel that I can now release my dearest brother Pete in greater confidence that he is well cared for and thriving along his own path.

THIS SIDE OF THE VEIL

We can see from these sessions with Pam and ARGO that even an event such as suicide which is defined as highly negative by our culture, the ultimate defeat if you will, provides opportunities for growth. This is true for the soul of one who has committed suicide. Such an act does not in any way sever the enduring flow of love and respect from the highest of spirit that we all abide within and that we can enjoy and trust if we can just open our hearts and perceptions.

The act of suicide provides a strong and sometimes crushing challenge for the loved ones left behind: and an opportunity for growth for them as well. I have tried, from the beginning of my grief at Pete's death to the present, to honor the experience, go with the flow and allow myself to experience the fullness of this dark gift. I was and am committed to learn from it and to create whatever positive aspects that I can from it.

Given my commitment to grieve consciously and create positive gains from this painful experience, I think that it is fair to ask, "From a twenty-five year perspective, how has this experience with Pete, his death, and tracking him on the other side changed me?" There has been an amazing richness of change and I will try to give the highlights.

Starting a few years after Pete's death I was feeling pretty good most of the time. But in early July I would begin to feel angrier and more depressed and would not know why. Then finally around July 15th it would hit me: this is the anniversary of Pete's death. Once I made the connection, the feeling would start to ease. It was a striking phenomenon that each year became slightly less intense and also shorter in time, until by fifteen years after his death, it disappeared completely.

The Thanksgiving-Christmas holidays generated similar feelings at first but I always knew as the feelings came on that they were related to missing Pete at these family gatherings and his birthday being on December 30th. Initial holidays were bitter and rough, then began to be bittersweet. I recall a Christmas morning about ten years ago, where Elena and I had tried to make the day really special for our kids, and then some minor glitches happened that set me off into a very uncharacteristic few-minute rage, which left my family shocked and me ashamed. The negative tinge to these holidays gradually also faded, occasionally increasing in the years when another loss occurred such as the death of my mother, father, and brother, but then continuing to fade away, allowing the holidays once more to be joyful occasions. About five years ago, we had a big Christmas tree and when one of my friends came over with his four- year-old child, she looked at it in wonder and said, "That tree is ginormous!" I laughed a huge belly laugh and remember that Christmas as free of heartache.

About eight years after Pete's death, I met a man in one of my first Inner Vegas Adventure workshops who became a close friend. Gary and I hugged warmly and often, spent money together like sailors on leave, and when in a casino playing, we would get to laughing so hard and be so silly that casino staff would come up to us and say we could not have any more to drink, even though we had never imbibed a drop. He named one of his pet wolves after me which I considered a high honor. It felt like he was an angel sent from heaven to give me back a taste of close brotherhood again. I took it as a sign that I was ready for healing at another level: not just releasing pain, but now ready to move back into joy. After a few years, Gary faded away from close contact. I handled this loss better than I expected and still treasure the oasis it provided during this long grieving process.

Not too long after this and about twelve years ago, my Brother John, who was closest to me in age, came from Rochester, New York to North Carolina. He was retiring and was attracted to the beautiful weather and mountains here. We sold him and his wife a few acres next to us and he built his home there. John and I began to visit a few times a week and became close. We brought home Labradoodle litter mates, John and I each taking one, and they played together nearly every day. John was diagnosed with an ALS-type illness and over the next ten years slowly became wheelchair bound, then lost swallowing and finally breathing ability. He remained cheerful and our visits continued to deepen in content and feeling as he approached death. My wife, his wife and I held him in his last hours at home. He passed peacefully and filled with light. I do miss John, but there was very little of the hard grieving that I had experienced with Pete. I often feel Pete, John, and my mom around as I play slots. While talking to them as the machine spins, I am filled with gratitude for having known them in this life.

In the first chapter of this book, I mentioned that as a kid I took Pete to be my model, as my admiration for him was great. I think now that I see that he lives on in me, in terms of much of what I admired about how he treated people. I can see him in me, particularly in how I relate to my kids and grandchild, with "his" style of playfulness, humor, and respect.

My own other-side communications with Pete over the years have moved mostly to a connection that I mentioned I feel most often when playing slots, but also on long woodland walks. They provide me with a blessed sense of connection with him. I did not have to lose or put away all memory of him to finally lose the heavy grief, which is what I had feared would have to happen earlier in the process. It is consoling and uplifting now to know Pete helps each of my loved ones acclimate when they reach the other side. I truly have friends in high places! I will look forward to seeing him when my time comes, without the anger and disappointment I felt in the early years of grief.

So the short answer to the question of how this event has changed me, I think is, while very difficult, it has changed me for the better. The biggest change, involves a shift in how I live both personally and professionally. It is fair to say that, earlier in my life and before Pete's suicide, I was a rescuer. I tried to help my mom out of her depression even as a little boy. I tried to fix anyone who I perceived as being in pain and this even extended to animals and plants. The desire to ease my own suffering and the suffering of others called me into the profession of psychotherapist. The yoga discipline of being a therapist provided balance to this trait and added respect for every individual's path; but nonetheless, deep down I wanted to wave a magic wand and have people's pain evaporate like mist. Believe it or not, often it appeared that I was successful in this mission. But of course this drive to rescue caused considerable stress and burnout when the person was unwilling or unable to conquer their dragons.

Pete's suicide was a huge wake-up slap-in-the-face, strong enough to bring me to my knees. I learned the hard way to respect forces greater than I can understand and pathways that people take that are more mysterious and magical than I can comprehend, even when such paths appear to be dark and futile on the surface. Now I have people come more quickly and deeply into my ocean heart, but more on their own terms with less of me having any idea of what they should be like. This has been most challenging with one of my own daughters who may decide differently than I would have her do, if I could live her life for her. Yet even here I think I have been successful at letting go of the need to rescue and instead hold an open loving space for her.

Surrendering the rescuer role has allowed me a much greater lightness and freedom in relationships and to take off a heavy mantle of responsibility. Life this new way is definitely more fun! This chapter has explored some of the ways that I have changed personally through the experience of suicide. It is written in the hopes of helping people freshly affected by suicide to see farther down the road to where they may be when the grief eases. I acknowledge and respect that each person's path will be different but do want to hold out the possibility that, even after experiencing a suicide or any other devastating loss, a person can thrive, laugh, and love, with the blessing of time, kindhearted support. and commitment to grow and live fully again.

INSPIRING CHANGE

The last chapter highlighted some of the personal changes that have happened for me. This chapter will look at the professional changes that occurred, once the need to rescue was released. It took awhile but I think that I have moved from being a rescuer to an inspirer—and it feels really good to have done so! This letting go of the need to rescue has unleashed terrific creativity, helped me to be in touch with wise guidance and support, and allowed me to discover tools of consciousness that invite a living into full potential.

One of my first steps was to make efforts to understand how such an event as Pete's suicide could happen. My thoughts on this have already been presented here. They can be summarized by, "It is not enough to be a good person, talented, and hard-working for good things to happen and be created around you. You must also experience self-love, trust in the lovingness of consciousness despite external events, and feel deserving of goodness." It is obvious that this stance can be highly challenging to develop and maintain given messages to the contrary and the massive amount of fear and stress that exists in our families, community, and culture.

Is it likely for most of us that past life, early childhood, and then community experiences all generate doubts and self-imposed limits that cloud our ability to see that we can be a successful creator of a terrific life. Further, such experiences cause us to question our own lovability and the goodness of the universe. I wondered how we could most reliably dissipate these illusions that drag down our energy. Much of my training as a psychologist and psychotherapist was designed to help find and ameliorate psychological damage. It was not designed to launch a person into the terrific life lived close to maximum human potential.

The early part of this search was attached to understanding what happened to Pete but it broadened into a general question of how we all could transcend the pitfalls of self-deprecation that consign us to living a life much smaller than we were designed to experience. At first, not much appeared to be happening in response to this question. Then some clues began to emerge. The spiritual states I experienced at The Monroe Institute confirmed that indeed the universe was grandly loving and available to help us. And the Hemi-Sync technology and inspired programs at TMI suggested that this shift in perspective to knowing that love abounds without limit was available without regard to previous beliefs and could be accessed without need to adopt any new dogma.

Then something happened for me that triggered insight into how to link our amazing-ness in spirit form to creating amazing lives while we are embodied here on this challenging planet. I discovered psychokinesis. In 1992, I began to investigate psychokinesis (PK), which is the ability to influence matter through non-physical means. PK can be used to illuminate light bulbs, bend metal and plastic, sprout seeds in your hand in minutes, influence computers, dice, and slot machines, and create healing and abundance—all just using the power of your human energy in a special way. Being able to do these things is incredibly exciting to me! Another great thing about PK is that it can be measured scientifically and results can be shown, often immediately, giving ultra clear feedback that "something important is happening." My book, *Inner Vegas: Creating Miracles, Abundance and Health* describes in detail my journey of discovery of PK, verification of PK in university laboratories, and the application of energy to influence physical reality in my own life, and then with my students.

By the start of college I was familiar with books that discussed abundance creation, including Norman Vincent Peale's *The Power of Positive Thinking*, first published in 1952, *Think and Grow Rich* by Napoleon Hill, first published in 1937, and Esther and Jerry Hicks' *The Law of Attraction*, recently popularized by the film, *The Secret*. In fact, these types of books go back at least to middle Egyptian dynasty times, in a work called the *Kybalion*. But for me all of this usually produced only weak or mixed results most of the time, until the study and practice of PK lit a fire under me by suggesting how to actually raise and focus the right kind of energy for results that often can seem miraculous.

With the discovery and exploration of PK and its application as a training tool I found the antidote, if you will, to the fear and limits which bind most of us to living a life that is restricted in some way. We may be great at finances but experience limits in relationships or health. Or we many have difficulty finding "right livelihood"—that occupation that fires up our passion and creativity and benefits the world. This antidote is also a great way to divert energy away from suicide, anxiety, and depression into a positive and thrilling direction. The discoveries about how we can create excellent life experiences and happiness answered directly the conclusion that, "It is not enough to be a good person. You must also experience self-love, trust in the lovingness of consciousness despite external events, and feel deserving of goodness."

Appendix One presents some of my creative projects that are designed to help people move into their full and joyous potential. They are examples of how Pete's suicide stimulated a search for answers on how we create a life filled with an abundance of health, meaning, connection, and ability to fully express each, our own unique passions and gifts. While we do not consciously control everything that happens to us and those around us, we can indeed powerfully influence just how positive and fulfilling our lives can be. It fact, it is even better than that—our power to create extends to often being able to generate what many would call miracles of healing and manifestation.

Hopefully I am conveying a sense of just how far my interest in these questions has taken me. I feel like I am truly exploring the spectrum from suicide to salvation in my own life, moving from deep depression to living in joy and abundance. We are free and creative beings and can create a life anywhere along this spectrum. If we find ourselves at the lower end of things and would like to change this, then with the right tools, work, and support we can transform and transcend negative and limited patterns, even if they are decades long. There are countless stories of human beings transforming weaknesses into strengths and challenges into opportunities. We are inspired by stutterers becoming great orators, shy people becoming famous actors and comedians, addicts and gang members becoming master teachers, and emotionally wounded people becoming therapists to help others conquer obstacles that they have overcome.

Once my own depression and then the grieving of my brother were lifted from my spirit, all the positive new energy in my own life began attracting to me the most wonderful people to work and play with. Literally hundreds have become what I would call friends and many have helped me in uncountable ways with my creative projects. These projects began to flow with amazing ease. I was used to the old model that had carried me through my years of depression—apply willpower and tremendous effort and slowly you will succeed. This old model worked but was often drudgery and required the type of energy that only a young woman or man has in surplus.

Now things began to flow with an inner lightness and with clear guidance on what was the next step—the main thing required from me was showing up and trusting the process. The next most important thing was to love myself enough to not overdo and take time from a busy schedule to rest, laugh, and enjoy the beauty that surrounds us.

In all my workshops and meditation CDs I talk about applying the energy of the heart. Going back to PK, but also true of manifestation and healing, many define PK as affecting matter with your mind. This principle is often promoted in manifestation work as "Just visualize it and you will make it so." I think this emphasis on the mind is a disservice to those who are attempting to create new more positive patterns in their lives. To me, the mind is important but more like the steering wheel of the car, setting direction or intent. But the car goes nowhere without fuel, and the most excellent fuel for this work is the energy of love or of an open heart. The focus on energy and how to generate it in ample quantities, and in a positive psychological and spiritual way, is what is missing in much manifestation instruction.

When the energy is absent not much happens. I value the phrase my friend and fellow Monroe trainer, Patty Ray Avalon uses: "The Universe cannot steer a parked car." I think she means we need to get going and act for the universe to help us manifest what we desire. I totally agree. But we need the high octane fuel of love to set out on the journey to transform our lives. That is how we un-park our car and get going with true power to complete our mission. We will even have trouble wisely identifying what we need and what the next steps are to create desirable outcomes unless fear and ego are quieted, and a strong flow of heart energy is the best way to do this.

So all these creative projects have been very healing for me. It has allowed me to finally express my deepest desire generated by my brother Pete's suicide, to help as many people as I can make the shift from depression and despair to the salvation of seeing and living life from a new perspective—one that celebrates how truly magnificent we are and how wonderful life can be. Along the way what I have been teaching also seems to have resonated with many who are just feeling a bit stuck—that feel that they are not yet living up to their full potentials for happiness and abundance.

When we don't positively influence our lives and, even worse, tend to manifest the exact opposite of what we want on a regular basis, we need to look at what would cause such a distortion in our life path and the consequent suffering it produces for us and those around us. We are not being tortured by some vengeful god but rather the playing out of the formidable energy of fear coupled with limiting beliefs. It does appear that we live in a free choice universe where we are free to think and feel negatively or positively. But the way we think and feel tends to become fairly habitual and when we do this consistently in one direction, that direction, whether negative or positive, begins to manifest and reinforce that particular direction. It was clear from my brother's experience that it is not sufficient to be a good person; one must also feel deserving of receiving goodness, learn to alleviate fear, and to be in positive energy.

It seems that most people actively try to influence their lives in a positive direction by applying things such as study, hard work, and hope to goals that they would like to achieve. But there is often a good bit of fear mixed in that they perhaps will not get the break, or are not good enough. This often results in a life with a mixture of good and bad things happening. This seems to lie near the center of the continuum of those who seem to be naturally lucky people, to folks where most everything seems to go wrong. When we look more closely at each of the opposite ends of the spectrum, and see the internal pattern of thought and emotion associated with them, this can guide us in the direction that we want to go. It can be tempting to feel powerless and that things just happen out of our control. It can seem a bit intimidating to embrace responsibility for the main direction of our lives.

As in my brother's case, because of ever-increasing fear that he would not make it, in context of mounting intolerable financial pressures, negative manifestation can result in disaster, at least from this earth perspective. On the other end of the continuum we see ever-increasing success. Most people are hampered to a greater or lesser degree by their fears, limiting thinking, and lack of quality heart energy. It is possible to make a great deal of money "on the backs of others" but this tends to come at a great personal cost in other important areas of abundance, such as happiness, health, nurturing relationships, and spiritual progress. I am advocating here for finding true abundance in all areas, including graceful ways to respond to life's challenges that can indeed be traumatic and tempt us to be demoralized. And most importantly, it is vital to be compassionate and passionate about helping others find their joy as well.

The tools I have designed are, in Pete's terms, "to increase your wattage." This is so because they tend to reduce fear and increase our flow of love. There indeed are a wealth of tools from many sources now available in the form of books, seminars, online classes, community support groups, etc. My hope is that more and more of us will connect with what we find to be empowering to move our individual lives and collective evolution forward. Also, these tools are best used holistically, meaning as part of a program that nurtures body, mind, and soul. In times of great personal challenge, physical healing and psychotherapy can be beneficial. Always, a great diet of organic food, plenty of fresh air and exercise, volunteering to help others, and positive fellowship serve to clear and raise our energy.

It is very helpful when working to increase abundance to realize and celebrate all the abundance that is already in your life, ready for your enjoyment. Just this morning, as I was editing this book on my screen porch, I looked up at the early morning sun streaming softly through the woods. What a beautiful view! I then realized that if I moved even an inch to the right or left, up or down, or closer or farther, that I was graced with a slightly different view. If in fact you are blessed with vision (meaning the physical capacity to see and an inner openness to perception) there are quadrillions of different beautiful views available on this planet in each moment, some as sweeping as the Grand Canyon and others as simple as a raindrop hanging off a mail box. And these views all change slightly with each second, minute, hour, day, month, and year, providing an infinity of beauty available to each of us throughout our lives, as we also change moment to moment. That is true abundance! Add to this all the sensations, feelings, and insights produced by music, animals, good food, laughter, and so many other experiences, and there is really an infinity times infinity of riches here on this planet. What a privilege to be alive here!

I feel it is very important to understand how we manifest our individual and collective lives because at this time there is a high degree of fear in our world that is pulling us toward manifesting a very negative world future. For example, because of fear of terrorism now, we see our privacy rights in the U.S. being diminished where much of what we do is monitored and we can be abducted without charges or legal representation to an unknown place for an unlimited time in the name of Homeland Security. The fear generated by the threat of terrorism has created an overkill response that takes away the freedom, privacy, and important rights of all our citizens. This shift has been dramatic. When I traveled in Europe pre-9/11, there was a palpable appreciation and desire for the "American" way of life. Now when I travel there, folks respectfully take me aside and express concern that the American dream is dying in the United States. And Europeans report fear of coming to visit what they see now as the American police state, particularly if they have experienced firsthand, the entry process for foreign visitors established at our borders after 9/11. And this distortion caused by fear saddens me deeply—the actual facts are that an average of six people a year have died in foreign terror attacks on U.S. soil in the past ten years (2004-2014). This is in contrast to an estimated 400,000 per year dying from medical mistakes and tens of thousands in car accidents and gun incidences. So we need to keep perspective.

I also see the immense reserve of good will, creativity, and love of freedom that exists in the United States and know we can get back on track if we can get our fear under control. I write this paragraph while the United States in the midst the 2016 presidential elections and fear is flying its flag high. Healing starts with the majority of us individually getting our own fear under control and beginning to envision a positive future. I used to try to meet fear with courage, now I melt fear with love. My new mantra is, "Fear is expensive, love is priceless, choose wisely!" Someone was kind enough to put my saying on a wooden sign and gift it to me. I placed the sign on the wall of my office where I see it many times a day. This is good because I need to be reminded of it often. From my point of view, we very much need to understand how we create our reality and master the tools needed for creating a positive future at this tipping point in our society.

One of the tools that I have used since its discovery in the first year after Pete's death that has served me the best in terms of "Love is priceless" and keeping an open heart, is my image of my heart as a vast ocean, unable to be broken, which was presented near the end of Part One of this book. Since its discovery, my heart is like water. If you come into my life, you're enveloped completely, like a hand submerged in water. If you leave, the water goes back to complete, perhaps losing a drop. This idea of an ocean heart as mentioned has allowed me to experience the death of my parents, my brother John, and close friends without closing off my heart and without the tearing grief that I had with my brother Pete's death.

My ocean heart has also served me well when I had a near-death experience with anaphylaxis from a bee sting about six years ago. I was without vision and blood pressure within minutes. Yet I was able to control my fear during the event, which may have kept me alive. And on many occasions since, when a bee buzzes close by me, I can keep my cool. My ocean heart helps me hold the pain of the chaos in the Middle East and other world problems that tend to overwhelm us, with a peace in my heart and little fear.

So of all the tools and insights that I have mentioned, I think I treasure the open ocean heart image the most. I hope to carry this image life-long and into whatever life may bring next here, and even after death of my body. I offer this image to you as my gift. When the peoples of the world know and experience that their hearts are joined as a vast ocean, we will truly be able to create a paradise here on earth.

THE JOURNEY ALWAYS CONTINUES

My journey has helped me know that with complete certainty that "Yes," there is much help and hope on the other side and no soul is lost, even after suicide. My hope is that this book will help many individuals veer away from suicide, not from fear of eternal hell but from understanding the pain that suicide brings to those left behind and that things can improve for them here on earth despite feelings of deep tiredness and discouragement.

If suicide does occur, that person is not lost, will not be condemned, will be greeted with love, be allowed to rest and then again have the opportunity to learn a better way through the challenges of life. Suicide does not solve anything. Neither does it result in an everlasting death or punishment sentence.

And to all those families and friends recovering from suicide I hope this book provides the comfort of seeing the act of suicide from a greater perspective and knowing that your loved ones are cared for in spirit with limitless compassion and understanding. If you are like me you will miss them deeply.

Even as you trust that your loved one is being cared for well, allow yourself to grieve fully. Let it out and express yourself. Counter the isolation often surrounding suicide by surrounding yourself with the beauty of nature and supportive friends that can go beyond platitudes and help you stay connected with life. Do your own research to find materials that resonate with the positive messages in this book.

Give yourself much time—this is not a quick process. Those in your outer circle may be ready to move on in a few weeks. If the person who committed suicide was close to you, your journey through grief may take years. This grief is your right and your sacred process. Loss, anger, and sadness are to be expected. Self-torturing "Would have, could have, should have" cycles of thought can be like birds of prey circling. Bitterness, blame, and harsh judgment of yourself and others may surface. Look at these things as symptoms of the storm—they will subside eventually. To the extent that you can, gently but firmly steer your life back to the light. An unfathomable weariness may weigh you down. When it does, get some rest, and if sleep will not come, at least rest in the form of a nature walk, listening to a meditation, or watching an old sit-com.

If you desire contact with your loved one on the other side, it can help to see them in their highest and finest and resting comfortably in angel wings, then think of some essential quality they possessed that you loved, such as their kindness, or sense of humor. Then reach out in love to them and release—a message may come then, or in sleep, or in the shower or on a walk. Let close friends know that you are open to messages, if they receive them, because sometimes your grief may have you in such turmoil that subtle messages from spirit are hard to hear and friends might be better able to connect with your loved one. It is fine to talk to the person in your head or journal what you want to say to them, even if you do not immediately perceive a response. It can help prime the pump by imagining what they would say and writing this down. Then after a few sentences it may start to feel like you are no longer making up the answers but they are coming from guidance. There are many psychics that can also help with contact but I would only approach one for help that was highly recommended by those you trust, and who then elevates your energy and respects your choices.

Much of your pain can be from attempting to close off and protect your heart so that you do not experience more hurt. This can make everything seem dull and grey, and you to feel even more isolated. It takes courage but keep you heart open if at all possible, and if not this week then try again next week, and the next.

I think it is appropriate to do something in memory of the person that you have lost. That may be as simple as planting a tree or more extensive such as volunteering for a cause that they would have been passionate about. To the extent you can, trust that you will be with this person again in spirit if you have that desire, and that while an earth life here can seem to go on for ages, from the other side perspective it is but a blink of an eye. And finally, after the grieving has eased, use your experiences to create something positive, something that brings a bit more light and love into this world. If you are grieving, I hope that joy and laughter return to you before much time has passed with the freshness of rain after a long drought.

To those who have escaped the experience of suicide, I hope this book shows you the depth of that experience and how to support those you love who may go through it. Remember that we all must die each day to what no longer serves us, in order to fully grow into who we can truly be. To do this takes melting fear with love and moving forward taking risks. The reward will be a great joy for you and those around you—of a life lived to full potential. Anything less is a bit of a suicide, now, isn't it?

Appendix One

LIFE-ENHANCING TOOLS

After five years of PK exploration, I wanted to share my discoveries. I began to offer a workshop called *Inner Vegas Adventure*™ in the casinos of Las Vegas where participants journey deeply into personal power. My students often achieve dramatic physical and psychological healing, strong influence over dice and slot machines, and many marvelous manifestations in their lives after they return home. The casino is an excellent classroom because with using PK to manifest abundance there, and the concrete feedback of win and loss, it is clear within minutes whether the person is being effective at applying the principles being taught. And with even small amounts of money being wagered, motivation and attention to the lessons is very high! This allows very rapid learning of the mental and emotional skill set required for the most effective manifesting of what one desires. As of this writing I have just completed my eighty-second *Inner Vegas Adventure*, so the workshop is still going strong after more than fifteen years.

I have been a facilitator at The Monroe Institute for twenty-five years. I currently train a spectrum of Monroe programs there. After my own discovery of PK and beginning the *Inner Vegas Adventure* workshops, I developed the Institute's *MC²* (Manifestation and Creation

Squared) program which teaches psychokinesis, healing, and manifestation. The MC² program is a six-day course in a relaxed retreat setting which allows us to meditate deeply, present much material, and play with PK in a greater variety of ways than in Vegas. MC² has now been running for more than a decade and we have offered it dozens of times at The Monroe Institute with excellent results. The program confirmed even further that we all have tremendous capacity to amplify our energy and effectively direct it toward dissipating any emotional or belief limits and creating an abundant life regardless of past experience. The PK process and results at MC² are being studied scientifically by the Department of Perceptual Studies (DOPS) at the University of Virginia and also I have participated as an individual research subject there. So the efforts to learn more about this process from a scientific perspective continue.

After a few years of teaching MC² I created *SyncCreation® a Course in Manifestation*, which is the home study version of the MC² program. This is currently my premier program in terms of the most in-depth tool for learning how to identify and release constricting emotions and restricting beliefs, and learning to do PK as a feedback device to practice and master the ideal energies for healing and manifesting. SyncCreation contains custom-designed Hemi-Sync meditations, extensive PK tasks, three sessions of individual personal coaching and many more tools to help accomplish its goals. I wanted SyncCreation to be very results oriented and practical and have been very pleased with peoples' reports of success with it. At the end of this Appendix is a summary of a survey as to SyncCreation's effectiveness.

The Inner Vegas Adventure, and MC² workshops and SyncCreation home study all require a substantial commitment of time and energy. So the next step along the road was to apply my energy toward developing some tools which would allow people to experience at least a taste of what was possible in a shorter period of time.

I first developed the CD called *Manifesting with Hemi-Sync*® with Monroe Products. As mentioned previously, Hemi-Sync technology uses binaural beats listened to over headphones that allow the listener to move easily into deep meditative states without years of practice. On *Manifesting with Hemi-Sync* a person can quickly relax and then be guided through a process that allows them to begin visualizing what they desire to create, while in an ideal energy state to do this—that is, free of fear and feeling of limits.

Next came the CD called *Partner's Meditation* which is designed to heal and raise the energy level in all our significant relationships (parents, children, partners, etc.), so that we have cleaner and more positive energy available to us to apply to creating abundance in our lives. *Partner's* unleashes the power of forgiveness and also changes the manner in which we relate to others. It is important to avoid toxic people in our lives but also to bring out the best in the relationships that we do enjoy.

In 2013 I felt called to develop an exercise available on CD and as a download that would capture the essence of decades of experience of what I had been learning about manifesting a magical life. I called this exercise *Liquid Luck: A Heart Based Meditation Designed to Increase Good Fortune.* It was an instant success with stories flooding in of houses sold in a hour after being on market for months, engineering problems being solved in a day after years of stumping an entire team, new inventions being discovered, scratch ticket lotto wins, businesses taking off, and soul mates being found.

These success stories were a joy to hear and confirmed for me that we as humans are now ready to take a significant leap forward to our ability to create wonderful things in our lives, often with just a short but skilled application of the correct energy and thought. I felt this was an important message, so in 2014 I wrote the book, *Liquid Luck: The Good Fortune Handbook*, wherein I shared the most inspiring stories that were being reported using *Liquid Luck*, and also why the principles in the meditation such as increasing happiness, gratitude, compassion, and love were essential in creating blessed lives. The book also provides exercises to expand on these principles. The *Liquid Luck* book was also a success, resulting in more inspiring reports of major shifts in people's lives.

When I speak of heart and love, most can agree that this energy is very important. Yet many are not sure exactly what I mean and are uncertain how to develop or increase heart energy or loving feelings. So for my next project I designed exercises that, with the help of binaural beat technologies, gamma wave stimulation technologies, beautiful music, and gentle guidance, address this important issue. In 2015 I released *The Healing Heart* and *The Abundant Heart* on CD and download. These two simple exercises have allowed many to gain a direct experiential understanding of the power of open heart energy. In *The Healing Heart*, it is applied for healing into your full potential and also sending healing to another person. In *The Abundant Heart*, the open heart energy is applied for tapping into deepest heart wisdom about what would be the most important things to manifest from your heart's perspective, and then while the heart is open, beginning to bring that creation into your reality.

Manifestation Successes

Sixty SyncCreation participants were surveyed. This is a partial list of the personal manifestations they shared with us.

Personal

- Virtually everyone experienced psychokinesis (PK) success.

- Virtually everyone experienced communication with ethereal, heavenly, and other-worldly beings; guides; unborn children; and/or loved ones who have passed.

- Virtually everyone received increased desire for love, life, health, and wellbeing.

- Twenty people manifested joy in everyday life.

- Eighteen people were able to lucid dream.

- Five people received answers to important life issues that had prevented forward movement.

- One person turned unusable well water into usable well water.

- One person received acceptance to a prestigious school.

Health and Wellness

- Ten people healed their pets.

- Eight people each healed children.

- Five people gained self-acceptance.

- Three people healed their ADD and no longer required medication.

- Three people manifested increased memory for studies.

- Two people healed organs, preventing surgery.

- Two people received healing of chronic headaches and migraines.

- Two people significantly healed their fibromyalgia.

- Two peopled healed their acne.

- One person healed a grandparent.

- One person gained freedom from sleepwalking.

- One person received increased vision.

Abundance

- Six people manifested abundant travel.

- Five people were given small fortunes.

- Four people received multiple checks for thousands of dollars that arrived unexpectedly.

- Four people manifested specific breeds of pets.

- Three people created the home of their dreams.

- Two people created money to buy homes.

- Two people manifested hot tubs.

- One person created a swimming pool.

- One person discovered jewels they did not know they had.

- One person created free airline tickets.

- One person experienced books they wanted to read show up in unusual ways, such as on a park bench.

- One person manifested a free vehicle.

Relationships (Including Family)

- Ten people gained friendship.

- Eight people received important connections for love.

- Five people gained companionship.

- Three people received peace regarding difficult divorces.

- Two people created engagements.

- Two people were reunited with lost family members.

- Two people manifested successful adoptions.

- Two people each received freedom from an unhealthy relationship.

- Two people created rewarding relationships with life partners.

- Two people created safe homes for their families.

Professional

- Fifteen people gained important connections for work.

- Ten people experienced contracts working out.

- Three people experienced the successful launch of new companies.

- Three people gained freedom from unhealthy work environments for much better positions.

- Three people received awards at work.

- Three people created multiple job offers.

- Two people obtained careers that cover living expenses plus health insurance.

- Two people received substantial promotions.

- Two people received an increase in profitable contracts to the point of nearing retirement.

- One person manifested a book offer, an advance, and three months in a cabin to write.

Get Lucky!

- Fifteen people manifested winning at casino craps tables.

- Eight people manifested winning at casino slot machines.

- Two people won raffles.

- One person won online poker tournaments.

- One person manifested winning at friend's poker nights.

What Will You Create with *Sync*Creation?

For more information go to www.SyncCreation.com
Or call (828) 698-4815.

Appendix Two

PAM HOGAN ON CHANNELING

In March of 1995 Pam Hogan graciously agreed to a phone interview about how she got started as a channel and what the experience has been like for her. What follows are edited excerpts from this conversation.

How did you get started channeling?
That is a bit of a story. The important pieces are this: In August of 1983 I was spending a lot of time walking in the woods close to my home. It was beautiful there, and I realized that when I walked I always watched my feet. I looked up one day and I started to cry about how beautiful the August woods were and the thought that came to me was that if I could appreciate beauty on that deep level then maybe I was beautiful too. Immediately a voice or a thought came to mind and showed me how it was all one—that we are all beautiful and of one energy.

At that moment, from the depths of my heart, I asked that everything that I touch from that moment forward be left in love. And that if I could speak with a high spiritual guide, I would share the teachings. This erupted from my heart at that moment and then I forgot about it.

In March of the next year I started receiving communications from ARGO. A loving voice, a strong mental imprint spoke to me, directing me on my spiritual path. Through many communications, many times . . . it is almost like many vis-

its, a relationship developed with ARGO. When I asked ARGO why he came, he said, "Why dear child, because you asked." I could not remember asking at first. Then I thought back and I remembered that time in the woods.

A couple of years later I was looking in a book on Ascended Masters' instruction and it stated that a Master will seek out his student and that initiates first must ask from their hearts that everything they touch in life be left in love. And so, not knowing it at that time, I was opening up to being a student of a Master.

All of this has been confirmed through the years. It is a process, like any relationship, of developing trust, love, working together, and growing together. So what ARGO and I have is a relationship that is really a partnership, as he explains it, with my higher self and ARGO.

The letters ARGO stand for Ascended Rays of God's Oneness. ARGO is a conglomerate. It is a very elevated group of Master consciousness. So this is a group of higher consciousness that communicates through my Higher Self. So I am the physical piece.

Some within this ARGO group have lived on Earth. Some have not. There are Master teachers in this group. When I see ARGO, it is an energy of love. The blending of that consciousness is a cosmic being who is ARGO that I relate to specifically as a guide. ARGO is an androgynous being, a wonderful blend of the masculine and the feminine who exists as the composite of that thought-form of love and stands as gate-keeper for me. ARGO works with me, with my clearing out my own personal issues, so I can heal in my own life and be a clearer channel in love, for them.

Have some of your past-life existences been within ARGO?
They have suggested that I have connected with them before but not in a physical life.

It is beautiful energy!
It is wonderful energy and they show me now as the extension of it in the physical dimension.

Now, I have seen channelers as they channel. At the beginning of sessions, their faces distort and they often talk in an accent of some sort. Did you go through a phase like that? Or was it more that the whispered voice would be there and you just say what the voice is telling you?

It was more like the whispered voice. But more than this, it is a very strong mental imprint. When ARGO first came, my face did not contort. I did not speak with an accent. I was aware in the beginning of really allowing energy to come fully through me, so that I could lose myself, and they could create. I could allow hand motion, which you would see typical of a channel, you know, some of the hand positions. When they would first come, my face would grimace for a moment and then go into a very peaceful state. That happened initially but there was nothing of an accent.

And you would be conscious of what was being said?

Very much so.

When you say conscious channel, that is what you mean?

Yes. I am awake. And I have said to them, "You know, I trust you so much that I volunteer to be removed."

Their answer was beautiful. They said, "No, dear child, you believe that if you were present, God's message would not be, and we have come to teach you of your own God-source. And so it will be a partnership between your higher self and us."

Because of that, I have been able to learn as I channel. I have to grow and expand in order to maintain the channel. I am not being used. I am expanded while they are expanding their words through the physical world. It is a gift to me. It is in no way a taking from me or a use of me. I am a volunteer. And they are very clear that I am not in any way to allow myself to become a victim of channeling. As a matter of fact, there are times when I have become really exhausted or overwhelmed. There was one point where they even threatened to leave because I was constantly going out and trying to help everybody. It never stopped. That was hurting me. And they would just not cooperate with anything that would damage me.

And it would hurt just because of a lack of balance in your life?

Well, energetically it takes quite a bit, so I was exhausted and I was finding that, no matter what the social situation, there was somebody that needed something and so I never had time off. It wasn't balanced. You know that it is all electromagnetic energy and ARGO exists at a greater vibration. In order to be able to hold that, you have to open to that level of energy. You are holding an unusual amount of electromagnetic energy. It can burn your rods. So you have to get clear and clearer—you know, the body, care of the emotional state, the mind, getting enough rest, balancing with play, having love in your life. All of those things raise your vibration.

Now, as I got to know ARGO, our energies blended more. At this point I can just put my head down and look off to the left a bit and just tell you what he is saying. There is none of the show of channeling in the sense there is no squeezed face even for a moment. Normally, what I will do is close my eyes, so that I will stay very focused and not get distracted. Then I can feel their energy enter. But we are more in sync now, so the communication is much easier. And I have also learned, you know, how to balance myself in my life.

ARGO's presence is so powerful. At first I asked that no one tell anyone, thinking that it would ruin my business. I just started reading for a couple of my friends and word spread so quickly that I soon had to choose between doing this professionally and doing my old work. I chose this because of obvious reasons, because of the dimension of expansion for everyone as well as for myself. This was the way to go and I have never regretted it.

Almost immediately, as a matter of fact, within three months, there was a color photo of me and an article about me in the Sunday paper. I was on television. ARGO is just that powerful. So I was public almost right away. There was a lot of work in balancing that and being comfortable with suddenly being public.

You know that I was trained in social work. When I look back at my life, I have been trained, I have been set up for this. Yes, that is the blend. I had started a business working with people with smoking cessation and weight control and I was doing one-on-one counseling out of my office, in Centerville, Ohio. That office then, of course, turned into my office for ARGO. So I was already set up in an office, it was all laid out for me. I just had to choose it.

And so at the beginning you did quite a bit in person. And now you do a majority of it by phone?

Now, because I have moved, I do a majority by phone. And also I have never advertised. It has always been word-of-mouth. The word spread to the East Coast and the Midwest, and even to Europe.

How far in training did you go in social work?

Just a B.A. I had applied to graduate school to pursue a Masters in counseling but duties as a mother and life changes interfered with more schooling.

Did you have a fairly traditional Christian background?

Yes. I was raised Catholic and went to Catholic girls' schools even at the college level. Very much a traditional background, although I had moved away from Catholicism for quite a while. I had done that toward the end of high school; although I studied at a Catholic college, I was removing myself rapidly from the religious philosophy and the ritual.

But you weren't real "New Age" when this started?

No. My husband David, who is now dead, was sick in the hospital. Suddenly, without understanding why, I began to move my hands over him to heal him. I asked him to visualize healing light moving through him at the same time. As we continued this process, his blood count, which was dangerously low, started to improve. Impressed by his progress, the physicians encouraged me to continue. At one point while David and I were working together, a minister walked in on us. He understood hands-on healing and directed me to a book, Agartha. He also gave me the name of a man in town who was starting a study group around these teachings. I read the book, which I found very informative and comforting, and joined the group.

For one year I met with them on a weekly basis and fundamentally listened and observed. The group members were respected persons in the community. They would discuss the fundamental principles of Agartha's teaching and apply them to their lives. I spent my time absorbing this new consciousness, changing my old perceptions of God and the purposes of life. After a year of this study, ARGO contacted me. What a surprise!

Interesting. With the Catholic background and then it happening to you directly, was there much need to say, "Well is this real?"
Well. I questioned it, of course. So much of what ARGO has taught me in this past eight years just flew directly in the face of my traditional thoughts and my upbringing. Yet when I trusted . . . because I trusted what I felt and I moved with this, flying in the face of all my upbringing, it brought me to a greater state of consciousness and peace, although through turmoil in the meantime. That's what takes courage.

Have you come across anything that would be helpful for the general public to better understand channeling?
Well, I think like with everything, you have to be very careful in who you are talking with as a channel, you know the way you would chose a doctor or a psychiatrist. I asked ARGO the question specifically, and his response was you can trust channeling when you can see a change in consciousness— when you feel a change in your consciousness and your life experiences support that change in consciousness. It is the inner shift, and this is that peaceful connected place to God's Source. This is coming to your spiritual power. This is knowing your divine self. And your life experiences are going to come to you to support connection.

Many people, I believe, mistakenly believe, "I'll go to a channel and then things will turn out the way I want them to. I am going to go to you so you will fix my life." And what a clear channel will do is work with the consciousness so the life adjusts around it. But there are times when what we would call a tragedy comes into your life so that you will expand your awareness. And that is not a negative, although we tend to judge it as that. So that was what ARGO answered as to how would you know whether to trust a channel. How has your connection with this channel affected your state of consciousness? Where is your heart? Anyone who comes through my office or calls me, I warn them, "Run this all through your own filter and make your own decisions."

Now, there are spiritual pests that you hear about in the Bible. Someone who is psychic can make a connection with a disembodied spirit that is not necessarily of light that can also give correct information about something. I think this is where channeling gets a bad name. You have to look to the message. Is that channel turning you to your own power, is that channel working on embracing your heart—bringing you to a point of true self-awareness and talking to you about God's source?

If you are with a channel who is bossy, is telling you what to do, or is not really directing your soul but just giving you general information, you are probably with somebody who may be very well-intended but connected with another part of their consciousness that may hold some truth and may have something valuable to say but it may not be all the way connected with the highest spiritual teachers you want.

Sort of the old Ouija board, where you contact an entity that gets its kicks out of drawing some energy from the physical?
That can happen with the Ouija board where you throw the energies wide open—something powerful and wonderful can come through or something that is the shadow of that. You are open. So either can come through. There can be an imprint of the energy, let's say, of someone who has died or a famous person—and a playful spirit can get into the imprint and come and say I'm Abraham Lincoln and you were me in a past life and have a great time playing with you. So, that is the thing about the Ouija board. It is not innately good or evil but that is something of which you have to be very careful. If people are using one, they need to white light it and be very careful that they are not with anyone who is holding a lot of negativity or fear to attract those kinds of energy.

One of the things I had to work with ARGO is clearing the channel because it comes down . . . I always see it literally as a channel, as a column of light, and if some of my ego fears are in there the message may be misinterpreted. So the channel owes it to the people she is sharing the message with to continue to do her personal work. You would want to be with someone that you know is doing that, someone with a higher mind. You know, there may be a disaster coming, but if someone is using scare tactics you obviously don't want to be around her. If someone is looking and saying, well, something unpleasant is happening but here is the higher viewpoint, stick with that counselor.

What was your pre-channel personality?

I think I tended to be rather skeptical. I was leading a pretty ordinary life. You know, I was very involved with my children and my family. Now a year after my husband David and I divorced, I was very stressed and saddened but nothing out of the ordinary. It was at that point I began walking in the woods. Certainly it was one of the lower points of my life. When I started to channel, I went to several therapists to get their impressions. Some said that I was the healthiest person they knew. None felt that I was mentally ill. They accepted the phenomenon of channeling in my life and supported me. They helped me cope with the changes occurring in my life.

So it sounds like you would describe yourself as emotionally balanced and level before this came along?

I guess as much as anybody. I wasn't hysterical. I would say that I am an emotionally-based person, but I tended to run everything through my logic—screen it pretty carefully.

Why does ARGO come to help?

Their purpose really is to help everyone find God's source. I think that is a very important statement to make. They don't come to fix our lives. They come to get us connected to our divine source. Our lives then start to reflect the connection. They have come to help. And apparently what I did was volunteer as a channel.

You have used in my channelings, as well as now, the term "God's source." Could you define it?

The divine spark, which can be termed also the creative spark, the God in all of us. This is the energy that we want to manifest through the physical dimension. It is love.

Thanks, Pam, for sharing all this personal information.

Sure. Hope it is helpful.

NOTES

1. Robert Monroe, *Journeys Out of the Body* (New York: Doubleday, 1971).

2. Robert Monroe, *Far Journeys* (New York: Doubleday, 1985).

3. Franz Bardon, *Initiation into Hermetics* (Wuppertal, Germany: Deiter Ruggeberg, 1976).

4. Thomas Budzynski, "Clinical Applications of Non-Drug-Induced States." In B.B. Wolman and M. Ullman (eds.), *Handbook of States of Consciousness* (New York: Van Nostrand Reinhold Co., 1986).

5. Recent scientific studies are establishing with certitude that these meditative states do exist and are dramatically different from normal waking consciousness in their neurophysiology and in how they are experienced. These meditative states can be monitored by using an electroencephalograph or EEG to find their associated brain-wave patterns. Also, current controlled studies confirm that the binaural beat sound patterns used by The Monroe Institute and others do actually change brain waves in a predictable way in the willing listener, more powerfully than placebos such as relaxing music. So we now have a technology that can aid a person in achieving states formerly obtained only through drugs or years of meditation practice. Michael Hutchison's book, *Megabrain*, provides a good overview of the consciousness technologies that now exist.

6. Bob Ortega, "Some Skeptics Become Believers After They Spend A Week Learning How To Get Out Of Their Bodies," *Wall Street Journal*, September 20, 1994.

7. Murray Cox, "Notes from the New Land," *Omni*, Vol. 16, No. 1 (October 1993).

8. Gari Carter, *Healing Myself: A Hero's Primer for Recovery From Tragedy* (Charlottesville, VA: Hampton Roads Publishing Company, 1993).

9. Joseph McMoneagle, *Mind Trek* (Charlottesville, VA: Hampton Roads Publishing Company, 1994).

10. Ken Eagle Feather, *Traveling with Power: The Exploration and Development of Perception* (Charlottesville, VA: Hampton Roads Publishing Company, 1992).

11. Guidelines uses reverse engineering (taking the brain-wave patterns of talented subjects and using them to create new Hemi-Sync signals) to enhance the meditator's access to his Higher Self, and also to assist the meditator in experiencing out-of-body consciousness.

12. Robert Jahn and Brenda Dunne, "On the Quantum Mechanics of Consciousness, with Application to Anomalous Phenomena," *Foundations of Physics*, Vol. 16, No 8 (August 1986); and Dean Radin and Roger Nelson, "Evidence for Consciousness-Related Anomalies in Random Physical Systems," *Foundations of Physics*, Vol. 19, No 12 (December 1989).

13. Charles Tart, Ph.D., "Compassion, Science and Consciousness Survival," *Noetic Sciences Review*, Spring, 1994.

14. Ronald Russell, ed., *Using the Whole Brain: Integrating the Right and Left Brain with Hemi-Sync Sound Patterns* (Charlottesville, VA: Hampton Roads Publishing Company, 1993).

15. Jane Roberts, *Seth Speaks* (New York: Bantam Books, 1974).

16. Pat Rodegast, *Emmanuel's Book* (New York: Bantam Books, 1987) and *Emmanuel's Book II* (Bantam Books, 1989).

17. Jose Stevens, Ph.D., and Simon Warwick-Smith, *The Michael Handbook: A Channeled System for Self-Understanding* (Orinda, CA: Warwick Press, 1988).

18. *A Course in Miracles* (Tiburon, CA: Foundation for Inner Peace, 1985).

19. The phrase "My body carries me for nothing" is paraphrased from "Finding the Father" by Robert Bly in *Iron John* (New York: Addison-Wesley Publishing Company, 1990), p. 21.

20. At the time of the final re-write of *Brother's Forever*, on January 26, 1996, we had to euthanize our Border collie. It was a tough decision brought about by extreme diabetes. My daughter, now eleven years old, witnessed the event and helped dig the grave, placing three heart-shaped objects on top, symbolizing our love for a dear and loyal pet. As we cried together it was clear that it was healthy grief for a good dog who had enjoyed a good life. Blackie was a champion Frisbee catcher. If you laid down a luscious steak and threw a Frisbee at the same time, she would go after the Frisbee. As we finished the funeral, my daughter specifically requested I add this footnote to my book, in remembrance of Blackie. I am happy to do so. I miss Blackie too.

21. David Feinstein and Peg Elliott Mayo, *Rituals for Living and Dying* (San Francisco: HarperSanFrancisco, 1990).

22. Brain L. Weiss, M.D., *Many Lives, Many Masters* (New York: Simon and Schuster, 1988).

23. Raymond Moody, Jr., M.D. *Life After Life* (New York: Bantam, 1975) and *Coming Back* (New York: Bantam, 1991).

24. The many books on the subject include: Melvin Morse, M.D., with Paul Perry, *Closer to the Light* (New York: Villard Books, 1990); Melvin Morse, M.D., with Paul Perry, *Transformed by the Light* (New York: Villard Books, 1992); Betty J. Eadie, *Embraced by the Light* (Placerville, CA: Gold Leaf Press, 1992).

25. E.J. Gold, *American Book of the Dead* (San Francisco, HarperSanFrancisco, 1995).

26. Michael Newton, Ph.D., *Journey of Souls* (St. Paul, MN: Llewellyn Publications, 1994).

27. Neale Donald Walsch, *Conversations with God: An Uncommon Dialogue* (Charlottesville, VA: Hampton Roads Publishing Company, 1995).

28. Robert Monroe, *Ultimate Journey* (New York: Doubleday, 1994).

29. Lucid Dreaming is the art of becoming conscious during dream sleep and then being able to take control of the content of the dream. Steven LaBerge is an acknowledged authority on this phenomenon and has developed a device designed to signal sleepers when they have entered a dream.

The author, Joseph Gallenberger, is interested in your reactions to his book. He is available for workshops and presentations. His website: www.SyncCreation.com contains many free articles, a free newsletter, and all his products can be purchased there. He can be contacted through:

Email: Joe@SyncCreation.com
Phone (828) 698-4815
Address: SyncCreation
120 Garden Hill Drive
Hendersonville, NC 28739

You may contact The Monroe Institute for more information about its research, tapes, and programs at the following address:

The Monroe Institute
365 Roberts Mountain Road
Faber, Virginia 22938
Toll Free (866) 881-3440
Email: info@monroeinstitute.org

You may contact Pam Hogan at the following address:

Pam Hogan
NDCBU 7041
Taos, NM 87571
(505) 751-3839
PamHogan@mac.com

Related Titles from Rainbow Ridge
Read more about them at *www.rainbowridgebooks.com.*

Conversations with God, Book 4: Awaken the Species
by Neale Donald Walsch

A Manual for Developing Humans
by PMH Atwater

God's Message to the World: You've Got Me All Wrong
by Neale Donald Walsch

Conversations with God for Parents
by Neale Donald Walsch,
Laura Lankins Farley, and Emily A. Filmore

*Consciousness: Bridging the Gap between Conventional Science
and the New Super Science of Quantum Mechanics*
by Eva Herr

Dying to Know You: Proof of God in the Near-Death Experience
by P. M. H. Atwater

Rita's World: Explanations from the Other Side
by Frank DeMarco

Messiah's Handbook: Reminders for the Advanced Soul
by Richard Bach

When the Horses Whisper
by Rosalyn Berne

Quantum Economics
by Amit Goswami

Soul Courage
by Tara-jenelle Walsch

The Cosmic Internet
by Frank DeMarco

God Within
by Patti Conklin

Liquid Luck: The Good Fortune Handbook
by Joe Gallenberger

Imagine Yourself Well
by Frank DeMarco

What to Do When You're Dead
by Sondra Sneed

The Healing Curve
by Sara Chetkin

Rainbow Ridge Books publishes spiritual, metaphysical, and self-help titles, and is distributed by Square One Publishers in Garden City Park, New York.

To contact authors and editors, peruse our titles, and see submission guidelines, please visit our website at *www.rainbowridgebooks.com*.

For orders and catalogs, please call toll-free: (877) 900-BOOK.